Families Behind Bars

*When someone is detained in a foreign prison
there is inevitably a family agonising behind the scenes.
This book is dedicated to them.*

FAMILIES BEHIND BARS

STORIES OF INJUSTICE, ENDURANCE AND HOPE

UPDATED EDITION

KAY DANES

Published in Australia in 2011 by
New Holland Publishers (Australia) Pty Ltd
Sydney • Auckland • London • Cape Town
www.newholland.com.au
First published in 2008
Updated in 2011

1/66 Gibbes Street Chatswood NSW 2067 Australia
218 Lake Road Northcote Auckland New Zealand
86 Edgware Road London W2 2EA United Kingdom
80 McKenzie Street Cape Town 8001 South Africa

Copyright © 2011 in text: Kay Danes
Copyright © 2011 New Holland Publishers (Australia) Pty Ltd

Front cover photographs: Patricia Gerber and her son, Johann; Schapelle Corby; Hakit Yang with his family; David Hicks.
Back cover photographs: Scott Hurford and his nephew; Michael Connell; Harry Bout; Eugene Debruin.
All rights reserved. No part of this publication may be reproduced, stored in a retrieval system or transmitted, in any form or by any means, electronic, mechanical, photocopying, recording or otherwise, without the prior written permission of the publishers and copyright holders.

A record of this publication is held in the National Library of Australia
ISBN 9781742571676

Publisher: Fiona Schultz
Publishing manager: Lliane Clarke
Senior project editor: Michael McGrath, Rochelle Fernandez
Editor: Victoria Fisher
Proofreaders: Niamh Kenny, Maria Sutera
Designer: Hayley Norman
Cover design: Erin Farrugia
Production manager: Olga Dementiev
Printer: Ligare Pty Ltd

www.kaydanes.com
www.foreignprisoners.com

Acknowledgements

I am grateful to the families who had the courage to contribute to this book and allowed me to highlight their experiences, despite the heartache they face on a daily basis. I hope that with the useful resources included, more support will be generated for them and for the particular issues their situations represent. Personal appreciation is extended to everyone who has privately encouraged me to persevere with this book. At times I wondered if I could get through all the unexpected obstacles that seemed to pop up from nowhere. I only had to remind myself a dozen times that what I was doing was worthwhile and would be a valuable contribution to others. That became my motivation.

I really want to acknowledge the support that I am given from my family, particularly my wonderful husband Kerry, and our three children, Jessica, Sahra and Nathan.

I would also like to salute all the humanitarian organisations, their volunteers, bloggers, individuals, forum administrators, civil libertarians, human rights lawyers and devoted advocates who selflessly give up their valuable time to assist families and their loved ones through difficulties, especially those representing such groups as the Foreign Prisoner Support Service, Cage Prisoners & Hhugs, Prisoners Abroad (UK), Fair Trials International, Amnesty International, Innocence Project, Prison Fellowship International and Reprieve. Also, the many that are listed at the resources section at the rear of this book. Your services are vital to the international community.

Heartfelt thanks to my closest friends for always encouraging me, particularly Tony Fox, Martin Hodgson, Murray Kidd and Aaron Mangraviti.

I wish to express my sincerest appreciation to New Holland Publishers for making this publication possible. It has been an incredible journey but one that has been made easier by their consistent support and guidance. Particular thanks to Managing Director Fiona Schultz, Diane Jardine and their wonderful team who work so diligently behind the scenes.

Foreword

Stephen Kenny
Lawyer and winner of the 2010 prestigious Justice Award for his committment to promoting access to justice, particularly for social and economically disadvantaged people.

Most of us lead quiet, peaceful lives in our safe suburban surrounds. On occasions however, individuals can find themselves trapped in a terrifying situation beyond their control, where their lives may be at stake. In moments like this, we are prone to making promises about things we will do should we ever become free of that situation. For those lucky enough to be freed and allowed to resume a normal life, many simply put the drama—and their promises behind them. A few, however, keep their promises. Kay Danes is one of those people.

While Kay was imprisoned with her husband, in Laos in 2000, she made a promise to her fellow inmates that—if she ever escaped the dreadful suffering and imprisonment that they endured—she would assist others who are imprisoned, rightfully or wrongfully, to ensure that they and their families would not be forgotten.

Since that time she has been the driving force behind the now world-renowned the Foreign Prisoner Support Service (FPSS) and has dedicated herself to assisting not only those in prison, but their families as well. She is well aware of the fears and anxieties of the families from her own experience and she is also aware of the difficulties of coping with foreign legal systems and governments who have no commitment to human rights.

Australians should all be proud of the work that she is doing.

Families Behind Bars reflects the experiences that she has had over the last ten years and is intended to assist those who are detained overseas. While there are some high profile prisoners, such as David Hicks and Schapelle Corby, who attract the attention of lawyers and at times the support of the general public, for each high-profile prisoner there are dozens whose stories are equally tragic but who remain unknown to the public or whose fate the public ignores. For those people and their families particularly, it is important that they have a point of reference, a book and a person they can turn to for help when all else fails them. By reading this book those families can prepare for the difficulties they face, knowing that others have faced them before and have found ways of coping, managing or simply surviving.

For those of us who do not find ourselves in this frightening situation, it brings a world of enlightenment and understanding of the difficulties that prisoners face and reminds us that human rights should be for all of us—that they should be respected and supported.

Paul Wolf
US Attorney at Law
Washington DC

Not everyone understands the motives of a person who defends criminals. Criminal defence is one of the least respected areas of the legal profession, which says a lot.

Many people see little difference between criminals and their advocates. The advocate is thought to be, at best, subversive. At worst, they are likened to a co-conspirator with a PhD in crime, promoting crime, getting rich through the loophole-ridden legal system—and all this undoubtedly at the taxpayer's expense.

So what are we to make of a person who does this kind of work *for free*?

It must seem a strange kind of charity to those who believe summary judgments and medieval punishments are the only things criminals can understand. It's the kind of work normally expected of the idealistic and well-meaning, but woefully naïve.

Yet the reader of this book will soon realise that its author is not naïve. She considers her views to be conservative. As an advocate for scores of prisoners locked away in the dungeons of the world, Kay Danes probably knows as much about this subject as any academic. She'll bring you to the dungeons and tell you stories right out of a gothic horror novel. Yet her characters are not the evil sociopaths you might expect. Their families, also trapped in a world of hopelessness and despair, are ordinary people just like you and me.

It may appear that the author has deliberately chosen extraordinary cases to evoke the reader's sympathy. Having worked with Kay Danes for several years now, I can vouch for the fact that many of the people who contact her do seem extraordinary. In this line of work, the extraordinary becomes the norm. After learning the details of scores of these cases, it becomes apparent that there are many people in foreign prisons deserving of our sympathy and help.

Some are guilty; some are not. Some are trapped in a bureaucracy or by a diplomatic dispute. Others are too poor to bribe officials with an entirely different concept of paying a debt to society. For the guilty, we may still find cases worthy of our sympathy. One particularly compelling category is that of the drug mule—the desperate or foolish person who risks their life for a few thousand dollars by swallowing a stomach full of packaged drugs then crossing an international border. If they survive the risk of toxic overdose, they may still face life imprisonment if caught in the act.

Most of these people are lucky enough to have families who support them. Families are the prisoners' first line of defence. They provide not only the material, but also the moral support so necessary to the prisoner's physical survival. They also bear a heavy emotional burden of worry and grief and share in the frustration of dealing with what may turn out to be an impossible situation.

Day-to-day issues like access to drinkable water, nutritious food, medical care and the use of the telephone and mail can be serious if not life-and-death problems for the foreign prisoner. Weight loss and illnesses like hepatitis and cholera are commonplace in some prisons. Normally, the food and medications a prisoner can receive are restricted, both as a punishment and because of the fear that the food or medications contain illegal drugs. There may be no way to avoid contaminated food and there may be no way to get medical assistance or life-sustaining medications.

Another serious problem is to find a competent and honest lawyer in a foreign country who can speak not only the defendant's language and the language of the foreign court, but will also refrain from sending every caring member of the defendant's family into bankruptcy. Due to the inbred corruption in many legal systems around the world, it can also be difficult to find an attorney who is not compromised by his relationships with the judges and prosecutors where he works. Some may view these relationships as beneficial, but aside from the illegality of bribing foreign officials, who will you turn to when a bribe doesn't produce the promised results? On the issue of competence, perhaps one in ten criminal defence attorneys has experience in international cases. Attorneys specialising in international law most often work in international trade. The field of international criminal defence is a small niche. Add to this the unique combination of countries, languages and charges involved, and it should be clear that there may be no attorney in the world competent to handle the foreign prisoner's case.

Court-appointed lawyers may be overworked, uninterested, unable to establish a relationship with the defendant or too constrained by the politics of the system in which they work. Even if they're inclined to do so, a court-appointed lawyer may not be able to speak to the family except in a three-way call with the family's interpreter. It's possible to find a good lawyer, but international cases are far more difficult than domestic ones and, unless the court-appointed attorney takes a special interest in the case, it may just be too difficult for the amount of work required.

Consular officials may be able to help, both in ensuring the health of the prisoner and—under the Vienna Convention—in assisting the prisoner to find an attorney. In practice, this kind of assistance varies from country to country and may be influenced by political considerations having nothing to do with the prisoner's case. Diplomats are in a difficult position, because not only do prisoners ask them for help, so do local prosecutors who need the assistance of their counterparts in the prisoner's home country.

For the curious and sympathetic reader, this unique book will show how the lives of entire families have been consumed trying to rescue their loved ones from impossible situations. For lawyers, foreign prisoners and their family members, it's a survival manual, full of indispensable advice. Other than this book, or an organisation like the Foreign Prisoners Support Service, there is really nowhere else to turn for help.

The people in this book are real. Until now, their stories were not known to anyone outside of their immediate families. Not a lot of people would have listened to them. Kay Danes listened, and has discovered a subject that no one else has ever really written about, especially in such depth.

What is it like to be a prisoner in a foreign prison where you cannot speak the language, cannot understand the situation you are in and no one you know, not your mother or even your lawyer, has any idea how to help you? What is it like to be the one waiting at home for that phone call in the middle of the night that changes your life forever?

Tony Wilson
Chief Police Reporter
The *Gold Coast Bulletin*

Only a crack Hollywood writer could create a scenario of such sheer and enduring hell as the one Brisbane couple Kay and Kerry Danes found themselves in at the beginning of the twenty-first century.

Living in Asia, Kay had created a successful personal security business while Kerry was beginning to come to grips with life after a career in the Army. Suddenly, all that was gone in a twinkling when Lao police kidnapped Kerry and later snatched Kay as she tried to flee Laos with her children in December 2000. The next 10 months were filled with the horrors of life in Phonthong Prison, dealing with physical and mental torture, a corrupt government and a tough battle from behind bars to gain their freedom, facing trumped up charges and even having to undergo a shambles of a trial. They saw terrible human rights violations in the gulag that was their prison, carried out by a paranoid and ruthless communist regime. They were lucky to survive at all.

Having gained their freedom, Kerry returned to the Australian Army while Kay battled to come to grips with her terrifying ordeal. Meeting a number of people in that horrible Lao prison, who did not deserve to be there was part of a life changing experience for both Kay and Kerry. Naturally, they had no previous first-hand idea so many people were locked up unfairly. Even those who were guilty did not deserve such inhumane treatment in sub-human conditions.

Apart from looking after her family, the treatment of people in prisons has become a cornerstone of Kay's life which she embraces without any remuneration, kudos or expectation of anything other than a thank you from the families she deals with. Families, more often than not Australian ones, who all have the same thing in common—a loved one locked up in a foreign jail somewhere.

It was in the pursuit of this cause that we met in May 2005. As a journalist, I had followed the Schapelle Corby case from its inception in October 2004, finally becoming personally involved in the plight of a fellow Gold Coaster I believe is innocent.

The Corby family had asked Kay to come to Bali and talk to Schapelle in Kerobokan Prison about how she dealt with life in an Asian prison.

Foreword

Kay and I met at Brisbane Airport and by the time we touched down in Bali we had become friends. Kay visited Schapelle on May 26, 2005—the day before her verdict—and although she has never publicly told anyone exactly what she said to Schapelle, her words are credited with the amazing strength and composure shown by Schapelle after she was handed a horrific 20-year sentence. I saw Kay a few hours after her visit to the prison and she burst into tears, such was the toll it took on her to step back inside an Asian prison. But Kay did it to help someone else and that is typical of Kay Danes.

We have spoken frequently on the phone since that trip and, while it is mostly to do with Schapelle's situation—with Kay doing a great deal behind the scenes in co-ordinating the Corby support group—she has often spoken of other prisoners in other parts of the world and the toll it has taken on their families and friends. I have listened with sympathy and frustration and, occasionally, I've suggested to Kay that she write about these people. The result is *Families Behind Bars*, an unusual book that looks at how tragedy can strike a family in an unimaginable way.

Since becoming involved with the Corby case, I have a far greater sympathy for families of those incarcerated in dreadful prisons around the world that are light years away from the standards of Australian jails. As a tough old police reporter, I used to think, let them rot, but having now seen them living in hell and seen the toll it takes on their families who are guilty of nothing, I have changed my mind. I realise that the work Kay does for these families, and the battles she has fought with foreign powers to improve conditions and visits for these often forgotten prisoners, is phenomenal. She is not really interested in their guilt or otherwise, she is more concerned about offering help, even if, on some occasions, it only amounts to a shoulder to lean on and an ear for people who often have no one else to turn to.

Kay's story takes readers to hellholes all around the globe; it allows them to meet ordinary people thrust into extraordinary situations, riding a rollercoaster of emotions as they learn how people cope with a world that was alien to them until their loved one was arrested. Some of it is inspirational, some of it will make you cry, but through it all, there is Kay Danes doing what she can.

I know firsthand of the pain the Corby family has been through and it is raw and powerful. Kay is working behind the scenes with some of the Bali Nine prisoners and their families. I have met some of these people during my visits to Kerobokan and I have some inkling of what they are living with. Yes, for the Bali Nine, their offspring are guilty, but to see the bedrock despair of a parent whose son is facing a death sentence is a terribly sad experience.

Amid all this is the indefatigable Kay Danes, dispensing help, humour and—sometimes even hope. She has an amazing plethora of stories: a father who spent 26 years in jail for a crime he didn't commit; a family who learnt their son was to be executed by firing squad and were expected to buy his body bag beforehand; a sister grieving for justice for her brother jailed for life without parole. *Families Behind Bars* is real life drama at its most potent, from one of Australia's top social justice ambassadors.

Contents

Introduction 15
1 Choices: life doesn't always turn out the way we expect 16
2 Negotiating the minefield: valuable information for families 27
3 Bad things do happen to good people:
   Kay and Kerry Danes, Laos 42
4 Holiday of a lifetime: Schapelle Corby, Bali 63
5 Where is daddy? Jody Aggett, Thailand 96
6 Gone without a trace: Sheng's story, Laos 113
7 Dicing with the death penalty: Australians in Bali 129
8 Shirley's anguish: Alan Hodgson, Ghana 142
9 Proof of life: Mohamed Abbass, Egypt.. 153
10 No time for second chances: Michael Connell, Thailand........... 161
11 Do you know where your kids are? Rachel, Hong Kong........ 170
12 Morocco madness: Kelly's brother, Morocco............................ 180
13 Death for 250 grams: Scott, Thailand 186
14 Madam Gin Gin: Mrs Outachin, Laos 194
15 Trading lives: David Hicks, Guantanamo 199
16 Invisible bars: Belmarsh 12, UK 211
17 It's only prescription medicine:
   American grandmother, South America 222
18 My brother Brad: Bradley Peake, Australia............................. 228
19 Fallen angel: Randy Sachs, Vietnam.. 234
20 Zambian orphans: Gilbert Mwamba, Zambia 257
21 Keeping the promise: Eugene Debruin, South East Asia 264
22 Our right to human rights: they affect our everyday lives 269
23 Exonerated: Rickey Johnson, USA.. 279
24 Waiting for a reprieve: Linda Carty, USA 287
25 Do the courts always get it right? Harry Bout, USA............ 269
26 A mother's love lights the way: Patricia Gerber, South Africa 299
27 Justice for Jock: Jock Palfreeman, Bulgaria............................. 313
28 Words Can light the way 324
29. Hope The key to endurance 327
Useful resources 331
Campaigns 332
About the author 333

INTRODUCTION

Families Behind Bars is fascinating, terrifying and heart wrenching to read and a poignant wake up call for everyone. It is about the resilience of families who endure despite the odds. It explores the journeys of families from all over the world who have experienced the trauma of having a loved one detained in a foreign prison. It's about how these families have coped and haven't coped. These are real life accounts that are uniquely inspirational, shockingly heartbreaking and will make you appreciate how fragile our lives really are. We may, without any warning, be plunged into a roller-coaster of despair. What happened to them may happen to you!

This book covers a broad range of topics that impact on whole communities. Most importantly this book reminds us that no matter who we are, the principle of rights and justice are worth defending. We are sometimes very quick to judge others. We condemn them before we know the facts or truth about a matter. With arm chair critics a plenty, there will always be varying opinions on a person's guilt or innocence, but what is worth remembering, is that for a society to remain humane and righteous, for the sake of protecting the integrity of society, it becomes vital that a person is dealt with justly, in a fair and transparent way. That the legal, human and civil rights of a human being are stringently defended. After all, the very concept of justice is not about what he said or she said but rather, the moral rightness based on ethics, rationality, law, natural law, religion, fairness, and equity, along with the punishment of the breach of said ethics.

When someone is detained in a foreign prison there is inevitably a family member agonising behind the scenes praying that justice will be served. If their loved one is guilty, then they have a valid expectation that the punishment should be reasonable and proportionate to the severity of the infraction. Equally if their loved one has been wrongly convicted, they have a valid expectation to seek justice through an equitable appeals process. Without rule of law there would be chaos and anarchy. It helps keep the balance in society. It's worth defending. It's one of the cornerstones of a vibrant democracy. It is one of our most precious inalienable rights as human beings.

To put the world right in order, we must first put the nation in order; to put the nation in order, we must first put the family in order; to put the family in order, we must first cultivate our personal life; we must first set our hearts right.
—Confucius

1
CHOICES

Life doesn't always turn out the way we expect

In December 2000, in defiance of international law, my husband Kerry, then the managing director of a British security company based in Laos, was abducted from his office by secret police. His captors stole him away to an undisclosed location. Their aim: to get a credible witness to support their illegal nationalisation of a US$2 billion sapphire-mining company—Gem Mining Lao (GML). If Kerry Danes said GML was unlawful, then the international community in Laos would believe him. No one would ask any questions and the rag-tag group of corrupt government officials would get rich quick. But when their attempts at brutality failed, I was next to be targeted.

The Lao secret police thought that with his wife, Kay, in custody, Kerry would have no other choice but to sign a false statement and they'd get rich. Little did they know Kerry Danes had spent the last 20 years in service to the Australian Special Forces, the elite Special Air Service Regiment (SAS). He was extensively trained to resist interrogation.

Taking the job in Laos had given my husband Kerry an opportunity to clear two years of long service leave from the Australian Defence Force (ADF). This on the back end of his return to Australian from military operations in Kuwait. The Army Chief of Staff granted him approval to work in the communist state of Laos, so long as he didn't train anyone in *Special Forces Tactics*. It would almost be like a sabbatical away from the hectic pace and danger of SAS life. At least, that is what it was supposed to be.

I worked at Lao Securicor with Kerry as his administration manager and I planned on staying with the company up until December 2000. Kerry was due back in Australia on 4 January 2001, at which time he would decide whether or not to return to military service or to join me in Bangkok, where my bodyguard company was now flourishing. I subcontracted former elite military and police officers to provide close protection for foreign executives operating in hostile corporate environments within South East Asia. From time to time, my Thai company even provided services to Kerry's employers, Jardine Securicor, when they needed a security capability of close personal protection. This was an area they had not tapped into, whereas I had access to the King of Thailand's own personal bodyguards.

Looking back on our hostage ordeal in Laos, I imagine that our captors regretted the day they ever detained us in their rat-infested death camp. After all, our case publicly exposed them and their corrupt dealings to the international community and to their own President. Our case had a significant impact on the country's economy. It caused some foreign aid donors to withhold aid and others to seriously question whether they would continue to give aid if the Lao government was going to allow such incidents to occur.

President Khamtay Siphandone agreed on the only solution that would enable us to return home with our integrity intact. He granted us an unprecedented Presidential Pardon.

Some months later, those corrupt officials who had orchestrated our detainment were expelled from public office, or were demoted from their once-prominent positions. They had underestimated our ability to endure their torture and ill-treatment of 10 months in prison. They had underestimated our strength and integrity to withstand false and very public accusations. They had underestimated our government too, which fully supported our innocence throughout the entire ordeal and stopped at nothing to bring us home.

We returned to our three children on 9 November 2001 and to a 200-strong media contingent wanting to understand why we hadn't just given in and signed the false statements, so that we could come home. Nothing could ever be as simple as that, especially for two determined people like Kerry and I, who are not, were not and never will be prepared to compromise our integrity for any reason. The fact that Kerry and I were granted an unprecedented Presidential Pardon did nothing to fully restore our reputations. Because of the one-sided media coverage and a general public who didn't have all the facts, some people believed we were involved in something sinister. The media reported what they thought would sell newspapers. To them a headline such as *Australian Couple Accused of Gem Theft* was more attention grabbing than the closer truth *Australians held hostage*!

Where there is smoke, there is fire, they say. This is surely a very lazy way of thinking and is responsible for many injustices in our world. I couldn't understand how anyone could believe what our captors released to the media: that I had attempted to smuggle 160 kilograms of sapphires in my underwear while dragging two frightened children across the border, and somehow passing this off without anybody noticing. As I said, lazy thinking and quite preposterous.

When Kerry and I finally made it home, our world had changed. I heard people talking about '9/11' and wondered why they got so upset over a telephone number. That was until we learned about the terrorist attack on the World Trade Centre. We also learned that my bodyguard company in Thailand was in financial ruins.

While we were in prison in Laos, I had entrusted the management of my company to Kerry's older brother, Leslie. In the space of 10 short months, my company's accounts were emptied. He and my former subcontractors and another close friend started a new company. They convinced my clients that I was agreeable to them signing existing contracts over to their new company. I was left with nothing except a set of company spreadsheets that revealed massive expenditures written off as 'loans' that were never repaid and one entry that made me blink twice, a $250,000 entertainment expense.

Losing the money didn't bother me nearly as much as knowing that we had been betrayed by family, by those we'd trusted and thought we could rely on in tough times. Being betrayed by my brother-in-law, at my most vulnerable, was more heart-wrenching, more soul-destroying, than any of the ten months of torture in a communist prison. It took me years to get over the hurt, anger and betrayal. At one point, I almost sought my betrayers out to inflict as much pain on them as they had on me. The only thing that stopped me was the fact that my children had suffered enough. Fortunately, I was married to someone who understood my pain; after all, Kerry was feeling similar rage towards his brother. To this day we have nothing to do with him. However, on the upside, I now have a much better understanding of just how far mental anguish can push a person. I was determined not to be knocked out of life by people who didn't matter and so began the long and painful journey of restoring my mind and what was left of my faith in the human race.

In October 2007, I received a telephone call from our local federal member of parliament, Andrew Laming. He informed me that the then Australian Foreign Minister, Alexander Downer, was arriving in Brisbane in the lead-up to the federal election. Andrew kindly invited me to introduce Mr Downer at a local community event. He knew how much this would mean to both my family and me. I was excited because I had been waiting six years for the opportunity to meet Mr Downer face to face and thank him personally for all he had done for us. I had written and spoken to him on the phone but it wasn't the same as expressing my gratitude and that of my family to him in person.

It was an amazing event and I was humbled when, after I had introduced Mr Downer to his constituents, he proceeded to tell them just how much effort the Australian government had put into securing our release and why. 'Kerry and Kay Danes were completely innocent, unjustly detained in Laos, and when innocent Australians are detained overseas, the Australian government will do whatever it can to bring them home' said Mr Downer.

My spirits and self-esteem soared when Mr Downer told everyone we were worth fighting for. It was a special moment for my children and me.

People often ask me now if Kerry and I are still married. Did the ordeal in Laos put a strain on our marriage? Do I blame him for what happened? What's he doing now? Have our children recovered from the nightmare of losing both parents for so long? What am I doing? I tell them that Kerry and I still feel the same way about each other as we did when we first met. We are soulmates. The Laos ordeal has not affected our marriage other than to remind us how fortunate we are to have such a solid marriage that can withstand such intense pressures. As for blaming him, I could never do that. What happened to us was unjust and out of our control. We could only control the choices we made in that situation. My husband is my rock. He's the most remarkable man I know and I don't know anyone who has more integrity. As for what Kerry is doing now, he returned to the Australian Special Forces, was promoted to the rank of Regimental Sergeant Major, and has more medals on his uniform than ever before. He's enjoying life immensely and that's about all I can say about that. Our eldest daughter, Jessica, works for a company as an IT technician. Our second eldest daughter, Sahra, is a senior hair stylist in a busy city salon. She and her partner are having a baby this September (2011)—our first grandchild. Our son Nathan graduated from Senior High School in 2010 with a fantastic result and is working towards a music career. As for me, I swapped the high-powered executive life as a director of a bodyguard company for something a little more sedate. After clawing my way back to life from the flashbacks and anxiety attacks, I found my old self bursting to return. I wanted to be able to go outside my door again without fearing that something bad would happen. So when Diana Tacey, the director of an American charity called The Childlight Foundation, contacted me and asked if I would like to accompany her on a Humanitarian Aid mission to Afghanistan, I accepted. I documented this journey in *Beneath the Pale Blue Burqa* (2010). We travelled the ancient silk route through Taliban strongholds in a dusty Toyota Hiace. Myself, Diana, John Dell, Judy Hutcherson and Chris Dickinson. We delivered life-changing aid to people devastated by war. It was an incredible experience and has reawakened my desire to live a full life, beyond fear. The western media tend to give a snapshot of Afghanistan that focuses only on one aspect, the war. I wanted to show people the other side, the progress being made, the hope, the courage and resilience of the people.

In my spare time I have addressed several US Congressional forums on democracy, the US National Press Club, and the Conference on World Affairs, with an audience of 91,000, previously attended by Eleanor Roosevelt and US Vice-President Joe Biden. I have provided consultation to many, including the Australian Institute of Export, the National Human Rights Commission of Australia on the treatment of people under arrest or detained in prison, the Joint Standing Committee on Treaties, and the secretary to the UN Special Rapporteur on Torture (promotion and protection of human rights and fundamental freedoms while countering terrorism and torture).

In 2011, I completed a Diploma in Professional Writing and Editing, a TESOL course (Teaching English to Speakers of Other Languages) and I was named number 9 of 50 of Australia's Iconic Women. So much for taking it easy!

I use my experiences whenever I can to help create awareness about injustice, social issues, personal safety and overcoming adversity. I believe that the choices we make have an indelible effect on the quality of our lives. It has certainly been the case for me. I no longer fear the unknown. We make choices every day to determine our future. Many Christians would say 'you reap what you sow'. I believe that while that may be true for many things, some people have very little choice in determining where they are heading. Not everything that happens to us is always a result of our choices. We do not decide our gender, race, culture, community, family and the status into which we are born. Furthermore, the choices others make can have an impact on our lives both positively and adversely. We are not merely individuals; we are part of the very complex web of humanity.

I used to think that everything in life happens because of fate or predestination and that we cannot change our destiny. However, Karma is not about fate or predestination—it's about intentional actions producing a particular effect. Nevertheless, some things are completely random.

Sometimes choices are quite difficult and sometimes they become impossible. Teenagers, for example, often want to join a particular social group but their friends don't agree with their choice. They become isolated. They might really want to hang out down at the shopping mall with the 'in crowd' but their parents rant and rave and they'll only get into trouble if they do. They become frustrated. Some teens want to smoke cigarettes or drink alcohol simply because their friends are doing it. They want to rebel against social constraints and conformity. Others might spray-paint their neighbour's fence to release some inner artistic demon longing to be born or because everyone will think they're so cool because they weren't caught.

Adults too make choices that aren't necessarily well planned. For example, Australians owe more than $30 billion on their credit cards. Without negating the impact of addiction issues, this is essentially adults choosing their own financial ruin through consumption beyond their income level.

More than 14 million people in America abuse alcohol, which is one in every 13 adults. MPs in Britain warn that the scale of the gambling problem in the UK could be as serious as that of heroin addiction. For every action there is an equal and opposite reaction. The choices we make always have outcomes; some intended, some unintended. The unintended consequences of our actions can sometimes cause the greatest upheaval in our lives.

As a survivor of torture and unlawful foreign imprisonment, I know first-hand what it is like to both endure and overcome. The experiences I have lived through enable me to empathise with others who endure or have endured tragedy and injustice.

Many of the families I come into contact with are just ordinary families from ordinary communities. They, however, each carry a heavy burden. They suffer in silence because they feel there is no one who could possibly understand what they are going through. Some families have very little support in their community. Many know nothing of international law, criminal investigation, arrest, foreign judicial process or government relations. Realistically, how many people in our community have in-depth knowledge and experience in these areas? Many families, whose loved ones are detained overseas, often struggle to cope. Their dilemma may not appeal to those around them. It may create fear in the minds of others, embarrassment, or simply a desire not to be involved.

Having been where many of these families are now, caught between uncertainty and disbelief, I feel I can help them through their dark struggles. Of course, I can't change what they have been through or are going through, but by caring and helping them to identify sources of support, it might just be that lifeline to get them through the toughest times. Maybe things would have been less traumatic for my family had there been someone like me, helping and caring for them. Going through an ordeal with someone who has had first-hand experience and is on the same level can be tremendously comforting. I have made extensive contacts in many government, law enforcement and security agencies over the years and I am proud to be able to use my experience and knowledge to help others, if they want my help.

I believe that people who do wrong should be held accountable, but that the punishment needs to fit the crime. It needs to take into consideration all the complex issues relevant to corrections and imprisonment, social justice, civil rights and human rights. There are many people sitting in prisons round the world, enduring terrible hardships, wondering how on earth they ended up there. At the same time there are many more people wondering how they were caught!

When I look at a person, I see them first and foremost as a human being, not as some label they've been given. While I don't condone criminal actions or support acts of aggression, I believe it is inevitable that humans will continue to make mistakes and poor choices and so too will others who make decisions that impact on us. We just need to manage this reality as best we can. I believe there is a continuum of wrongdoing from innocent to guilty. There are those who have every intention of doing evil and simply don't care who they hurt and no form of rehabilitation has proved effective. These people need to be isolated from society and closely monitored, not necessarily as a punitive measure, but more to protect the innocent from harm.

One of my aims has been to create greater awareness about human, civil and legal rights and how they impact on our everyday lives. People must be prepared for possible personal risks which they may encounter abroad, perhaps on a visit investigating new markets for business or simply travelling on holidays. Through my experiences, coupled with my extensive security background, I am well qualified to impart valuable insight that will help prepare others and alert them to the inherent risks when travelling or working overseas.

Each year, over 30,000 Australians require consular assistance from overseas missions. Each year almost 1000 Australians are arrested overseas and about 220 are in prisons overseas at any one time. Being detained or jailed overseas, or having one of your relatives or friends arrested and in prison overseas, can be very traumatic, distressing and frightening. Prison conditions in many countries can be significantly harsher than those in Australia. According to the Universal Declaration of Human Rights, there are rights and freedoms to which all humans are entitled, but what does this mean in REALITY and how does it apply to everyday citizens? Chances are, most of us will never face the terror of being held hostage, but for aid workers and travellers, the risks are increasing. Whether someone's next journey is prison or paradise, I would like to encourage people to think about the choices they make before they risk the unintended consequences. A split-second decision or failure to really think about the consequences can change their lives forever.

With my own experience of surviving unlawful detainment and torture in a foreign prison, I would like to inspire those I come into contact with on a more personal level. To those seeking support, I wish to help them find a way to accept that while the struggle seems insurmountable, it can be endured. I believe that we each have the ability to prevail if we truly dedicate ourselves to that aim. The measure of a humane society is how it treats its most vulnerable members. We should care about those in our community who are less strong, those who are persecuted, those who are sick, the lonely and those who for whom every day is an enormous uphill struggle. No, we are not our brothers' keepers, but we should take the time to care. As humans, we should never lose sight of who we are, where we have come from, what we have endured, and what we can offer to others.

Sadly, some people, as a result of the choices they have made, may never have an opportunity to make another choice. Some people face a frightful legalised death because of their choices. I know of a 19-year-old on death row who thought he'd only get six months for drug trafficking. It's horrible to think that this kid may lose his life because of his own stupidity. Like so many 'drug mules' he was a pawn in a much bigger game, a game that will not even falter as a result of his death. As the researchers keep telling us, no prospective 'drug mule' will be deterred by this young man's impending death. What an unforgivable waste of a promising young life. And how tragic for the family of the person who buys into the death sentence that the dealers of death are selling. There are no winners in that game.

I've known many young kids who have fallen by the wayside. Some of them on death row and some of them already dead. What might happen overseas, in a far off court, inevitably has an effect back home, particularly on those left behind to pick up the pieces. Easy money always comes at a price and it's important to share this message with others. It's important for others to truly understand that to lose your freedom (and in many cases your life) to make someone else, who is not prepared to take those same risks, rich, is dumb. The families they leave behind, or are separated from for years, always pay a heavy price. These people are ordinary mums and dads, brothers and sisters, who cannot understand why things turned out the way they did. They don't know how they'll face another day, knowing their loved one is gone forever. Maybe their loved one faces a 50-year sentence for a first offence. Maybe their son, brother, husband, daughter, whoever, has disappeared without a trace, in the absence of a crime. The family sits and wonders—'Why?'

Every parent's worst fear is losing a child. That your child is branded a criminal is just another knife in your heart. To some people the fact that your son has been sentenced to death and will be shot through the heart or pumped full of potassium chloride in an execution chamber is not the issue. Ordinarily compassionate people when they hear the words 'prison,' or 'criminal,' tend to harden their hearts. Regardless, parents agonise when their child hits rock bottom and are deeply hurt when others ridicule them for believing that their child may still be capable of getting back up and contributing to life in a positive and meaningful way. We all make mistakes and the majority of us can and do learn from them. That is human nature. We can also learn to put our troubles aside for a moment and extend a helping hand to someone who is down on their luck or in way over their head. It makes the world not as cold and harsh as it sometimes seems.

Life requires us to make the best choices we can.

Personally, I am inspired by people who know what it is like to walk in the shadows. I've walked there too. I have endured the same frustrations that many in this book describe and it is a terrifying dark place to have to live in, day in, day out. These families have spent many thousands of hours walking in the shadows. Their lives have been shattered and they wonder if they will ever be normal again. These families often question over and over whether they could have done something to prevent the nightmare they now face. If they could have helped their loved one make a different choice with fewer consequences, they would have. If they had paid the ransom money then maybe their loved one would be home. If they'd not protested against a totalitarian regime. If they'd stopped their son from boarding that plane. Their hope, and mine, is that more people will try to understand what it is like to endure hardships that most do not ever face, to walk a mile in their shoes, and to remember that 'there, but by the grace of God, go I.'

2
NEGOTIATING THE MINEFIELD

Valuable information for families

> *Metaphorically speaking, in life we are always crossing bridges, always paying tolls, always heading towards someone or something. There may be detours, sending us off in other directions, and yellow signs saying Caution. Other signs say Dead End, Go Back! What if there's no going back? What if we miss a turn and head off in the wrong direction? What if our tyre blows out and we swerve to avoid danger and find ourselves in a ditch?*

Our lives are pretty much like that. It's easy to accept that things like this happen because they happen all the time to us or to people we know. However, are we humble enough to apply that same sort of scenario to those who falter, veer too far left, end up in a ditch and in need of some assistance? Can we manage to care enough for others to look beyond the wreckage and see the victims inside, even if it is by their own doing?

Punish the *prisoner* if you must, but don't abuse the *prisoner's family*, after all, you never know when someone you love falls foul of the law, or is taken hostage, or kidnapped by a foreign government.

Not all prisoners are criminals. Some like the former South African prisoner Nelson Mandela or pro-democracy Burma leader Aung San Suu Kyi stood firmly on the principles of justice. The belief that all human beings are born free and equal in dignity and rights. That all humans are endowed with reason and conscience and should act towards one another in a spirit of brotherhood. This is the inherent dignity of being human. The equal and inalienable rights of all members of the human family is the foundation of freedom, justice and peace in the world. All humans are deemed to be equal before the law and should be entitled, without any discrimination, to equal protection of the law. No one should be subjected to arbitrary arrest, detention or exile. No one should be subjected to torture or to cruel, inhuman or degrading treatment or punishment. Everyone should be entitled to full equality, to a fair and public hearing by an independent and impartial tribunal, in the determination of their rights and obligations and of any criminal charge against them. Everyone charged with a penal offence should have the right to be presumed innocent until proved guilty. Everyone who is judged should be judged fairly.

These are the principles supported by our great leaders, by our clergymen, by our governments and to which I espouse, whenever helping families navigate their way through the diplomatic minefield of foreign internment.

When a family learns that one of their own has been detained in a foreign prison, they feel like they've been caught in a car wreck. Suddenly, they are surrounded by carnage. They stumble around, disoriented and confused, looking for a hand that will guide them to safety. They suffer shock and guilt. The shock of finding out that their loved one may not be who or where they thought they were. In fact, they're half a world away and the family has no idea how or why they got there, or the details of their arrest.

Hearing that someone you love has been arrested, often thousands of miles from home, can turn your world completely and utterly upside down and inside out. Families may experience a number of physical responses to this distressing news. They may experience dizziness on hearing that their loved one may face a firing squad for their crime. They may even lose consciousness as the mind denies reality and refuses to face the facts because these are too painful. Common physical reactions are nausea at the very thought of what the loved one may have done, panic at wondering how they will deal with the emotional and financial impact this situation will present. However, the survival mechanism kicks in. The little voice inside their head tells them that they have to act. Now is not the time to fall apart.

Politics and diplomacy play a large part in any prisoner's life. Learning to understand unfamiliar systems and procedures can be distressing and frightening for both prisoner and their family. They need to know when to move, how to make that move, know what to say and how to say it most effectively. Foremost, the family of a prisoner abroad should familiarise themselves with the various protocols and policies relating to overseas internment. These can all be found in the Consular Services Charter which is available through any foreign affairs department.

Why do you need to know all this? Most governments, not all, act in accordance with certain protocols consistent with the Vienna Convention on Consular Relations. There is a general process that is set in motion whenever a person is arrested in a country other than their own. If the detaining state abides by international law then its government will uphold its obligation to report to the prisoner's country, generally within 24 hours, that they have detained a foreign national. Not all countries/states have embassies in every country. They have to be invited and then accept to operate in a foreign state. They also need to abide by the protocols set by both foreign state and their own respective governments.

What if there's no embassy in the country where your loved one is detained? Sometimes other embassies have mutual assistance type agreements. For example, there is no British embassy in Laos. However, the Australian embassy provides support to all Commonwealth citizens, including New Zealand and Canada. Consular officers (consuls) are assigned to each embassy. As the diplomatic arm of the embassies and governments they represent, they are bound by strict protocol. Without good bilateral relations, gaining consular access to prisoners would be even more difficult, if not impossible. The strict protocols keep these more macro-relationships manageable.

When consuls are notified by the detaining state that it has detained a foreign national, Consuls are usually, although not always, granted access quite soon after the arrest. In the course of their interview with the prisoner, consuls ascertain such things as:

How the prisoner is being treated?

Does the prisoner have any immediate medical or other concerns?

Who is their next of kin? Is there any information the prisoner does not want released to them?

Does the prisoner have a lawyer?

Do they have someone they wish the consul to contact to liaise with authorities on their behalf?

Consuls are responsible for custodial matters relating to their client, the prisoner, not the family. Consuls who have permission to disclose information to families do so in 'consular reports'. These reports are still considered privileged information and are protected under the Privacy Act.

Consuls do not have extensive powers, but they can offer a wide range of consular services in a detaining state and those services are vital. They can provide advice and support in the case of an accident, serious illness or death and sometimes even some limited financial assistance in real emergencies (subject to very strict criteria). During crises, such as civil unrest and natural disasters, consuls can provide a list of local doctors and lawyers. They can also provide the latest consular travel advice, which includes information about security and health conditions in many parts of the world. They can witness and certify signatures, provide certain other services relating to the preparation of applications for pardons, transfers and the like, and issue passports, including emergency passports.

Equally, there are services that consuls cannot provide. They cannot arrange visas, work or residence permits for other countries, or help a person to obtain them. They cannot give legal advice, intervene in court proceedings, provide funds to pay legal costs or fines, get a person out of prison, or obtain special treatment for them in prison. They cannot pay or guarantee payment of a person's hotel, medical or any other bills, including the cost of returning lost luggage.

They cannot act as a travel agent, bank or post office, store luggage or become involved in commercial disputes, take up complaints about local purchases, provide translation, interpreter, telephone or photocopy services or pay pensions. They cannot investigate crimes in foreign countries. This is something that only law enforcement agencies can do because it also comes down to jurisdiction. The Privacy Act prevents embassies from disclosing information to others without the express permission of the prisoner. The family will need permission from the prisoner to enable the embassy to waive specific privacy rights. Even if a person has a valid interest in a prisoner's welfare, like all citizens, prisoners' rights are protected under the Privacy Act.

Sometimes the prisoner does not want family or friends notified (for any number of reasons). In such cases, consuls are required by law to maintain that prisoner's privacy and can alert only the appropriate government and law enforcement personnel. Sometimes the next of kin are frustrated, 'The department won't tell me anything'. Sometimes it's not that 'they're not doing enough' but more about what they can and cannot do. Not everyone seeking information about a prisoner has good intentions. Drug dealers may be looking to contact their wayward drug mules. I often get emails from people asking me for case details on their cousin detained in a foreign prison (only they can't remember their cousin's full name). In such cases, I always alert the prisoner's embassy just in case something is going on that I don't know about. An exception to the rule of disclosure may be if a prisoner is seriously ill and is incapable of giving their consent or is not in a rational state of mind, injured or hospitalised and is not able to give consent. Then the consulate may inform the next of kin, if it feels it is essential to do so.

Consular officials understand that families are unprepared to deal with the emotional trauma of having a loved one detained overseas. Those officers I have met over the years in various embassies appreciate the failings and frustrations relating to the process of prisoner support and empathise with the family's frustrations dealing with foreign judiciaries. I've often heard families say how frustrated they have become when dealing with their government's foreign affairs department. With something as complex and emotional as the detention of a loved one overseas, frustration with bureaucratic processes is often amplified. The family of a person detained abroad needs to learn how to understand 'diplomatic speak' and how to speak it fluently. For example, 'we are dissatisfied with the process which resulted in the conviction and sentencing' translates as 'they never had a fair trial and we know it'. Hopefully the matter can be resolved at the appeal process. Part of understanding diplomatic speak comes from knowing what to listen for, and hearing what is important. What a diplomat doesn't say can be more revealing than what they do say.

Families cannot and should not be expected to have all the answers. After all, without prior experience of such things, it is very difficult for them to know which way to turn and who to trust.

As they will discover, many will offer advice but too few will offer the right advice. Given the tremendous pressure that the family is under, it makes sense to appoint an experienced, independent advisor to act as liaison between government and family. Choosing the right legal representation is vital. The family lawyer who has helped over the years to arrange mortgages and draft wills may be a good choice as an independent advisor, but he/she may not have any experience in undertaking an international legal proceeding. This type of service is a specialty and finding the right lawyer can be difficult. The family needs to be very careful who they choose as legal support for the detainee. They need to do more research than merely scrolling down a list and signing with the first lawyer who answers the phone. The best advice for the family is to consider getting a personal referral from another lawyer. There may be a lawyer in your hometown whose specialty is in foreign investment in the detaining state. They may be able to recommend a criminal defence attorney, and this may be a good place to start.

Don't ever just select a lawyer on hearsay. Check out their credentials, try to contact their former clients if possible and learn as much as you can about them to see if they are suitable to your situation. There is never a shortage of in-house prison lawyers. That is an inmate who has a certain amount of legal knowledge. They may have been a practising lawyer at some stage but it is highly doubtful that their licence would be current. Then why are they in prison? Maybe they have no formal legal training but think they know the system.

The embassy can provide a list of lawyers who are approved by the country's judiciary to represent prisoners. However, be aware that just because the embassy has given details of their service, is not in any way a guarantee or endorsement of that service. The embassy assumes no responsibility for the professional ability or integrity of the lawyers on their lists. There are literally hundreds of thousands of lawyers practising law internationally in various fields ranging from human and civil rights law, corporate and commercial law, criminal law, tort law, intellectual property rights, immigration law, and tax law, just to name a few. The family may think they are getting the best lawyer in the world but then discover that they cannot guarantee the outcome the family were hoping for, or justly deserve.

Sometimes governments and judicial authorities of a detaining state don't always play by their legislated rules. Any lawyer promising a good outcome because of their abilities and special connections alone is not one I would hire. What is essential is that the lawyer has the humility, flexibility, cultural awareness and wherewithal to adjust to the legal environment of the jurisdiction in which the detainee is held. Arrogance and cultural myopia on the part of the legal representative will not benefit the detainee. The lawyer must evaluate the strength of the prosecution's case before deciding how best to proceed.

Granted, a prisoner may still do some jail time but an effective lawyer may have secured a better result. It's important to remember that when charged in some foreign states, securing a minimum sentence is often better than the alternative. But it's inevitably the choice of the prisoner just how much humble pie they are willing to eat.

I've made it my business to personally get to know as many top lawyers as I can in a variety of countries. Finding the right one for your situation may seem difficult because everyone appears suitably qualified but have they had any experience operating in the country where your loved one is detained?

Have they succeeded in bringing forth successful outcomes to similar cases?

Do they have in-country networks?

These are just some of the questions you need to ask. However, no one can guarantee results. It is impossible to guarantee anything when dealing with foreign entities.

When Kerry and I were unlawfully detained in Laos, we weren't able to appoint a lawyer because we were isolated from everyone, including our embassy. So it was up to someone else to engage a lawyer on our behalf and quite a few who raised their hand did so with high expectations. The lawyer we ended up with told us 19 times we were going home. He said he was optimistic. As you can imagine, each one of those 19 assurances that were made and broken were a rollercoaster of hope and despair for us and our family.

A valuable lesson I learned from that experience is to remember that lawyers are not psychologists. They deal in cold legal arguments, not mental health. They have little or no appreciation of how their optimism affects the mental psyche of a prisoner. Despite everything, however, our lawyer effectively put together a summary book of evidence 317 pages long that overwhelmingly supported our innocence. He had it translated and presented to the court. Sadly, the judges never bothered to open it. No one, except the Australian foreign minister, realised at the time that the Lao judicial process did not allow for adversarial proceedings. No one was ever acquitted once charged.

Base your choice on expertise and experience. Choosing the wrong lawyer may complicate an already untenable situation. US Attorney at Law Paul Wolf once told me that when offering advice to families seeking to engage legal support to always tell them to shop around. He concluded by saying: 'Buyer beware!' I've seen many cases, as Paul has with his extensive case load in South America, where families are asked to pay 'compensation' to the lawyer prior to any court proceedings.

The lawyer might say, 'I have an uncle in the department who can fix this quietly' or 'I can guarantee your son/brother/ husband/daughter will be released, but we need to pay the police!' These promises sound good to the desperate, but they are false promises to fill a greedy person's pockets on the misfortune of others. Bribery is recognised as a criminal offence in nearly every country in the world.

Rule number one in any emergency is ensuring your own safety first—and families need to ensure they don't land themselves in hot water trying to get their loved one out. Bribery only leads to more bribery. Those involved in it often don't honour their agreements because as a general rule they have no honour to begin with. (Note this is different to payments sought in some countries where compensation to families is a legal requirement).

Families and prisoners struggle with the thought of putting their lives in another's hands. After all, there are no guarantees that things will work out the way they expect. Even seemingly simple matters are often complex. Sometimes it is not possible for an embassy to gain regular access to a prisoner. This may be for a variety of political, practical or geographical reasons. Prisoners may decide to appoint someone who has earned their trust power of attorney to enable that person to make certain decisions on their behalf. However, to appoint a power of attorney, the prisoner must understand the implications and consequences of what they are doing. If they do not have the capacity to understand this, the appointment will not be legally valid. There are several types of powers of attorney and a prisoner may opt to give full or limited powers to one or several persons. For example, they might give general power of attorney to a person or persons for a specific period of time, to make financial and/or legal decisions on their behalf. They might appoint enduring power of attorney to someone to make long-term decisions where they think they may not be able to continue making decisions themselves. They might appoint someone to have enduring power of guardianship to make lifestyle decisions, for example, where a child is involved. In any case, the prisoner should appoint someone they trust, who knows them well, can make decisions in their best interests and can access information that is not accessible to the general public.

One of our fundamental human rights is the right to freedom of information. I find it ironic that it is so often overlooked, a right which is the touchstone of all the freedoms to which the United Nations is consecrated. This right is enshrined in the Declaration of Human Rights, and numerous countries throughout the world have implemented some form of legislation regarding it. Freedom of Information (FOI) legislation defines a legal process by which government information is available to members of the public. Privacy and data protection laws also form part of the freedom of information legislation. The basic principle behind most freedom of information legislation is that a person requesting information does not usually have to give an explanation for their request.

If, however, the information is not disclosed to them, then a valid reason has to be given. The right to access information underpins all other human rights. It supports the view that where there is transparency, corruption has less opportunity to exist. FOI aims to help hold governments accountable to the people who elect them. It also bolsters the capacity of the media to seek out the truth and expose corruption. In some cases, FOI has provided invaluable evidentiary support to prisoners. In other cases, it has enabled questions to be raised to ascertain the treatment of the prisoner. For example, the requester seeks information on the legality of a prisoner's detention. It also enables families/prisoners to gain access to copies of some, but not all, correspondence from third parties to government relevant to their particular case.

In submitting FOI applications, usually via a lawyer, families can better understand the workings of their case. Sometimes they think they know what happened as their case proceeded to a conclusion but it is often to the contrary. False impressions are inevitable when people don't have all the facts. FOI documents enable families and prisoners to see a much bigger picture. They discover who supported whom, who didn't, who blocked, who facilitated, who tried to help, and who said what, including government to-government dialogue. It's truly astounding what they might learn when they apply for information under the Freedom of Information Act, and more than a little revealing!

You can get more information on FOI from your local state and federal members of parliament (members of congress) or senators. Generally, your government member has responsibilities to three main groups: constituents; the parliament and their political party. The most effective way for the family of a detainee to find the help they need to support their loved one is to be able to convey their needs specifically and appropriately. Too many people rush like a bull at a gate and head straight to the media. What they should do is lay a good solid foundation for when the road gets rocky. Make an appointment with your state and federal parliamentarians and explain your needs. Do not just show up on the off chance that they'll be available to see you. Plan your visit, be focused about what you want and be very clear about what you want your MP to do. Prepare a brief summary (a chronology of events with dates and brief description) and leave that with your MP. And I mean brief! Don't hand over reams of paper as they are seldom read.

Be prepared for politically generic responses and don't be put off or disheartened by them. Staying calm and being diplomatic can increase your chances of winning over those you need to win over to improve the situation of your loved one. Putting a face to a family of a loved one detained in a foreign prison is an important step and should never be underestimated. It's important because the government's representative gets to see your pain, not just read about it in a letter sent a week or so ago.

It is in the family's best interests to at all times be gracious for the time given by others, regardless of the outcome. Sometimes having a federal MP in your corner can unload a lot of the emotional burden from a family. Sometimes it's easier dealing with the local federal MP and having him or her making representations on your behalf than dealing with the bureaucracy itself. Your MP will be able to advise you on how best to lobby government to get the support both you and the prisoner need. In foreign relations a government has three main priorities: to maintain good bilateral relationships; to protect favourable trade relations; and to ensure regional stability. A government is rarely going to be prepared to jeopardise these priorities for an individual prisoner, even if that prisoner is innocent.

The media can be a useful tool if used the right way. It can help raise public awareness where needed about the plight of the prisoner. For example, it may generate interest from influential people who can apply pressure on your government to act quickly and in the interests of protecting a prisoner's rights. It may highlight the consequences of being detained overseas, the conditions and treatment. Remember, however, that with every positive there is also a negative. Unwanted public scrutiny could negatively affect the economics of a country and damage much-needed tourism.

If you do decide to engage the media, then appoint a media advisor. It needs to be someone who can calmly articulate responses and preferably someone outside the family i.e. a lawyer or professional advocate. An advisor can ensure that the appropriate information is accurately conveyed to the media in accordance with a proper legal strategy. They can ensure the family is not overwhelmed or bullied into terms with which they are not comfortable. The advisor can deal with the complexities of diplomacy and campaigning and, where a case is high profile, can negotiate contracts associated with exclusivity and organise settlements, where practical, that might assist families with travel and ongoing legal costs relating to the case. Before families get involved with the media they should certainly weigh up the pros and cons. They must decide whether or not they truly want to have their lives put under a microscope and made public. More often than not, that is exactly what happens.

Always remember that the job of a journalist is to get the best story they can. They can print anything the family says, whether they want them to or not. Generally, the more sensational the story, the greater interest they have to dig deeper. The media may not portray your loved one in the way you want them portrayed. Remember too that nothing is ever 'off the record'. People have found that they have been quoted when they thought they were talking 'off the record'. Some have seen their story sensationalised, all for a good story or attention-grabbing headline. You may be disappointed with what is actually printed.

You might have signed off on a headline: 'Couple Held Hostage by Corrupt Government' only to read the actual print on the front page the following morning: 'Couple Caught in Million Dollar Gem Heist'. Or perhaps you never signed off on anything at all. Most stories are written without the prisoner's involvement or consent. Labels have a tendency to stick and your family and your plight will become public property. You will be on show in your community. This may be all to the good and may generate support. Remember, however, that the publicity may be so negative and destructive that you may have to relocate, as has been the outcome in some cases.

The sad fact is that prisoners and their families have no control over the amount of media coverage they receive. The repercussions of this may affect the prisoner and not always for the best. Media pressure will rarely get their loved one liberated. Shouting the loudest doesn't always work. In fact, quite often it has the opposite effect. It can escalate to become a highly charged, political profile which will then guarantee government-to government negotiations with no guarantee that the decisions made will be in the prisoner's favour. Any campaign is best conducted with the utmost of integrity. Maintain the high moral ground and seldom can you go wrong.

Without exception, a family's trauma will be met with a mixed response by those around them. People you have never met will come and offer selfless assistance or prey on your vulnerability. New relationships will form, relationships will crumble, but some will survive and be the stronger for it.

Today you can cross international borders with the click of a mouse. Network in whatever way you can to get the help you need. Use every resource you can lay your hands on—the library, the internet—contact human rights organisations, prisoner advocacy groups, civil liberties groups. Google for help and advice. If you are a church-goer ask your local priest or minister if they can put you in touch with local resources. Many churches have prison missions and overseas programs in place in most parts of the world. Their services might include liaising with prison staff to arrange a visit and, where possible and if appropriate, establish in-country support. They might also provide funds to send literature into the prisons. Others may offer to include your loved one on 'prayer chains'—praying for their continued endurance. It is a steep and terrifying learning curve for the family, which can often seem that you have to learn it all overnight. Something as simple as making a phone call or writing a letter can be fraught with difficulty and obstructions. In many cases, prisoners are not allowed to write letters or make phone calls. Very few people tend to consider these practical elements.

The financial impact on a family, struggling to provide basic care to their loved one thousands of miles away, accused of a crime, is often enormous. These families usually discover the hard way that few people genuinely care about their plight, especially if their loved one has been accused of drug trafficking and the like. To the family it can feel like more isolation or being ostracised when they are already facing a nightmare.

We haven't even got to the practical hurdles of providing basic care to their loved one detained in prison. We haven't even discussed that they might be detained in something far less functional than a modern, hygienic prison and one that is not close to consular services. Aside from facing social difficulties, providing basic care is more difficult than most people think. Food and clean drinking water become luxuries. In some prisons they don't provide them at all or only at inflated prices that are almost impossible for prisoners to afford, especially those who have little to no access to financial support. In most prisons in developing countries, the tap water is undrinkable. It's often not considered safe enough to bathe in or wash clothes in. Hot water for drinking is not always available either because the prisoner may not have access to funds to pay for the heating. A simple bottle of drinking water each day can equate to thousands of dollars over a lengthy incarceration period, and that's just the tip of the iceberg.

'Here in Bangkwang Prison, water is heated for drinking and cooking over primitive charcoal stoves which must be purchased by prisoners from the prison shop. There is no hot water provided for washing, showering or laundry. Cold, filthy brown river water is pumped into a communal trough and is the only water available for showering or laundering clothes. Money, that is, cash, is essential in a Thai prison. Yet possession of cash is illegal and a punishable offence, which is convenient for the guards when they want to relieve you of a little of it.' —UK prisoner **Steve Wilcox**.

Prisoners who have access to money will always be better off than prisoners who don't. Prisoners might access funds via their embassy, i.e.: a prisoner loan scheme whereby their government may provide limited funds to them during their internment or the prisoner might have family who send them money via their embassy (generally via Western Union transfers). Depending on the prison regulations, family members might visit the prison and deposit funds directly into the prisoner's account or, if they are lucky to have in-country support (i.e. friend or missionary), then that person could act as the conduit for funds transfer. At no time should anyone attempt to send cash via the mail because often mail is read before it reaches the prisoner and any cash would in all probability be confiscated. Similarly, money orders, personal cheques etc. generally, if accepted, should be produced in the local currency. International postage coupons are not always accepted.

Depending on the prison regulations, prisoners may be able to arrange limited telephone contact or the delivery of mail (care packages including clothing, medicines, reading material, etc) via the prison or via their embassy. Usually the embassy will not receive care packages but they may advise an alternative. Some embassies are also located a considerable distance from prisons and it may not be practical for them to make regular visits.

In those instances, family members must seek to establish local contacts and, as you can imagine, this is often fraught with difficulties. The best and safest way of engaging local support is always through referral from a reliable source such as an embassy, law firm, human rights organisation or church group. In most instances, prisons have their own in-house prison stores where prisoners can purchase food and drinking water. Sometimes this must be the sole source of purchase for security reasons. There is a standard minimum treatment of prisoners that most countries have agreed to uphold, so food and water are usually provided as a basic need. (More on this can be found at: http://www2.ohchr.org/english/law/treatmentprisoners.htm). Having said that, the document is only a guide.

As for telephone access, prisoners may or may not be allowed access. Some prisoners have been known to find ways of getting phone access. In one case, a prisoner in Indonesia gained access to a mobile phone by purchasing it directly from a prison officer. The prisoner was able to access the internet and telephone family and friends on a regular basis. Another prisoner in the same jail attempted to do likewise, but when a raid on the prison occurred, that prisoner's phone was seized. The prisoner lost their right to a later sentence reduction, as per the usual end of year remissions for foreigners. Prisons can be complex places. Prison guards might allow a prisoner phone access one day and then deny them the very next day.

Life in a foreign prison presents many additional challenges for prisoners who are usually unfamiliar with language and culture, but it doesn't end there. I once knew a Muslim prisoner who refused, for religious reasons, to eat the prison ration of pig fat water soup. He would have starved to death had the other prisoners, who had access to money, not shown him mercy. They purchased food he could eat that was not offensive to his religion. Without family, embassy or someone on the ground to assist with the provision of practical essentials, prisoners detained in foreign prisons can indeed find themselves in particular life threatening situations. The financial implications of an arrest abroad can be devastating on families too. Families soon discover that they need, at short notice, air tickets, visas, travel insurance, vaccinations and accommodation. That's simply to travel to wherever it is that their loved one has been detained—assuming they are allowed to enter the country and assuming the prison is accessible. Unlike hotels, prisons don't have an open door policy.

Sometimes prisoners are not allowed visitors for months. Others may only be allowed a visit once a week for 15 minutes and, even then, perhaps a complete stranger is granted a visit which may mean that a family member misses out that week. Imagine travelling thousands of miles to see your son then finding out you can't because some Norwegian tourist, who doesn't even know him, was given a visit on the off chance. The tourist may have had the best intentions and might even have taken fresh vegetables and a tin of tobacco, but it doesn't make it any less stressful for a family member who now has to wait for the next available visit. Generally, the family can pre-book visits through their embassy which often prevents these sorts of mishaps from occurring. It's not surprising that many families run into a great deal of debt in a very short amount of time. One family I know spent over $100,000 in a single year just travelling back and forth supplying their loved one's basic needs. Another family were forced to mortgage their house to pay the court imposed fine to the amount of US$150,000 and another family paid $600,000.

Where does the money come from? It is unlikely that families can rely on fundraising dinners or proceeds from raffles because their plight is so unpopular and very few people care. Some are forced to file for bankruptcy when they can no longer sustain the cost of supporting their loved one. Maintaining a prisoner in any jail is a very expensive exercise. It all takes time, so exercise patience. Serious criminal cases take months, if not years, to come to trial, and during this time the prisoner is dependent on their family for the necessities of life. This can be emotionally and financially draining for the family, particularly over the long haul. They'll need to adjust their lives and learn to cope with this new burden. If it seems too difficult at times, that's because it is difficult.

One moment your life seems set and safe and your future guaranteed. Then that phone call comes and your life will never be the same again. Some families find courage in a simple quote, while others find courage in religious texts. Whatever it takes to keep the mind focused. These journeys are distracting, frustrating and at times indefinite. However, one has to remind oneself at such times, as in the words of Abraham Lincoln: 'One of the best things about the future is that it only comes one day at a time.'

3
Bad things do happen to good people

Kay and Kerry Danes, Laos

> *My daughter Kay asked me if I wanted to contribute a chapter for this book from the perspective of having a loved one detained in a foreign prison. Having endured such an experience and knowing that Kay dedicates much of her time trying to help other families throughout the world, I was more than happy to write something about how we did and didn't cope during our ordeal.*

That experience in 2000 and 2001, changed our lives forever. Even today we still sometimes find ourselves reminded of those moments that seemed to last forever. Of course, the gripping details of Kay and Kerry's journey can be found at her website www.kaydanes.com but as Kay says, it's also very important to know another important side of that story—our side. I hope that other families might learn something from our ordeal that might help them endure their own journey. I hope that they come through the struggle which at times feels overwhelming. They say: 'What doesn't kill you makes you stronger.' Sadly, there are times when it just isn't true. Quite honestly, I don't feel stronger, but perhaps we were when we were in the thick of it.

In 1999, my son-in-law, Kerry, took two years extended leave from the army with permission to work in Laos, South-East Asia, as the managing director of Lao Securicor, a Jardine Securicor subsidiary. My daughter Kay joined him a few months later with my three grandchildren, Jessica, Sahra and Nathan. Five months later, Kay was given the job of administration manager, an appointment that was approved by Kerry's employers. I didn't really know much about their work, other than that they provided security services to investors, banks, multi-million dollar corporations and foreign government agencies. They employed local people as static guards and as Kay wrote, some of them had never worn shoes until they issued them a pair. She talked about things like 'risk management' and 'supporting the economic growth of Laos' which went completely over my head. She said they were doing great things and their bosses were really happy with their progress.

A whole year or so passed and our eldest grandchild, Jessica, returned to live with us in Australia because the International School in Vientiane (the capital of Laos) didn't include the last three years of senior high school. Jess said that while she thought that living in Laos had been great, it was pretty boring for teenagers. Sahra and Nathan loved it. They were content to raise their pet Lao ducks and make frequent visits to local markets, the Settha Palace swimming pool and the all-you-can-eat buffet at the Lao Hotel Plaza. Jess, however, missed shopping malls and video arcades.

Being woken in the early hours of the morning two days before Christmas by an international phone call from a stranger telling me Kerry and Kay had been taken by communist secret police, left me completely speechless. What the hell was this man talking about? Was it a prank call? In my dazed state I struggled to form rational thoughts. He must be mistaken! Yet this stranger, who definitely knew my daughter and son-in-law, said they were in grave trouble.

The caller, Mr Jepesson, explained that his company, Gem Mining Lao was being taken over under an illegal nationalisation order. Somehow Kerry and Kay were caught in the middle of this dispute. He said it wasn't a hoax. He said he was deadly serious and that I needed to get them help and do it now!

My mind raced as I tried to make sense of everything. I couldn't understand how Kerry could possibly have been kidnapped. He was a highly trained soldier in the Australian Special Forces—the elite SAS (Special Air Service). Despite this, Kerry had been abducted, and my daughter had been detained by secret police near the border between Laos and Thailand, while trying to get out of the country.

My husband Ernie stood beside me in the dining room of our small three-bedroom home. We lived in the quiet suburbs of Brisbane. The man on the phone spoke slowly as I scribbled his name and contact details on a sheet of paper. Afterwards I hung up the phone, rather shakily, and returned my husband's bewildered expression with my own look of shock. Ernie listened intently. We weren't quite sure who to call. We didn't have the telephone number of anyone in the Australian Army because we had nothing to do with that aspect of Kerry and Kay's life. Then Ernie decided to call the Australian embassy in Canberra. They'd know what to do. He dialled the Australian telephone operator to connect us and as you can imagine, we were confused to learn that there wasn't an embassy to assist us. We were dumbfounded. It must have been some mistake! The wall clock ticked loudly in the background. It's a wonder we could hear it at all, above the blood pounding through our veins. We'd never been in a situation like this before. We were just ordinary people going about our ordinary lives. We were completely out of our depth. We didn't know anything about how our government or its departments worked in these situations, but we knew they must have some idea what to do. The telephone operator then quietly asked us the nature of our problem.

We told her politely that we couldn't give her any specific details, other than that our daughter was overseas and needed assistance urgently. That's when we were told about the Department of Foreign Affairs and Trade (DFAT). Apparently they help thousands of Australians overseas each year and are available 24 hours a day. Imagine how relieved we were to hear about these 'DFAT people'! The operator gave us their hotline number.

Ernie called it immediately. DFAT had already been informed of the situation through their embassy staff in Laos, who were with Kay when she was detained at the border. It was a relief to hear that Australian government officials were with Kay at that time. It offered some comfort that they knew what was happening to Kay at least, however little comfort that no one knew where Kerry had disappeared to. They also advised that the children were being cared for by Kerry's sister-in-law Marina, who also lived in Laos at that time. I knew of Marina from conversations with Kay. We were relieved that the children were with a relative rather than strangers. DFAT staff explained that the Australian embassy in Laos had informed them of Kay and Kerry's abduction and were taking the matter very seriously.

Throughout the days, weeks and months that followed, DFAT, in particular Keith Gardner and John Judge lifted a great burden from our shoulders. Australia's foreign minister at the time, Alexander Downer, appointed Keith and John to assist our family directly. They seemed to be available to us whenever we needed them. Their calm demeanour and experience put us instantly at ease. It was good to know that help was only a phone call away. We must have driven them crazy with all our endless frustrations, emotional outbursts and constant demands for more information, but the DFAT staff always seemed to understand. They rang frequently to keep us informed, even when there was nothing much to report. To me they were like our very own lifelines to Kay and Kerry. I appreciated that they even talked to my husband about fishing and other trivial things he liked to do. In many ways, it helped take his mind off things, which was tremendously thoughtful of them.

On 25 December 2000, the Australian government secretly evacuated Sahra and Nathan out of Laos. Kay's phone call on Christmas morning was extremely distressing. She'd made the call using Kerry's mobile phone secretly hidden during her first two days of detainment. Her eldest daughter Jess spoke to Kay, 'It's okay, Mum. It will be okay. Don't worry I will look after them when they get here. We will be okay. Don't cry, Mum.'

Kay told Jess that her brother and sister, Sahra and Nathan, were being secretly evacuated by Australian embassy staff. When Jess handed the phone to me, Kay's last words before the phone went dead were: 'I think they're going to kill me ... oh, and Happy Birthday Mum!'

It was a difficult and tense Christmas Day. Ernie suffered terrible anxiety. He couldn't eat or sleep, and I wasn't doing much better. We needed some time to adjust to everything, to get it all into perspective but there wasn't any time for that. I thought about my grandchildren travelling all the way from Laos by themselves, especially on Christmas Day. It was a dreadful thought and one which kept me awake all night.

In the morning, Ernie and I felt as if we'd aged ten years. Our grandchildren were due to arrive at Brisbane Airport by 8:30 am (26 December 2000). We were at the arrivals gate by 8 am. We sat with my granddaughter Jess and my eldest daughter Karen waiting anxiously for the plane to arrive. DFAT had called Ernie late the previous evening to advise us that Sahra and Nathan were entrusted to his care upon arrival, so he had to literally sign for them like taking delivery of a postal package. While waiting, he took Karen aside to give her the latest information from DFAT, which didn't sound very promising—Kay was no longer being detained at the immigration building. She had been moved, but no one knew to where. She'd been taken to wherever Kerry was and that was still 'unknown'. We later learned they were taken to Phonthong Prison.

As a mother, I found the stress of not knowing unbearable. I had to know where my daughter was. Had they hurt her? Had the other prisoners hurt her? Did she have food and water? Years earlier, I had watched a movie called Bangkok Hilton, starring Nicole Kidman. It was about a young Australian woman who went in search of the father she never knew. Her trip took her from Australia to England and then on to Bangkok. There she met a charming young man who asked her to carry some luggage through Thai customs for him. She found herself arrested for drug smuggling and was sentenced and imprisoned in the horrific 'Bangkok Hilton'—a notorious prison. The plot and the characters were completely different and my daughter's situation was real, not some Hollywood movie, but I couldn't help wonder if my daughter was enduring those same primitive conditions.

I remembered times that Kay would ring home and tell me that the Lao people were really friendly and always smiling. She had a great affection for them. She never once had a bad word to say about them, but she did mention that at times it was distressing for her to witness their daily struggle under such an oppressive regime. She was at least glad that what she and Kerry were doing there was making a significant difference to many lives and to the economic development of the country, which was very important to them both, she said. Kerry and Kay had always been dedicated charity workers in Australia, always raising their hand to help someone in need. Were those now detaining her friendly and smiling? I doubted it.

The airport arrivals board showed the plane had landed. Jess and Ernie moved closer to the gate to await their arrival. The rest of us stayed in the background. We thought it would be less overwhelming that way. After all, we hadn't seen our grandchildren for a number of years. Considering the traumatic events they'd recently endured, we all agreed it was a good idea to take things slowly. Our grandchildren appeared relieved to see their elder sister. They hugged her tightly. Sahra and Nathan then turned and hugged Ernie. Of course, Nathan must have felt like he was on a holiday to see his Nan and Pop because at seven years old, he was too young to understand what was going on. Sahra on the other hand was eleven and knew everything that was going on and, as she told us later, she was very reluctant to leave her mother and father in Laos.

Our house was small and Sahra and Nathan had to share a room, but they didn't seem to mind. I think they were just happy to be off the plane that had taken them from Laos to Thailand, on to Sydney and then to Brisbane. Sahra said she was exhausted and needed to sleep. What a brave little girl she was!

As the weeks passed, my anxiety about Kay and Kerry grew so much that my blood pressure went through the roof! By mid-January my doctor wanted to hospitalise me, fearing I'd have a stroke. I refused, so instead I was medicated and confined to bed. I regretted that this created more stress on the family, especially for my grandchildren. They were now burdened with concern about my health too. The children often sat around my bedside just chatting and making sure I was okay. I guess the blessing was that my health concerns distracted us from our other problems, at least for a short time. However, in moments like these, time is your biggest enemy. It goes by so slowly. Every minute is like an hour.

The Australian Ambassador to Laos, Jonathan Thwaites, announced that they had finally secured consular access to Kerry and Kay. It had taken a while to arrange and under normal circumstances, access should have been granted within 48 hours. The usual 'once every three month' visit was extended to once a week, so we weren't complaining. The Ambassador had tried hard to get twice-weekly visits, but the Lao government said it was too much of an overload on their resources. Of course, embassy staff were only ever allowed to see Kay and Kerry separately, but at least that was something. I watched the television that evening for the first images of my daughter and her husband. One of the ABC's foreign correspondents, Geoff Thompson, had managed to get permission to film Kay and Kerry as they arrived at Lao Immigration. Kerry looked rather annoyed and slightly defiant as three armed police officers escorted him to immigration. Geoff told us later that Kerry had told him to tell our family that he was well. When Geoff asked Kerry about the allegations, Kerry responded by telling him they were all lies. Geoff Thompson also reported the first words my daughter uttered to the world since her arrest: 'I love my children. I've never broken the law.'

We had the video recording it all and later, young Nathan sat for hours looking at the frozen images of his mother and father on the screen. 'I want to give Mummy a kiss,' he said, hugging the television.

That was the one and only time that Geoff Thompson ever filmed Kerry and Kay. He wasn't allowed back into the country after that.

The embassy told us that every Thursday Kerry and Kay would be taken by police escort from the detention centre to the immigration bureau where they would see them in succession for 15 minutes each. The embassy said that they would meet in a roomful of Lao officials and had to be guarded in what they asked. They said that Kay and Kerry were equally guarded because they'd been told before leaving the prison that if they mentioned anything about the conditions then all future access would be denied. We just knew that the conditions were very harsh. We knew that they were distressed because the embassy told us. We only found out about the way in which the interrogations were conducted by degrees and in many ways I'm glad that we didn't know more because my blood pressure was already too high.

In the coming months DFAT rang every Thursday night at 7pm like clockwork. But there was never any good news. I began thinking that they should be doing so much more. They should have had Kay and Kerry out of that country by now. I couldn't, at that time, appreciate everything the government was doing for Kay and Kerry, which appeared to be a far greater effort than any other Australians overseas received.

The months passed and the tensions in the house grew between family members. Everyone in our household was getting on each other's nerves. Our small three-bedroom house wasn't big enough for so many people. I felt like the referee caught in the middle, trying my best to keep everyone from getting too carried away. Everyone seemed to have an opinion, but the only people who really had a clue were Kerry and Kay. We began to unconsciously take on roles within the household. Ernie became the spokesperson, I looked after the household and our other daughter, Karen, became the on-call helper/organiser. She also helped organise media interviews. Most of these were held at our house. Karen divided her time between her house and ours. She was wonderful. How she coped with everything and studied for her university exams still amazes me. Karen and Ernie sometimes clashed because they had different ideas on how to handle the media.

Karen wanted to keep things quiet on the advice of the lawyers, while Ernie wanted to storm the Lao prison walls with a '60 Minutes' producer and free Kerry and Kay. The news of the proposed media trip reached Kay and Kerry and prompted them to request Ernie to stay in Australia. It was far too dangerous.

'I don't want the added burden of watching my father getting tortured if the Lao authorities decide to detain him too' Kay told the Australian Ambassador.

It angered the '60 Minutes' producer because he'd organised Ernie's visa and flights, but finally, whether we agreed with it or not, we had to trust Kerry and Kay's judgement on the matter. It was after all, their lives at risk. In those early days, Sahra also did some media interviews. She wanted to be involved in fighting for her parents' freedom. Now that the embassy knew where Kerry and Kay were, it made it a little less stressful, but we still weren't out of the woods. I wasn't sure about allowing our youngest granddaughter to be questioned by media but Karen said that Sahra had experienced something more traumatic than we could possibly imagine, and that it was perhaps important for her to feel as if she was doing everything she could to help her parents. Sahra was feeling guilty for 'abandoning them'. Reluctantly we agreed and were all surprised at how grown-up she appeared on camera. How calmly she handled the interviews. It seemed to help her cope with the situation. I'm not sure other children of her age would have been able to handle such a situation or the media interviews, but Sahra was always confident that she could do anything she set her mind to do. It was a trait she'd obviously inherited from Kerry and Kay.

My impressions of the media turned out to be far different from what I'd heard from others. They were seemingly protective of the children. The media respected the privacy of our family and never insisted on speaking to us. They never hounded us to make statements and never tried to photograph the children without our permission. We greatly appreciated the support offered to us by all media, but especially Derek Moore, a photographer for the *Courier Mail*. Derek would visit us to genuinely see how we were and offered some suggestions on how to handle certain media situations. He told us not to do exclusives (paid interviews) because that would isolate Kerry and Kay from getting support from all the media. We had no intention of seeking payment for any interviews anyway. We just wanted them home.

Derek was a godsend and our grandson enjoyed searching for frilly lizards in my front garden with him in tow. Nathan also enjoyed walking around with Derek's very expensive camera equipment draped around his neck pretending to be a photographer. My grandson wanted to be either a journalist or a photographer from that moment on. Sahra decided she wanted to be a lawyer, not surprisingly, to help people like her parents get their freedom when they were innocent. Jess had no idea what she wanted to do after high school. Quite frankly, I don't even know how she got through the 11th grade with all the stress that was going on at the time. She showed great determination, courage and strength for a young 15 year old.

Two journalists we came to know well went undercover in Laos, despite the fact that foreign journalists weren't allowed into the country without government approval. They risked their personal safety to try and find out firsthand what was going on. Of course, they wanted the story too, but we felt their concern was genuine. We learned from them that the Lao government owned the radio, newspapers and all television and everything they put out was censored.

The stranger who had initially called us with the news, Bjarne Jepesson, was the reason Kerry and Kay were detained. He said that the Lao government was trying to steal his investment, a US$2 billion sapphire concession, and that Kerry and Kay were being used to try and force his return to Laos. I couldn't really blame him for wanting to stay out of the country, but I didn't like the idea of my daughter and her husband being made scapegoats.

Although it all sounded like something out of a James Bond movie, with talk of secret police and abductions, none of it was imagined. Jepesson's story was confirmed by the Australian Embassy and later by a New York judge, Mr Corretore. He had heard about Kerry and Kay's arrest through his contacts in America and Laos. One evening he rang our house and told Ernie that the Lao government had a history of this sort of thing. He put Ernie in touch with someone who was formerly in the Central Intelligence Agency (CIA) and he told us more about Laos and its history. It didn't give us any greater peace of mind.

Whenever the Australian media had news we heard it, even before the Australian government shared it with us. The media covered the story for the whole 10 months and camped outside our house for the entire time Kerry and Kay were detained. Each night at 6 pm we would tune into the latest news update and when that finished we would change channels to the ABC for the next hour's edition. Kerry and Kay's faces filled the corner of our television screen as the presenter informed the nation that they were still detained in Laos and that under the legal system, no one has ever been acquitted once charged. We took little comfort in that fact despite their newly appointed lawyer guaranteeing that they would never even see the inside of a Lao courtroom. I couldn't understand why it was constantly reported that my daughter and my son-in-law were involved in sapphire theft. I knew without a doubt that Kerry and Kay would never do anything illegal. It simply wasn't in their nature to be dishonest. Not only that, Kerry was still a current serving member of the Australian Defence Force. There's no way that he would put at risk his unblemished 20-year military career or jeopardise the respect he had earned over the years.

One of Kay's best friends, Norma Jamieson, was the wife of a former army chief in Western Australia. Norma gave an interview to the ABC and when asked what she thought of Kay going to Laos she replied 'It didn't surprise me that she was running a security company. It was not unusual for Kay to tell me the most astounding things that she was planning to do. Everything that Kay Danes did was larger than life. That's how I found her and I think this is what attracted me to her. She dared to be different, but she didn't know she was being different. It was just Kay. It seemed to me an extraordinary place to go, an extraordinary thing to do. But on the other hand, that was sort of the Danes—they did extraordinary things.'

Most people who knew Kerry and Kay stood up publicly and defended them. As a mother, I always felt proud that my daughter and her husband were thought of so favourably. But the whole situation was a nightmare. None of it made any sense. The owners of the sapphire mine said that the only people trying to steal anything from them were some corrupt officials from within the Lao government. The Lao government, however, used everything it could to discredit Kerry and Kay. They told one journalist that Kay had tried to hide sapphires in her dirty underwear. According to embassy officials who were present at the time that Kay offered her bag to be searched, the only thing she seemed upset about was the fact that her children were traumatised and that complete strangers, men in particular, were handling her underwear. Another journalist reported that it was highly suspicious that Kay had been detained with so much cash in her possession. Kay's lawyer countered this by explaining that in addition to the services she provided to Lao Securicor, she had also established, with her employer's knowledge, a legitimate bodyguard business in Thailand and the cash she was carrying was for paying wages and other expenses in the business. It was that cash more than anything else that created an impression, a false impression in Australia, that Kay was guilty of some corrupt crime. Her lawyer pointed out that it was perfectly legal and quite common for businesspeople to travel across the border with large amounts of cash for the purposes of transacting business.

The television, the phone and the internet became our world. We hardly left the house, always waiting for the phone to ring or for a story to air, in the hope that it was good news. DFAT's calls every Thursday evening helped us all remain calmly informed about the situation. More often than not, however, it didn't appear as if there was much of anything going on, apart from a great deal of tail chasing. I struggled to comprehend the amount of money this ordeal was costing the Australian government, let alone Kerry and Kay. Their Australian-Greek lawyer looked as if he'd just stepped out from some executive magazine in his Armani shirts and gold cuff links. Did Kay's company in Thailand really have enough money to cover his initial $50,000 retainer? The lawyer, of course, said it was all necessary.

He added that he was in the process of having their employers reimburse Kay's company for his retainer, and assume responsibility for their ongoing legal costs. He also said it was critical for him to work behind the scenes to build a defence on the basis of what he anticipated the charges might be even though no formal charges had ever been mentioned. It was nothing to do with the legalities, because the legal system in Laos was not developed, he said. So how do you fight a legal battle when no crime has been committed? The lawyer said that it was more of a persuasion exercise, 'You have to persuade the government officials, not the judges'. I really didn't understand any of it. He promised to bring Kerry and Kay home and that's all that mattered.

While the legal manoeuvrings were going on, the embassy spoke to a whole range of Lao authorities, up to the most senior levels. The Australian Ambassador said that, while it wasn't really his place to make any formal statements, it was the opinion of those who really knew what was going on that Kerry and Kay had no case to answer. Meanwhile, Ernie and I were doing our best to keep our heads above water. We had gone from a family of two to a family of five. The food bills alone swallowed my meagre wages. The phone and power bills were more than my husband earned. We struggled with the mortgage payments. Fortunately, I had put all our savings into the mortgage prior to this happening, so we were in front with the repayments, but that slowly began to dwindle as time passed. I had reduced my hours at work during the year and was forced to take my long service leave and stress leave to cope with the crisis our family now faced, as well as trying to recover from my dangerously high blood pressure.

My husband and I worked hard all our lives. We never had much money, but we had never had to ask anyone for financial help before. It was humiliating for us to literally beg the multi-million dollar security firm for which my daughter and son-in-law worked for financial help. They grudgingly gave in. It was the least they could do since it was their joint venture partners detaining Kerry and Kay. The lawyer said they wanted to put corporate water between themselves and what was happening in Laos. Obviously they didn't fully comprehend the situation either, but at least they'd agreed to become the 'cash cow', as Kerry and Kay's lawyer labelled them. We hated being a burden to anyone but money was scarce and as the months passed, the struggle became more difficult. One day we received a money order from a stranger in Central Queensland for AU$150 with no return address. Gratefully, but also reluctantly, we used the money towards our grocery bill. Eventually, Kerry was able to instruct his employers, via the embassy, to send us some of his salary. This was a huge relief.

By this point Ernie had to take time off work because he was on the verge of a nervous breakdown. Fathers are so protective of their daughters, and Ernie and Kay were particularly close. They always had been when she was growing up. They shared the same passion for music, and when Ernie used to perform at various clubs around town, little Kay would be the first one up on the dance floor, singing along to her father's Elvis renditions. Ernie found it almost unbearable that he couldn't go to Laos and get Kay out of that prison. He promised her before that very last phone call that he wouldn't leave her there. It ate away at him that she was still sitting in that filthy prison so many months later.

Young Sahra was very upset one night. 'I knew I should have stayed there.' she said 'If I had stayed there, I could've got my mum and dad out.' She decided she'd write to the Prime Minister of Australia, John Howard. He wrote her a nice letter back telling her that he and the Foreign Minister, Alexander Downer, were very concerned for her parents and doing all they could to bring Kerry and Kay home. That helped keep Sahra's spirits up for the rest of the week. 'I've been to the top. He knows about it. He will do something,' she said.

In fact, Mr Howard was doing a great deal behind the scenes and had already written to the Prime Minister of Laos, Mr. Bounnhang Vorachit, who agreed to consult with the Australian government to reunite our family. Mr Howard wrote to Sahra and explained to her that this was most encouraging news and that Mr Downer would be meeting his counterpart in the next few days to ask the Lao government to release Kerry and Kay.

'The Australian government will not give up. Our ambassador in Vientiane is working every day on your parents' case. We want your parents to be able to come home very soon', said the Prime Minister.

Foreign Minister Alexander Downer sent his top advisors to our home not long afterwards. They brought a special edition Macquarie World Atlas as a gift to the children. Mr Downer had even taken the time to inscribe a personal message of encouragement to them. His advisors confirmed that Kerry and Kay were caught in the middle of some political power play between the Lao government and Gem Mining Lao. They explained that the secret police were trying to force Kerry and Kay to make false statements against their client. We had to be patient they said.

News of the ongoing detainment spread far and wide. Ernie and I got offers of support and letters of encouragement from all sorts of people: Members of Parliament, defence personnel and even a United States senator, Jesse Jackson, from the White House. The Governor General of Australia, Sir William Deane, wrote to his counterpart, President of Laos His Excellency Khamtay Siphandone, urging him to return Kay as quickly as possible for the sake of the children. Staff at a United Nations project office based in Laos wrote to Kay and Kerry urging them to be strong.

The Danish government had apparently cancelled foreign aid to Laos upon hearing two 'Danes' were arrested. The Danish Government had been through a similar experience with the Laos Government previously. They weren't happy that it was happening again. I guess they'll find out soon enough that Kerry and Kay are actually Australians. The Japanese government too were putting pressure on the Lao Government. Kerry and Kay had a great working relationship with several Japanese investment companies in Laos.

It seemed like everyone was supporting Kerry and Kay and this support encouraged us to continue to cope with the distressing situation. Despite feeling completely out of our depth there was still the stress of getting the children settled in at school, fixing the hot water system that blew up under the strain of so many people in one tiny house, and the countless other little things that went wrong that kept us grounded. The months dragged on. Some days seemed normal and we laughed and had a good time until our grandson Nathan would innocently say 'I wonder what Mum and Dad are doing now'. The moment of joy would turn solemn.

I never doubted that Kerry would survive their ordeal, due to his specialised military background, but I was gravely concerned for my daughter.

Things improved slightly. Kay was allowed to speak to the children each week for five minutes. It seemed too short, but it was a lifeline to Kay that we greatly appreciated. It was frustrating not being able to speak to my own daughter, but it was more important that she and the children could finally communicate with each other. Eventually the calls were gradually extended to ten minutes. I think this was mainly due to Kay's pleading with the immigration officer in charge, Mr Khamkit. Perhaps he felt some compassion for her and the children. As Kay said, 'Mr Khamkit is really quite sweet!' Of course, we didn't know if she was just saying that in order to get longer chat time. It didn't matter.

Six months passed and contrary to their lawyer's assurances that they would never see the inside of a Lao courtroom that's exactly where they were taken. It was only two days before Nathan's eighth birthday. Their lawyer explained that it was merely a formality and that Kerry and Kay were booked on a flight out of Laos that afternoon, following the proceedings. He said it was all for show as arranged by his 'people' and they would never be convicted. We didn't know what to believe. He'd already told us 19 times over the last six months that Kerry and Kay were on their way home. Each time it didn't happen we were all devastated—especially the children.

When the telephone finally rang late that same evening it was our Foreign Minister Alexander Downer. He advised Ernie that Kerry and Kay had been sentenced to seven years on trumped-up charges. The shock hit us like a tidal wave. Mr Downer assured us that the Australian government did not accept the ruling and would take the matter further.

The following morning their lawyer called and told Ernie that the trial lasted five hours. A trial such as that in Australia would take at least four weeks. He was bewildered that his plans had been foiled. He said the judgment was delivered within 25 minutes after the court went to recess. It was already typed! He further explained that the Lao court unlawfully convicted Kerry and Kay of embezzlement of state assets, saying that Lao Securicor staff had moved state assets without first seeking permission from the Lao government. He explained that the assets were not even owned by Laos. They were still at that time in the control of Gem Mining Lao, to which Lao Securicor was contractually obliged. Ernie listened as the lawyer continued. He said the assets were office furniture, a lounge and two computers stored safely at Lao Securicor's security headquarters and returned when eventually the Lao authorities seized Gem Mining Lao. Their lawyer said that no one in the court could believe that the Lao prosecution had come up with such ridiculous charges. Evidently, no one bothered to ask why the Lao authorities had ever arrested Kerry and Kay in the first place, or make any complaint at the way in which the assets were secured, if in fact they had ever thought Kerry and Kay acted inappropriately.

The court ordered that in moving the two computers into storage that the data had been destroyed. The court charged Kerry and Kay with the destruction of evidence. Their lawyer explained that this was yet another trumped up charge because the data from the computers remained intact. A back-up copy was stored at Lao Securicor's office. His legal submission was thorough and he substantiated that Lao Securicor staff had returned the computers at the request of the Lao authorities long before Kerry and Kay's detainment, and long before the seizure of Gem Mining Lao.

What I couldn't comprehend was how the Lao authorities could use that same computer data as so-called evidence to convict the Gem Mining directors of stealing their own assets. If the data was destroyed then how could they still use it and why would you steal something you already owned?

Jepesson had previously explained that it was all smoke and mirrors and that the Lao government was trying to 'force the nationalisation of Gem Mining Lao because he had refused to sign a new agreement with them, giving the Lao government 51 per cent ownership of his investment, as opposed to receiving revenue from tax as with the current agreement'.

In short, he said, they just got greedy. He told us that other foreign investors were also being targeted but no one in the World Bank or UN was doing anything about it.

The final charge against Kay related to the violation of Lao tax regulations, even though Kay's lawyers showed evidence that contradicted their charges. Kay had not violated any Laos tax laws, Lao laws or even Thai laws. The Lao court falsely ruled that it was entitled to collect revenue from Kay's international bodyguard company, despite the fact that it was a company established and operating entirely outside the jurisdiction of Laos. The lawyer presented evidence that showed that all taxes were rendered to Thailand and a full audit by KPMG chartered accountants in Thailand refuted allegations of tax evasion.

What did this situation have to do with Kay's company in Thailand? Thai tax is paid to Thailand and Lao tax is paid to Laos—isn't it? I know my daughter worked closely with a Thai lawyer, studied the tax rules and rules of business operations in Thailand thoroughly, before even considering starting a company in Thailand. Why didn't the Lao authorities know their own laws? Or if they did, why didn't they follow them?

Of all of us in that small suburban house that night, Jess was the most upset. I think that months of holding everything inside had taken its toll on her. She sat on her bed, weeping. Sahra sat with her until she eventually fell asleep. Nathan was oblivious to it all. Surprisingly, Ernie was calm, not agitated. He was being strong for the children. I was expecting him to erupt like a volcano, but he remained calm. It helped us all tremendously knowing that our government knew that Kerry and Kay were innocent. I knew if the Australian government let them down then Kerry would take matters into his own hands. He would find a way to bring my daughter home. I had total confidence in Kerry.

Australian Foreign Minister Downer made a statement to the media in a special news edition:

> *I am deeply disappointed and I have spoken to the families of both Kerry and Kay myself. The Australian government is dissatisfied with the process which resulted in the conviction and sentencing of Kerry and Kay. I have had a personal briefing from the Ambassador (Jonathan Thwaites) and have asked him to explore avenues for further action and to report back to me. We will pursue all avenues to enable Kerry and Kay to come home.*

Three more months passed and we began to wonder if we would ever see them again. Three months felt like three years. Then we got a phone call from the lawyers telling us that the Australian government had come up with a plan to get Kerry and Kay home through diplomatic negotiations. They would need to withdraw their appeal to the Supreme Court and pay $1 million dollars in compensation to Laos.

I knew that Kerry and Kay would never agree to those terms. There was no way they would sell their reputations that cheaply, but where did that leave them? Mr Downer said it was pointless to appeal to the Supreme Court because no one had ever been acquitted in Laos once charged. He said it was just best to get them out of there any way possible. The Australian Ambassador said that the Lao government wanted specific compensation, but when the offer was put to Kerry and Kay, they flatly refused as advised by their lawyer. Paying compensation, in lieu of signing a guilty statement, was still a form of acknowledgement that they were somehow responsible, when in fact, everyone knew they weren't.

The Australian Ambassador said to the media:

> *It's very difficult for the Lao authorities to accept that there's anything much wrong with a situation where people may take the rap for something that they didn't do. As they said to us on a number of occasions, if the Danes had been released, where does that leave us? How can we get the compensation for all the damage that has been done to the Lao people over the years by Gem Mining Lao? Don't be too fussed about the connection between the Danes and Gem Mining Lao. The Danes are all we've got left.*

As it turned out, the appeal to the Lao Supreme Court was dismissed before it was even submitted. The Lao Foreign Minister said they had no right to appeal. The writing was on the wall. It didn't look like Kerry and Kay were ever going to get out of Laos without making some sort of compromise. They insisted that the Australian government renegotiate the 'form of words' of the agreement. Mr Downer agreed and sent a special envoy to do this. The wording on the document was changed. Kerry and Kay signed an acknowledgement of their conviction but, importantly to them, not guilt. They remained incarcerated until 8 October 2001 until, through intense negotiations, the Lao government agreed to release them into the care of the Australian Ambassador on the condition that they remain at his residence until things could be finalised.

I went to bed that night thinking that it was a huge relief knowing that Kerry and Kay were both finally together and sleeping soundly under the protection of the Ambassador's roof. The end was now in sight. Over the next two weeks, Kay spoke to the children every day for as long as she liked. Ernie, Karen and I spoke to her too and she kept telling us that we ought to be patient and only believe that she's free when she tells us herself. We started getting excited with Christmas approaching and thinking that this year would be the best Christmas ever!

Kerry and Kay's lawyer had been forced to take a back seat to the negotiations at their request. He continued to keep us informed, however, and explained that the President of Laos had agreed to grant them a Presidential Pardon. It was the only way to resolve the matter without Kerry and Kay retaining a criminal conviction.

I thought it rather ironic that the President of Laos' grandson had sent my grandson a hand-made greeting card, along with many others made by the children attending the Vientiane International School, the school my grandson once attended. It was sent before Kerry and Kay had been released from the prison, but we were late receiving it. The young boy wrote: 'Dear Nathan, I hope your Mum and Dad get out of jail soon!'

After three weeks of house arrest, the Lao government requested a show of goodwill. They wanted Kerry and Kay to sign over US$150,000 from their local bank account, frozen shortly following their detainment. It was all the money they'd saved while working in Laos. 'Let them have it. Most likely they've spent it already,' Kay told the Australian Ambassador.

It seemed a lousy deal to have to part with so much money, especially when it was enough to buy a big new house in Brisbane and a fresh start after all they'd endured. But as everyone agreed, the Lao government wanted money. That was all this case was ever about and it was the only way they would ever let Kerry and Kay go and save face. The money was paid and Kerry and Kay were granted a Presidential Pardon soon after. On 6 November 2001 they were officially free and warmly invited to return to Laos at any time.

I doubt they ever will.

Kerry and Kay flew home to Australia on 9 November 2001. I barely recognised them when they stepped into the private suite at the Conrad Treasury Hotel where we were all anxiously waiting for them. I was shocked at the sight of my daughter because she had lost so much weight, but was extremely happy to be home and that's all that really mattered. We were a family again.

Kerry and Kay eventually bought a house around the corner from ours and life slowly began to assume some sort of normal routine. Kerry resumed work at a military post in Brisbane on compassionate grounds instead of returning to his Perth-based unit. We were all relieved that they weren't moving back to Perth. Not that Kerry and Kay had any intention of doing so because it would have created too much distress for the children.

Kay was suffering severe Post Traumatic Stress Disorder (PTSD) and depression and needed to remain in a stable environment. It was awful watching my daughter in such a state.

Six years have passed, yet the nightmare still sometimes feels as if it were only yesterday. I read a comment posted on the internet by someone in our community who was upset that the Australian government was seizing the proceeds of a book written by an Australian detained in Bali for drug smuggling. New legislation now prevents convicted prisoners from benefiting from the proceeds of a crime. 'Are they now going to take action against Renae Lawrence for all her magazine articles, Chopper Reid, Warren Fellows, Kay Danes and now Pauline Hanson, who have all been convicted of crimes and who have wrote books?' the writer said.

I was furious and hurt that my daughter and son-in-law were being labelled criminals, alongside convicted drug smugglers and murderers. It was disappointing that people were still so misinformed about their horrific ordeal and unlawful imprisonment. Do people seriously believe that the Australian government would have invested so much time, money and resources and risked a 50-year bilateral relationship for criminals?

'If Kerry with all his SAS training, with all his discipline, dedication and patriotism, is ever going to break, it's not going to be for physical reasons. It's going to be because he doesn't feel he can restore his good name, and that he has somehow been judged by his own people to be guilty of something that he absolutely didn't do' said Ambassador Thwaites.

This was true, of course. Kay told me that when Kerry returned to the Special Forces, he endured all sorts of hurtful innuendoes, not so discreetly said behind his back. One person had the audacity to say that Kerry shouldn't even be in the army because he was a criminal. Of course, when Kerry confronted that person, he was quick to deny it. Kerry was promoted to Regimental Sergeant Major of an elite Special Forces Unit. We were all immensely proud.

My daughter, Kay, has never returned fully to the security industry although she has a consultancy and offers advice to corporations about working overseas. Nowadays, she has dedicated a great deal of her life to writing and helping others who have loved ones detained in foreign prisons. I know she misses her high-powered executive lifestyle, but she accepts that we must all keep moving forward.

In January 2008, Kay was nominated in the Australian of the Year Awards and was congratulated by the Australia Day Council 'for setting high standards of excellence and contributing in ways that inspire us all'.

In 2011, she was named number 9 out of 50 of Australia's iconic women. I am so proud of my daughter's achievements. She is indeed an inspiration and has turned a very negative experience into something quite positive. Not everyone is able to do that.

My husband and I moved to the country. We no longer felt able to work as we once did because the stress of everything had taken its toll on both of us. Ernie continued to suffer terrible anxiety and chest pain, but the countryside is quiet and we love the peacefulness of it. The most demanding choices we have to make now are which native bird species we'll feed first. We visit Brisbane occasionally and whenever I see that familiar Gateway Bridge looming across the Brisbane River, I feel my heart skip a beat. It feels very much like coming home.

This ordeal has taught me many things and I hope that by reading this book, others might gain something useful or even some solace in their time of despair. The separation from a loved one feels hopeless, but never forget that there is always hope. There has to be. We endured the nightmare of Laos by taking one day at a time. We told ourselves, 'let's wait and see what happens tomorrow'. We learned to focus on what we could control: going to work, looking after the children, doing the housework. We left the complicated legal and political stuff to the lawyers and government and faced the things we knew we could face. We tried to take each day without getting too overwhelmed. Some days we succeeded and many days we failed, but we kept trying to focus on small day-to-day tasks rather than thinking too far in the future.

It's important to let off steam and hopefully your family members will forgive you as we forgave each other. I learned that we need to stand together. Often I felt that our grandchildren handled the situation much better than we adults. So never underestimate the power of young people to endure the seemingly impossible. Finally, I wish you peace in your own struggle and trust you continue to have faith. There can be miracles in your life when you believe, just as there were miracles that happened throughout our ordeal that eventually reunited our family. I will pray that somehow you will get through those dark times and you will find peace. Until then, never give up!

Read Kerry and Kay's story *'Standing Ground' – An Imprisoned Couple's Struggle for Justice Against A Communist Regime*
www.newholland.com.au
www.kaydanes.com

4
Holiday of a lifetime
Schapelle Corby, Bali

'When I flew to Bali on 8 October 2004, I imagined my biggest problem was going to be deciding which sarong to wear with which bikini ...' says Schapelle Corby, an Australian currently detained in Kerobokan Prison, Bali

Schapelle Corby, born 10 July 1977 in Brisbane, lived on the Gold Coast in Queensland where she was enrolled in a beauty therapy course and worked at her mum's fish and chip shop. She was from a working-class family, an ordinary girl from the suburbs who loved the beach and hanging out with friends.

On 8 October 2004, Schapelle Corby, Katrina Richards, Alyth McComb and Schapelle's 17-year-old half-brother, James Kisina, checked in their suitcases and Schapelle's bright-yellow boogie-board bag at the Qantas counter at Brisbane Airport. The total weight of 65kg was recorded under Schapelle Corby's name. The group were flying on a domestic flight to Sydney and then transferring on to an international flight to Denpasar, Bali. They met Jodie Power, a friend of Schapelle's older sister, Mercedes Corby, at the Sydney airport. Jodie was flying to Bali on a later flight.

All bags were transferred to the international terminal before the party boarded their flight.

Approximately seven hours later, their plane touched down at Ngurah Rai Airport, Denpasar. It was around 3:30pm. Schapelle and her companions passed by the giant signs that read: Death Penalty for those who carry drugs to Bali. None of them took much notice.

Schapelle went to collect her boogie-board bag but it wasn't on the carousel with the other bags. Dismayed, she found it lying on the ground several metres away. The handle was broken. Her brother James helped her drag it, along with his bag, over to the counter for Bali Customs Officers to inspect. Alyth and Katrina had already gone through customs. They were excited. Bali—one of Australia's number one travel destinations. It's like Las Vegas is to Americans.

Bali customs officers searched James' bag first then asked if the boogie-board bag was his.

'No, it's mine ... here you go,' said Schapelle then reached for the zips to open it. She says she paused when she saw the zips were done up in the middle instead of the side as she always did them up. Without any further thought, she opened the bag to the unmistakable smell of marijuana. Panicking, afraid of how it would look she says, she quickly re-zipped the bag, hoping the customs officer hadn't noticed.

He had.

Inside the boogie-board bag was 4.2kg of marijuana, in two vacuum sealed plastic bags.

Schapelle's sister, Mercedes, who was holidaying in Bali at the time with her Balinese husband and two small children, was contacted by Katrina. She arrived on the scene shortly after the arrest and tried to convince the Bali police to at least release her brother James. He was only 17 years old. The Bali police, however, insisted he accompany them to Polda police station. Mercedes says she felt helpless as she watched the distraught faces of her brother and sister fade into the distance as the police car took them away. Schapelle's two friends, Alyth and Katrina, were allowed to leave the airport.

Mercedes contacted the Australian consulate in Bali and was given a list of lawyers. Most of them had closed for the day. Their answering machine messages simply left instructions for callers to call back on Monday. Mercedes managed to get through to one woman who couldn't personally take the case but said that her sister would. As Mercedes waited for the call back from lawyer Lily Lubis, it didn't register at the time that Ms Lubis wasn't on the embassy's approved list of lawyers. What did that matter anyway?

Schapelle's young brother James Kisina was released from Polda station as the Bali police turned their sole attention to Schapelle, as the owner of the boogie-board bag. This was when her nightmare truly began. Schapelle Corby would be facing the death penalty—execution by firing squad.

For someone to get a strong-smelling, pillow case-sized bag of marijuana through both Brisbane and Sydney airports undetected, they would have to bypass check-in staff, x-ray machines, scanners, sniffer dogs, police, customs and baggage handlers. Who would even attempt such a thing? Surely not a young would-be beauty therapist from the Gold Coast? Why take the risk of trafficking 4.2 kilograms of marijuana overseas when there was already a market for it in Australia? Unless of course, you thought you'd get a higher price for a higher-quality product. Even then, surely not?

In this case, Schapelle was adamant the drugs weren't hers. In fact, research shows that marijuana is usually distributed throughout a domestic market by road, not air, because of the inherent risks involved. It's not usually exported, although there was a case when a customs detector dog at the New South Wales international postal centre in Mascot detected the largest attempted export of marijuana—110 grams destined for Vanuatu. (Australian Crime Commissions Illicit Drug Report 2001–02.) Again, the attempt was made by post.

Why would Schapelle plant drugs in her own luggage, use her own name and address on the tag and run the risk of getting caught? Why not plant the drugs in someone else's luggage? Could Schapelle Corby be so confident that no person or security device would detect such a large quantity of drugs at any of the three airports she passed through? Logic would suggest that it was madness to ever consider that you would get through undetected.

'I swear as God is my witness I did not know marijuana was in my bag,' said Schapelle.

Her new lawyer, Lily Lubis, agreed that it defied all logic. Her associates Erwin Siregar and Vasu Rasiah agreed. Siregar was baffled 'If the marijuana did not belong [to] Schapelle then how can the boogie-board and the bag with the marijuana be exact the same [shape]?' he said.

Bali customs officer Nyoma Winata said much the same thing: 'The evidence I first found was so different to what we saw in court. It was packed in transparent plastic, shaped as a boogie-board. It is pressed in a plastic bag, air tight. When I pulled it out, the thickness is similar to the boogie-board. The evidence is now different. It has already been handled by many people. So from what I see it, it was intended to look like a boogie-board. If we had not been careful we might have missed that.'

Customs officer Winata also told *60 Minutes* reporter Liz Hayes that at the airport Schapelle was reluctant to open her bag. He says that he is sure she knew she had some illegal substance in her bag because when they opened the second zipper, he claims that she was already trying to stop him from opening it. He claims she said 'Oh no, I have something inside'. Schapelle adamantly denies this.

Over the coming weeks her legal team, which consisted of Australian lawyer Robin Tampoe and Gold Coast entrepreneur Ron Bakir, met to discuss these possibilities. Certainly Schapelle could have brought the marijuana to Bali and then just denied it being hers. She could have said that the bag is not locked so anyone could have tampered with it. Her legal team engaged the advice of a leading criminologist who firmly believed Schapelle was not capable of that degree of planning.

'I just do not think that that is the sort of woman that she is. I don't think she's that intelligent ... she's not dumb ... I'm saying she's average ... average intelligence, average person ... with average ambitions. Very ordinary people, in my experience, do not smuggle drugs, do not courier drugs.'

Except that the 'Bali nine', the name given to a group of nine Australians arrested for drug trafficking on 17 April 2005, in Denpasar, were of average intelligence and very ordinary people. It's a known fact that the masterminds don't courier the drugs, they pay others to do it for them—people with less intelligence. One could reasonably argue that Schapelle fit the mould. But that alone doesn't mean that she was guilty and it doesn't support the claim that all ordinary people are drug mules.

The criminologist also made comparisons between drug mules in Thai prisons, saying that generally speaking they have an addiction problem. That's a pretty broad generalisation. There are many drug mules in Thai prisons, whom I've had dealings with, who are not addicts. They were more economically motivated and though not as common, there have been reported cases of unsuspecting drug mules. In 1997, a Melbourne couple, known as Steve and Dee, arrived at their Bali hotel to find a large block of compressed marijuana in their luggage. It was in an airtight clear plastic bag and was about the size of a loaf of bread. When they rang the Australian consulate for help, they allege they were told to flush the drugs down the toilet or 'you'll be eating nasi goreng for the rest of your life in jail'. No one from the Australian Federal Police interviewed the couple—nor did Australian authorities inform Schapelle's defence team of the case. Why was Steve told to destroy the drugs and why has no police agency ever sought to interview him?

Baggage handling, drug syndicates, unsuspecting mules. Australian Federal Police Commissioner Mick Keelty said that the AFP could find no evidence to support that key Corby Defence claim that Schapelle was the innocent victim of a drug smuggling ring. He told journalist Laurie Oakes on the *Sunday* program on 24 April 2005, 'If people use that as a defence, they've got to understand that it needs to be corroborated, and we will follow down every lead to corroborate as best we can, that sort of allegation'.

Mike Phelan, the AFP's National Manager told Schapelle's lawyers the AFP believes, 'it is extremely rare to encounter a genuine "unsuspecting" mule and that in the vast majority of cases that the AFP encounters, where people deny knowledge of drugs found in their possession, there is other compelling evidence that supports their guilt.'

Schapelle's lawyers responded by saying that there was no compelling evidence of her guilt. If it was 'extremely rare' then that means it was possible. So why was it so impossible for Schapelle to be an unsuspecting mule? Was it simply too hard to believe that it actually happened? Was it easier to just let it go and save themselves the effort of investigating how the drugs came to be in her bag? Why did the AFP not search her home for further evidence if they believed she was guilty or had some connection with the drug trade? Former Australian Customs officer Allan Kessing wrote several damning reports about security at Sydney Airport. He expressed a number of concerns in relation to poor screening procedures of staff and processes, access by staff to restricted or sterile areas, and in particular, access or staff working at the baggage handling areas. His report showed that there were people working in the baggage handling sterile areas who had criminal records.

Qantas Head of Security Geoff Askew was reported to have said 'It's never been reported to me that any Qantas passenger has had their bag used to transport drugs.' But in another interview, Qantas told *60 Minutes* that it alone gets approximately 400 complaints a year from passengers about baggage tampering. Tampering yes, but it was not reported that customers complained about finding drugs in their bags which is something else altogether. Either way, Schapelle was in a situation where she could not prove the drugs found in her bag weren't hers. Indonesian law places the burden of proof on the prosecution and provides for a presumption of innocence similar to that which applies in Australia. So in other words, Schapelle was to be considered innocent until proven guilty. Unless of course, the prosecution could establish a prima facie case against her. According to Professor Tim Lindsey, director of the University of Melbourne's Asian Law Centre, being caught with drugs on you, whether strapped to you or in a bag that is your property, is probably going to be sufficient in most instances for the prosecution to establish a prima facie case.

The Indonesian Prosecutors stated that there was no dispute that the cannabis was in her bag when it was opened at Bali's Ngurah Rai Airport. Their witness, an Indonesian Customs Officer, said that Schapelle admitted it was hers (despite her denying this). With a prima facie established, the case then took on a different set of rules and it was then up to the defence to counter the prosecution's case. What evidence did they have? Did the Corby legal team expect Schapelle to convince the judges that she just simply didn't do it? There was no investigation into where or how Schapelle intended to sell the marijuana. There was no history of her doing this before.

Sceptics would say there's always a first time, as was the case for some of the Bali nine. A number of them did not have criminal records, came from good families and weren't addicts. Her legal team argued that Schapelle didn't use an alias on her baggage tags, as drug mules do. But neither did the Bali nine. Her legal team argued that Schapelle intended to stay two weeks instead of doing a quick turnaround. Again, the Bali nine were in Bali almost two weeks before their arrest.

Her legal team argued that she wasn't carrying a large amount of money. But if the allegations were correct that she was importing drugs to Bali, she would have no need for large amounts of money. No need to buy drugs if it is alleged you already have them for supply. It was also suggested that she travelled with her family which would be a very unusual thing to do. But this was a ridiculous statement since thousands of drug family syndicates operate worldwide and tens of thousands of siblings are arrested in drug and crime cases. This still doesn't prove that Schapelle was guilty, however.

The head of Bali's drug squad, Bambang Sugiarto, claimed the marijuana was 'high purity and quality and would sell in Bali for about 14 times the price of locally grown marijuana.'

The Bali police, prosecutors and court accepted this.

Schapelle signed a formal document requesting that the drugs be forensically tested.

Fourteen days after her arrest, an officer checked the laboratory that contained the evidence (marijuana). The lab report listed as 'Brief of Criminality Laboratory Check No Lab: 262/KNF/2004 dated 22 of October 2004 confirmed the dried flower to be marijuana. This supported the initial test that was done at the airport at the time of her arrest. But no DNA testing was ever done. Schapelle's lawyers wrote to a doctor at the Centre for Forensic Science at the University of Western Australia:

> *We have obtained a sample of evidence (marijuana) from the Bali Police and would like to send this sample to the government laboratories via (name withheld) and to be tested by you for the following; the THC value to establish the strength of Marijuana thus to establish the street value of the substance in Australia; Pollen/DNA testing to establish the location of growth of the Marijuana; Any other information pertaining to the sample to establish a fair trial to Ms. Schapelle Corby. We would appreciate it very much if you could please obtain any necessary permits from the Western Australian State Police, to import the evidence sample of Ms. Corby to Perth and be tested without any legal implications.*

Advice provided to Schapelle's lawyers from the doctor confirmed their willingness to test the sample. However, they received subsequent advice from the AFP in Perth that the proper protocol would be for the Bali police to contact them, to have the sample sent to Australia for testing.

The doctor offered to travel to Bali but could only do that upon written permission from the Bali police, so that they would be immune from prosecution for handling the sample. AFP Commissioner Mick Keelty confirmed the Corby defence team had approached his officers about conducting the tests, but he said it was the same lawyers who later backed away.

In an interview three years later, a member of Schapelle's defence team, Vasu Rasiah, told his version of what happened. He said that Bali police were going to allow a sample of the marijuana found in Schapelle's boogie-board bag to be tested, but Schapelle and her sister Mercedes wouldn't allow it.

'She [Mercedes] manipulated the entire situation,' Vasu said. 'We had the privilege of requesting from the Bali police a sample to be tested. We had all the correspondence from these people. We put forward testing the drug for DNA and a lie-detector test. But it was never done. They would never do it. What we wanted was for them to tell their actual story so we can build a case.'

AFP Commissioner Mick Keelty told the *The Australian* 'I think the reality was if it was tested and the tests didn't come up with what the defence counsel expected, then it may, in fact, assist the prosecution and not the defence'.

It was a risky move too because Schapelle claimed she didn't know where the drugs came from. What if they came from Australia? What if they were inserted into her bag in Australia by someone else? She would still look guilty. She would still be in the same position of having to prove where they came from and who's drugs they were! There was no guarantee the AFP would be thorough. There was no guarantee they would have been able to track down the network that her lawyers claimed were exporting drugs from Australia. The people who grew, cured and packed the drugs would have dropped hair into the sticky resin. Such forensic testing might have meant that real clues would have been found to convict those responsible if it wasn't her. But it was all a risk and Schapelle was facing a death sentence. It could also be easily argued by the prosecution that Schapelle simply wasn't there when the drugs were grown, cured and packed, as is often the case with drug mules.

No one insisted on weighing her luggage until it was well after the arrest. Her sister, Mercedes, asked but was told that such weighing was 'unnecessary'. It was most likely because the Bali Police had an open and shut case. Schapelle's bag contained drugs and she'd admitted owning the bag. To them, that was all they needed. But if someone had had the foresight to weigh all the bags, and match the weight against the recorded weight on Schapelle's ticket, then perhaps it might have been different for Schapelle. Or not.

Was Schapelle Corby innocent or guilty? Frankly, it didn't bother me either way because 98 per cent of the cases on the Foreign Prisoner website are guilty as charged. But just imagine being in a foreign jail for a crime you knew you didn't commit. It does happen. In the United States, there have been 111 people exonerated (freed) while waiting on death row, and a dozen or so found innocent after execution.

I had no idea if Schapelle Corby was innocent but her story was hot. All sorts were out to profit from her incarceration. Within weeks of her arrest she was front page news and there were lucrative media exclusives on offer, Free Schapelle T-shirts, Schapelle mugs and Free Schapelle wrist bands. Even Schapelle Corby G-strings went on sale. Websites were being registered using Schapelle's name and countless variations of it, and some collected funds that never went to the lawyers to fight for her freedom as promised. Everyone was looking for their own little piece of Schapelle. It was the worst case of prisoner exploitation I'd ever seen. Schapelle suddenly had so many new best friends that it must have been impossible for her and her family to trust anyone. It became a feeding frenzy. People she didn't even know were queuing at the prison to see her. One guy, Eddie Hutauruk advertised 'Schapelle Corby Tours'.

His advertising read 'Schapelle Corby is a convicted Australian drug runner, and my tours allow people to see Schapelle in her cage at Kerobokan Prison in Bali. Tours can be arranged for most days of the week and pickup is possible from most Bali hotels ... Have your photo taken in front of Schapelle in her cage. Small gifts can be given to Schapelle to encourage her to pose and smile in your photos. Watch Schapelle being fed at either lunch or dinner. Optional extra: for just $10 AUD more you can feed Schapelle yourself—watch her face light up as you throw various pieces of food to her. Actually get inside Schapelle's cage, and spend up to 30 minutes just metres away from her. This tour is recommended if you want to take up-close photos of Schapelle, or if you want to try and talk to her on a personal level. For safety reasons Schapelle must be chained up during all cage visits, and should not be approached under any circumstances. Although it is almost certain that you will see Schapelle on the tour, sightings cannot be guaranteed—if Schapelle is sick, she may not be on display. Please do not hit the bars of Schapelle's cage to get her attention as you may annoy other people on the tour.'

It was disgusting!

Watching this circus unfold from the sidelines, I remember thinking how horrible it was for her and her family. Schapelle's idea of spending two weeks in Bali, surfing and celebrating her sister's thirtieth birthday had turned into a nightmare beyond belief. It was then I decided to contact her lawyers to offer them some free advice.

I spoke with Robin Tampoe, Schapelle's lawyer on the Gold Coast, via telephone and told him my background and, more importantly, that if he challenged the Indonesians with any fist waving, that Schapelle might very well face a 20-year sentence.

Rumours had already begun circulating about Bali Customs officers planting the marijuana in her bag. Again, it was possible but did it make sense? Why would they go to so much trouble to make a hoax bust when there were plenty of willing drug traffickers attempting to transit Bali every day of the week? Or why not just plant a small quantity of cocaine, which would have been far easier than trying to find a bag that matched exactly the dimensions and weight of what was eventually discovered in her bag? And what would be the purpose behind setting up innocent travellers? Were they hoping to extort cash? It's plausible. Why bother with the drugs at all if that's the case? If the suggestion is that Bali police are that corrupt then they can easily detain a person without any reason or cause. Why draw attention to themselves by creating a media frenzy? There's nothing to be gained by it. There's no bilateral leverage. It just doesn't make any sense. Or maybe there was someone who was supposed to be working at the Bali airport that day, airside, who didn't show up for work to remove the drugs from her boogie-board bag. It all seemed illogical but certainly not impossible. Did the Bali police set Schapelle up on the behest of the Indonesian government, to diminish Australia's bold outspokenness on their domestic affairs? This was another ridiculous theory. For one, Indonesia didn't need to deliberately plant drugs on Australians travelling through Bali when there are so many willing traffickers already. More precisely, the Indonesian Government is well aware of its sovereign rights and knows full well that international law prevents the Australian Government and any other Government from interfering in its domestic affairs. No, these are the ill-informed rantings of fanatics who want others to believe they know something on the subject when clearly they don't.

There were conspiracy theories after conspiracies. The trouble with conspiracy theories is that they are based on the common need to find a scapegoat for all that is wrong. To the untrained mind or the unqualified ear it gels with whatever it is that person came to the issue with. Some blindly accept their theories as fact. They may even sound incredibly knowledgeable. Then they spread their conspiracy theories to others, while all the time they have no real idea what they are talking about. They are perhaps seeking attention, wanting to be needed, have an axe to grind or some other agenda. In Schapelle's case, there was no room for conspiracy theories. Her lawyers would have to deal with what they could and could not prove. The conspiracy theorists would go round and round endlessly. Which they did then and are still doing even now.

♓

I didn't at the time believe the Indonesians would actually execute her but they would certainly deal harshly with anyone accusing them of foul play. It was important for her defence team to know exactly what they were up against. Who better to inform them than someone who had experienced wrongful conviction, someone who had credibility and the full support of the Australian Government. Granted our cases were as different as night and day but the process of putting together a case, against a hostile prosecution, would be similar. I spent an hour telling Robin Tampoe all that I knew about foreign internment and how to engage our Government to effect a diplomatic solution in the event the legal one failed. At the end of the phone call he thanked me. He said he would be in touch if he needed me. I never heard from him again.

Simultaneously, Mercedes Corby contacted me out of the blue via a friend in the UK, who I was helping, in the hope to secure the release of her son detained in a Japanese prison. Mercedes and I maintained regular contact through emails and phone calls. I gave her pretty much the advice that I gave Robin Tampoe and told her that if she needed me, to call. I also visited her mother to give her some insight into foreign judicial process and internment. I did not meet her father until later.

My repeated advice 'Don't anger the Indonesians' and 'Do this diplomatically' always seemed to fall on deaf ears.

Schapelle went before the judges on 28 April 2005 and delivered an impassioned plea of innocence. She appealed to their humanity and belief in God and, finally, warned them she could not continue to live as she had done for the past seven months.

'My heart and my family is being painfully burdened by all these accusations and rumours about me and I don't know how long I can survive in here,' she said, her voice rising as tears fell. 'And I swear by God as my witness, I did not know the marijuana was in my bag. Please look to your God for guidance in your judgement of me. For God speaks only of justice.'

At the end, she said 'Saya tidak bersalah', I am not guilty.

The very next day, John Patrick Ford took the stand. Ford was on remand in a Victorian prison charged with a range of offences including rape and aggravated burglary. He testified that he had overheard a conversation in a

Victorian prison between two prisoners. He alleged that one of them claimed to have planted the marijuana in Corby's boogie board bag in Brisbane, with the intention of having another person remove it in Sydney.

Ford claimed the drugs were owned by Ron Vigenser, who had been a prisoner at the same jail. Ford claimed that a mix-up resulted in the marijuana not being removed and subsequently being transported to Indonesia, all without Schapelle's knowledge. He refused to name the man who he claimed planted the drugs for fear of his life, he said.

It didn't matter. It was all hearsay according to the judges. John Ford's testimony was later dismissed.

Did anyone honestly believe that the testimony of a prisoner, who claims he overheard a conversation between other prisoners, would carry any weight at all with the judges? John Ford had no credibility as far as the Indonesian judges were concerned. Ron Vigenser strongly denied any connection with the drugs and reportedly gave a statement to that effect to the Australian Federal Police. John Ford returned to Australia and at his trial, a Victorian County Court jury found him guilty of 11 charges, including rape and stalking. They sentenced him to eight years. Subsequently, in prison, he was beaten and stabbed and then held in solitary protective custody. Ford's wife stated that this was a consequence of evidence he gave at Corby's trial.

On Wednesday, May 25, 2005, I flew to Bali with Schapelle's father, Mick Corby and *Gold Coast Bulletin* journalist, Tony Wilson. I'd spoken to Tony by phone and he was very sympathetic to Schapelle's plight. In fact, he categorically believed her to be innocent. He had been investigating the case since the very beginning and for every sensational headline, he found a plausible alternative.

Arriving at the Brisbane airport, I asked the Air Paradise airline check-in staff to make sure any media travelling on our flight were seated as far from us as possible. Poor Tony Wilson ended up down the back of the plane too. We didn't count on a female journalist recognising me in flight or that she wasn't travelling on a journalist visa, which she was supposed to be. So when the seatbelt sign went off, she approached us. I told her that I had only just met Michael. She asked him to confirm this and being slightly deaf in one ear, Michael turned to me and yelled, 'What did she say?'

I repeated that she wanted to know if we had met before. He laughed spontaneously and replied: 'No, I've only just met her now!' The journalist looked confused. We managed to avoid her questions but it was quite obvious she was dying to turn on her mobile phone to alert her film crew in Denpasar. Tony Wilson stood guard over Schapelle's dad while I went to the bathroom. We dared not leave Michael alone.

I'd bought a sausage roll at the airport cafeteria and didn't have time to eat it. It had been sitting in my handbag throughout the flight. I told Michael that it was there and I would have to find some way of getting rid of it before we touched down in Bali. He said: 'Why don't you just eat the damn thing?'

I wasn't hungry. Were you allowed to take sausage rolls into Bali? As every moment passed and we drew nearer to Denpasar, I couldn't help but think of Schapelle sitting in that prison cell while her father sat beside me. About an hour before we landed, the hostess announced that the toilets were out of service and we'd have to wait until we reached Denpasar to use the bathroom. A few groans were heard among the passengers, followed by a moment of complete silence in which Michael Corby blurted out rather loudly: 'You stuffed your sausage roll down the bloody toilet, didn't you?'

I hadn't, of course. It was simply a coincidence.

We arrived at Denpasar Airport. During the time it took us to transit, by bus, to the busy airport terminal, half the sausage roll that had been sitting in the bottom of my handbag ended up in Michael's hand, the other in mine. We giggled as we devoured it in haste. Quite a few things happened after we made our way through customs. For one thing, the media was on to us. Michael disappeared. The speed with which that man could move was incredible. One minute he was there and the next when I turned around, he was gone. Tony and I took to the crowd and tried to hide so we could avoid being on the six o'clock news. It was rather difficult for me to hide with the six-foot giant that is Tony Wilson, but somehow we managed. About 20 minutes later, Schapelle's sister, Mercedes, sent one of her friends back for us. Apparently, Michael was already on his way safely to the secret rendezvous point. We would meet him there.

The next day, Tony Wilson was going to the court to see what arrangements had been put in place. He asked if I wanted to tag along, so naturally I did. We were allowed inside the courtroom where the big show would be televised across the country and back home in Australia. For a long moment I stood with my back to the wall of the room and silently observed the scene. They'd even placed a chair in the middle of the court where Schapelle would be seated. It was just a brown wooden chair but it signified so much more to me. I felt a terrible sense of déja vù being in that room. Another time in another place, I too had been presented before a three-judge panel. Quickly I pushed those painful images from my mind and focused instead on a time when I had stood beneath the heart-shaped leaves of the Bodhi tree (wisdom tree) in Laos. I had searched for inner peace from all the turmoil that surrounded me. I learnt from the Thais that 'making merit' (to perform an action or ceremony that increases one's virtue—according to the Buddhist doctrine of Karma) brings happiness, a peaceful life and many other good things, like gaining merit for strength to overcome any obstacles or misfortune. I closed my eyes and thought of Schapelle and her family. I silently wished for all good things for them, especially strength and endurance.

When I visited Schapelle on 26 May 2005 in Kerobokan Prison, the day before her trial, I did so without any preconceived ideas. I simply thought of her as a young woman caught in a terrible situation with a family suffering because of it. Mercedes thought it would help Schapelle to see me; after all, no one ever thought I'd survive unlawful detainment in a communist prison. Many people had been telling Schapelle that she would go home. By sitting there holding her hand, I think that I was able to give some reality to those hopes. I told her that it could happen, but that it wouldn't happen overnight. Such cases are often fraught with complexities and difficulties that are beyond people's understanding. I told Schapelle to prepare for the worst and hope for the best.

I told her that it was looking like a 15-year sentence and she should be prepared. She, of course, refused to believe it and laughed, saying her sister was working on getting her home.

As I sat with her on a scrappy straw mat that only partially covered a small section of the dirty tiled floor, Schapelle didn't strike me as a person who had anything to hide. She put on a brave face and smiled, but you could see she was frightened. I saw her emotional struggle to come to terms with what was going on. She had the look of a person who didn't quite believe where they were. I've seen that look before. Dazed. Shocked. Unable to come to terms with the reality of their situation. I'd been there myself. Schapelle's Balinese legal representatives were hoping, for her sake, that the sentence wouldn't be too high but surely they knew? In my opinion, her Australian legal team were way out of their depth, despite their passion for justice. They didn't possess the necessary experience or high-level connections, in my opinion, to deal with such a case. But it was too late to change tact. They'd tried their very best. I knew Schapelle didn't believe that things could get any worse. She was still hopeful. Her family were busy making plans for her return to Australia after the trial. Mercedes was organising her exit visa. It struck me that no one was considering the alternatives. Schapelle's family and close friends truly believed that she would be set free. Was I the only one who knew she was about to be hit hard?

Tony Wilson knew what I was thinking but like the rest of them, he too was hoping for a miracle. I believe Tony was one of the few journalists who truly cared what happened to Schapelle in that court room. The rest were just in Bali for their story. Tony and I sat for many hours together at various little roadside restaurants in the days preceding the trial, discussing Schapelle's plight and what might and might not happen on the actual day. As I told Tony, when it comes to saving face, these situations rarely turn out in favour of the foreigner. On top of that, Schapelle can't actually prove the drugs aren't hers. It's pretty much an open and shut case. She will be found guilty. Just how guilty is about to be determined.

No one really wanted to hear what I had to say. Sometimes the truth is too difficult to comprehend. Everyone just wanted to remain in the safe cocoon of their fantasy and who was I anyway to try and pry them from it. I was merely there to give an opinion when asked and to maybe give Schapelle a little strength. So many times I longed to take charge when I saw how much Mercedes was struggling. I longed to say 'you should be doing this' but my compelling arguments would have been lost in all her emotion. She wanted to be the one to save her sister. She didn't trust anyone else.

It was actually quite difficult for me to make the journey to Bali. I had never stepped back into Asia since my own horrific ordeal in Laos. I had no idea if my name was listed on Interpol computers for breaching the Lao agreement because I'd testified against the regime at a US Congressional forum. It was the first time too that I had set foot inside an Asian prison since leaving Laos. It unsettled me a great deal. The sound of prison doors banging shut almost had me jumping out of my skin a couple of times, although I hid my feelings well. The sights and smells were, of course, completely different in Kerobokan Prison. Watching people visiting their loved ones completely threw me too because the only people visiting prisoners inside a Lao prison were those coming to inflict torture. The Lao police said that if your family wanted to visit you then they could join you.

Kerobokan prison was cleaner by comparison to a communist prison and was not blanketed by oppression. Quite honestly, however, one can't draw any comparisons between a Balinese prison and a communist one, except to say that in both you have no freedoms. I wondered if at night, Schapelle was forced to listen to the screams of the damned. I wondered if she wore her smile during the day to hide the fear, as I once did, and sometimes still do.

My visit with Schapelle was private and walking with her to the green gates left me feeling quite sad for her. I knew only too well that feeling of wanting to go through the door, yet knowing it was impossible. In some ways it's quite cruel when you think about it. Watching your loved one or friend walk through the door without you, knowing that at any time they can go to the beach, to the market or just home to watch television. Being so close to freedom and yet so far. Feeling that if only you could pass through to the other side of that wall that you stare at every day, or wishing it would crumble. I felt torn leaving Schapelle because part of me remembered just how bad that feeling was to be left behind.

'I'll be okay,' she said, before I hugged her one last time.

The next day the sun shone brilliantly in the sky. The frangipani bloomed and children laughed. It was indeed a tropical paradise, but in another part of Denpasar a dark cloud loomed over the life of a once-vibrant, beach-loving slip of a girl. Schapelle went to court. We were already there when she arrived.

I'll never forget that day, 27 May 2005, and how I worried about how her family would cope, as I sat with them in the front row of the Denpasar District Court. I prayed I was wrong and that Schapelle would be dealt with justly but in my heart I knew she was about to be given a big dose of reality. I asked the Australian Embassy to have the embassy doctor move to the front row just in case Schapelle fainted. They responded immediately. I sat and watched Schapelle's obvious anxiety as she sat before three Indonesian judges and a throng of media snapping away every time she moved her head.

It seemed like such a violation of her rights, only it wasn't. Her case was open and transparent. She wasn't being subjected to a closed court where there were no adversarial proceedings. Her verdict had not been pre-typed.

She had the right to object.

But none of it mattered when Schapelle was found guilty of drug importation. The sentence was harsh.

She would spend the next 20 years behind Indonesian bars!

In fact it was the harshest sentence to be handed to a foreigner in Bali in recent times. Others had been convicted of trafficking twice as much marijuana and got far less. One Mexican women trafficked 15.22kg and was sentenced to 15 years. I watched the Corby family's world crash down around them. Mercedes was devastated and on her feet. Her mother was horrified, screaming at the judges, 'Liar. Liars' and then at her daughter 'I'm taking you home'.

Mercedes was screaming and waving her fist 'She is innocent. This is not fair.' Schapelle was visibly upset and cried 'Mum, stop, it's okay,' holding her hand up in the air in a motion for her mother to stop yelling. It was terrible. The courtroom was filled with the pain and longing of close friends and family, all trying to absorb their new nightmarish reality.

Schapelle's emotional plea 'I'm not guilty' had fallen on deaf ears.

'Every inmate would say "I'm not guilty",' said one of the Judges later. He said he was unmoved by her emotion in the court. 'It's normal because it's not only Corby who is like that, in other hearings many of the defendants cry. We can't be influenced by crying, we treat her just like normal. But of course, we don't consider the accused as guilty before the verdict is delivered.'

Judge Sirait also confirmed an ominous pattern to his past judgements. 'I've handled many cases, not a hundred or 200, but over 500 since I became a judge. As far as I remember in a drugs case I haven't yet set anyone free.'

Schapelle was forcibly removed from the chaos that descended on the courtroom and taken back to Kerobokan prison to begin her 20-year sentence. Her family were left reeling from the shock of her conviction while the three judges, seemingly unconcerned, simply called it a day. Her Australian lawyer, Robin Tampoe, and advisor Ron Bakir, stood at the back of the courtroom, dejected.

Both slumped against the wall. Robin's hands were cradling his head as if he was trying to come to terms with the reality of what had just happened. His best laid plans in ruins. Ron Bakir actually wept. Then in the next moment I was on my feet and heading towards Schapelle's father. The plan was to get him out of the media spotlight to the vehicle parked outside the courthouse, then off to the secret villa paid for by *60 Minutes*. Liz Hayes was meeting us back at the villa where the family would give them their exclusive.

Later that night we managed to get a phone call to Schapelle inside the prison. Everyone was filling her head with hope: 'we'll get you out on the appeal' and 'it's going to be fine ... we're going to fight this!' I simply told Schapelle to stay strong and keep her head in a positive place because nothing is ever certain, especially in Indonesia.

I returned the next week to Kerobokan prison to visit with other westerners, taking them soap, food and basic supplies as promised. I had a hard time accessing the prison because of the media. I had no intention of meeting with Schapelle because her sister had insisted that we not contact her. I gave my word. Inside the prison I did see Schapelle from a distance. She was being visited by the Australian Consul. I waved to her but she was dazed. She probably thought I was just another visitor which of course, I was. I met in the courtyard with several other western prisoners. They enjoyed the cigarettes I'd brought, however cheap. They also spoke of Schapelle's sentence and said that it was steep. They said it could have been a whole lot worse. I never doubted it. I spoke to Schapelle the next day and again told her to stay strong, that miracles do happen and she has to be patient. This was the advice given to me by political prisoners in the Lao camp. 'No matter what, Schapelle, you just have to keep going!' I said as I hugged her goodbye.

I flew out Bali a few days later with the promise to help Mercedes if she ever needed my help. I had no idea if I would ever see Schapelle again.

On 29 May 2005 the headline of the *Sunday Age* read: 'It Could Have Been So Different, But The Offers Of Help Fell On Deaf Ears'—Phillip Hudson and Eamonn Duff. The article revealed that Australian Attorney-General Philip Ruddock, Justice Minister Chris Ellison and key advisers had just finished a meeting with members of Schapelle's defence team— Ron Bakir and Vasu Rasiah. Clearly they were concerned that Schapelle was not getting the experienced legal support she needed and her team were 'out of their depth'. The article went on to say 'There were also concerns about her Indonesian lawyer, Lily Lubis, and questions as to whether she

had ever handled a drug case before.'

From this meeting, the Australian Government offered two Queens Counsels to assist in the appeal that was to come. Mr Tom Percy QC and Mr Mark Trowell QC.

'Downer, Ellison and Ruddock all expressed genuine concern for her (Schapelle Corby's) welfare and were frustrated about what they could do and that they could not interfere,' said Mr Mark Trowell QC. 'Ruddock approached me and said he wanted to do something to help. He said, "Would you be prepared to offer some advice to the Corby legal team?"'

Trowell made a phone call to Schapelle's Australian lawyer Robin Tampoe. He left detailed messages explaining how he could help and naming some of his Indonesian contacts. He kept his phone on but no one called back. The Australian Government did not contact Schapelle's Indonesian lawyers or Schapelle Corby herself at the time because they believed the messages had been passed on. Schapelle's legal team claimed that no offer was made, but on 21 April 2005 Robin Tampoe revealed in an interview with Brisbane's *Courier-Mail* that Mr Trowell had in fact left messages.

After Schapelle was convicted in the Denpasar Court, again Trowell and Percy offered to look over the appeal. Schapelle's lawyers would not even let Percy and Trowell see the draft 21-page document that they intended to file with the Bali High Court. Even though the eminent QCs had agreed to work on the case pro bono, there wasn't anything they could do when they weren't even being included in the legal discussions. Schapelle's Indonesian legal team then did the unthinkable and recruited an Indonesian soap star, Anisa Tri Hapsari, to act as an information officer to persuade ordinary Indonesians of Schapelle's innocence and help influence Indonesian judges.

Mark Trowell QC questioned the sanity of doing this and said in the media that it was an insult to suggest that public pressure could in any way influence Indonesian judges in their decision. What it did do was enrage the Indonesian Prosecutors to the point where they called for Schapelle Corby to be punished more severely. They accused her of being involved in a transnational crime. The waters were getting murkier by the minute.

Then allegations of bribes came out when Trowell told the media that Schapelle's case co-ordinator (Vasu) had asked him to request $500,000 from the Australian Government to bribe the appeal judges. In actual fact, it's probably the only thing that would have realistically secured Schapelle's freedom but it's one thing to know this, and another to expect a prominent

QC to participate in such illegal activity. Vasu said rightly that they should forget the merits of the appeal. 'All you have to do is put in the appeal and if you have got money to bribe the judges, you win the appeal'.

With talk of bribery in the news, Mercedes acted on the advice of Walter Tonetto, a German lawyer based in Indonesia, and fired Schapelle's entire Indonesian legal team and broke all ties with Tampoe, Lily, Vasu and Bakir. Tonetto was to take the place of Vasu as strategist. Following his suggestion, Mercedes re-hired Erwin Siregar and Jakarta lawyer, Hotman Hutapea, who was as flamboyant as they came, with his bejewelled hands and chrome-plated pistols. Walter Tonetto didn't generate much media attention back in Australia but he and the new legal team would file an appeal against Schapelle's 20-year jail term, demanding her case be reopened and new evidence heard. Earlier, Indonesian prosecutors filed a separate appeal demanding she be jailed for life.

If anything, Walter Tonetto made a lot of sense. He said that the whole idea of Australia flying its own silks in (Trowel and Percy) and telling Indonesia how the legal process should have been done was counter-productive to Schapelle. He also said that there should be a lot of bowing and apologising to Indonesia for the cultural insults and Australia's arrogance. He promised to remedy the flaws of the defence efforts and said that they would look for new evidence, as required, that had not been brought before the previous judges. He said that the way the defence presented evidence about Indonesian police not fingerprinting the bag containing the 4.2kg of marijuana found in Schapelle's luggage, and the Australian investigation into corruption among baggage handlers, could have been done much better. He questioned the wisdom of calling an Australian criminologist as a witness, as opposed to calling for an Indonesian one. He also said that the new legal team would withdraw from the spotlight to focus on tackling the legal aspects of the case and mending the damage done to Schapelle's image in Indonesia. Tonetto expressed concern over the way many senior politicians in Indonesia had been offended; he said this lowered Schapelle's chances of a compassionate hearing.

Walter Tonetto made a whole lot of sense and it seemed to me that finally, Schapelle had someone on her side who understood the Indonesian way! But then 72 hours later, his services were no longer required. He too was out of the picture. Mercedes let him go and went with Hotman Hutapea.

By 4 July 2005 Schapelle's case was appealed. This created a wave of fresh media attention in Australia. Diehard Schapelle supporters wanted to rally and some did. Crowd sizes were rather small, and their online presence had fallen significantly from the initial campaigners calling to 'bring Schapelle home'. Nevertheless, Schapelle supporters were determined. I kept my word to Schapelle and told the general public what I could tell them about her, and her plight. I did what I could to make sure she wasn't forgotten, in the hope that a better outcome could be negotiated at her appeal. I didn't think much of Hotman Hutapea but he was Mercedes' choice. It was her show. I was simply there to rally support, to create awareness in Australia that regardless of guilt or innocence, the sentence was extremely harsh, even by Indonesian standards. I aired a message that translated to 'this could be your daughter' and focused on due process issues. I never crossed the line, however. I never said that I believed her to be innocent. I always said it didn't matter, which it didn't. Schapelle, like anyone else, was entitled to her human, legal and civil rights. This put me at odds with some of her more fanatical supporters, but for a while, that didn't matter either. And for a while I believed that I could actually help Schapelle.

Tony Wilson's gut feeling was that she had been set up as mentioned in his book titled *Schapelle*, published by New Holland in 2008. He believed in the baggage handler theory put forth by her lawyer Robin Tampoe.

Since September 11 and the Bali bombings, Australians had been repeatedly assured by the Australian Government that security measures and checks at Australian airports were heightened, but, on 1 August 2007, a former rugby league star, Les Mara, pleaded guilty to involvement in a 2004 baggage-handler drug importation racket at Sydney Airport—the same time that Schapelle Corby's bags were in Sydney Airport. The Australian Federal Police (AFP) reported that the same drug syndicate had been intending to import a further 20 kilograms (illicit drugs) from Argentina in May 2005 with the cooperation of some baggage handlers at Sydney Airport, but had abandoned the plan after discovering listening devices in the homes of some of those involved. It was as the former Australian Custom's officer, Alan Kessing, said, that criminality was systemic at the airports, particularly Sydney airport. However, his reports had been quashed. The Australian Government said it was unaware of report's existence.

Australia's Homeland Security spokesman at that time was Robert McClelland. He questioned why the report was kept from Schapelle's lawyers, since it had been available and indicated systematic criminality.

As McClelland said, 'that is a material fact that at the very least should have been disclosed to her defence.'

No answers were given and by now it was too late. Would it have made a difference? Probably not, unless it could be determined who exactly put the drugs in her bag. It might have created reasonable doubt, but in this case, they needed more than reasonable doubt. This was, after all, Indonesia, not Australia. Fourteen articles of the International Covenant on Civil and Political Rights (ICCPR) were breached in principle; Indonesia only ratified this agreement in 2006. Therefore, the breaches didn't technically apply to Schapelle's case. An experienced lawyer might have argued that the Indonesians had agreed in principle—a legally enforceable, but incompletely specified, agreement between parties that identifies the fundamental terms that are intended to be or are agreed upon. It's been argued before in other cases but was not considered in Schapelle's case.

The Indonesian Chief of Police admitted that, in the prosecution of Schapelle Corby, the investigation that led to her conviction was not only flawed but only 50 per cent complete. The judges contaminated evidence before them in court when they handled it. Customs officers contaminated it before that. Mercedes had screamed at them to put their gloves on when she first raced to Schapelle's aid at the airport. But all to no avail. Indonesian authorities failed to weigh the total luggage at the time of arrest and the failure of customs officers to follow basic investigative procedures, made it impossible to mount an effective defence.

By 12 October 2005, Schapelle supporters were expecting Schapelle to be set free. The Bali High Court reduced her 20-year sentence by five years.

Days after, flamboyant Hotman Hutapea quit. By 19 January 2006 the Supreme Court reinstated the original 20-year sentence. Schapelle was back where she started.

Twenty long years! She would be 47 years old by the time she walked from Kerobokan (less remissions)!

The evidence was destroyed in March 2006. The Indonesian police had the usual ceremonial burning with the prosecution's boss, police chiefs and the local mayor all in attendance. Erwin Siregar had implored the prosecutors to keep a sample for testing, for the extraordinary appeal they were hoping to submit at a later date. But it was too late. It was over. It didn't matter. They had their man or in this case, Schapelle Corby.

The handful of diehard Schapelle supporters that remained were outraged but it did neither Schapelle nor them any good. Then the media began searching for the next great story. They began digging about in the family's closet and, as with any family, they found a few skeletons. Despite the family's denials that any of them had ever been involved in drugs, it was revealed that Schapelle's father had been fined for possession of drugs, years before Schapelle was even born. 'I received a $400 fine for about two grams of marijuana which wasn't mine. Some girl had it and they busted the whole joint and I had to go along for the ride,' Michael Corby told *The Weekend Australian*.

Queensland police confirmed that there was no recorded conviction against him but the media followed up that story with another. This time they played on the fact that the Corby family repeatedly maintained they had no association with anyone linked to the drug trade.

A month before Schapelle's arrest in Bali, Queensland police raided a property in central Queensland where they allegedly found a sophisticated and well-established hydroponic cannabis-growing operation. They also allegedly found 5kg of high-quality marijuana in vacuum-sealed plastic bags, along with thousands of dollars in cash hidden throughout the property. The owner 'Tony' was charged with producing a commercial amount of illicit drugs.

ABC investigative journalist John Stewart uncovered the fact that Schapelle's father, Michael Corby, had purchased a property next door in 1998, two years after his accused neighbour bought his farm in 1996. And it wasn't the first time the two men had been neighbours. They were neighbours in the mining town of Middlemount in Central Queensland several years before when both men worked at the German Creek Mine. Then John Stewart revealed the flight records for Michael Corby showing he had travelled to Bali on 4 September 2004, just four weeks before his daughter Schapelle was arrested at Denpasar airport. The ABC reported that sources close to the AFP viewed photographs of the cannabis found inside Schapelle's boogie-board bag and said that it was most likely to be hydroponically grown. Though without DNA testing, this was simply hearsay.

As John Stewart pointed out, the fact that Michael Corby knew 'Tony' and lived next door to him, or that he travelled to Bali four weeks before Schapelle, did not make Michael Corby or anyone else in his family part of any drug trade. But it certainly created enough smoke for the public to get an impression that there might have been more to the story than what was aired on the ABC. It was a case of 'where there's smoke there's fire' that got people second guessing, regardless of whether there was a fire. Had the Queensland police been able to make a connection, surely they would have arrested Michael Corby?

Schapelle's father's cousin, Allan Trembath, came out of the woodwork and told the media that Michael Corby Snr had been 'involved in drugs for three decades'. He told *Lateline* that in the '80s Michael Corby was known as 'the local drug dealer' in Mackay. He said that Michael Corby had once offered him $80,000 to ship marijuana from Cape York to Mackay. He also talked about Schapelle: 'Honestly, I don't think Schapelle would have known any different, you know, because she would have been around drugs all her life.'

Why would Trembath make up such a story? What would motivate a relative to go on national TV and say such things and risk a defamation case when it's a known fact the ABC don't pay for stories like other TV networks do? Queensland police refuted the claims and said there was no evidence linking Michael Corby to the drug trade.

It was then revealed that Schapelle's older brother, Clinton Rose, had been jailed for drug-related activity and was serving a 15-month sentence in Queensland for breaking and entering and fraud. This was his second time in prison. In January 2002, he was convicted of drug possession. He had pleaded guilty to what the Southport District Judge, Robert Hall, described as a 'campaign of crime'. Clinton Rose pleaded guilty to a total of 62 charges accumulated over a six-month period. He was sentenced to three years' probation. In August 2004, he was sentenced to 12 months' jail for breaching conditions of his probation.

Schapelle's young half-brother, James, who travelled with her to Bali, was arrested in Australia on drug charges, a year after Schapelle was arrested in Bali. He appeared in court on drug possession and assault charges, along with two friends who allegedly invaded the home of a well-known drug dealer, tied up the occupants and bashed a male occupant before fleeing with a quantity of cannabis and cash. It was reported that the Queensland police found cannabis in Schapelle's mother's home. James' lawyer claimed he had broken into the home of the well-known drug dealer, believing the home's occupants may have had information that could assist in Schapelle

Corby's sentence appeal.

Months later, James Kisina pleaded guilty in court to eight charges: two counts of deprivation of liberty, two counts of assault occasioning bodily harm, and one count each of producing a dangerous drug, possessing a dangerous drug, possessing an item used in a criminal offence and entering a dwelling. He was sentenced on 16 October 2006 to a four-year suspended sentence with a 10 month non-parole period.

There was one story after another until an even bigger bombshell dropped on the Corby family. Photographs of Schapelle with a man from Adelaide identified as Malcolm McCauley surfaced in the media. McCauley claimed to be Schapelle's father's marijuana supplier. He claimed that drugs were regularly smuggled into Bali by Michael Corby. Police in two states refuted the allegations as baseless. They said that there was no evidence to link Michael Corby with involvement in the drug trade. The detectives in Adelaide further claimed the allegations by convicted drug dealer Malcolm McCauley were 'laughable' and that an extensive investigation found no links between the man and the Corby family. One of the police officers said the photographs of McCauley and Schapelle Corby together did spark an extensive investigation to determine if there were any links between McCauley's smuggling syndicate and the Corby family.

'We have found no links, nothing at all, no evidence linking the two situations,' the officer said. 'If he had any further information, it would have been advantageous for him to have told us at the time. There is every likelihood he could have used that as a bargaining chip and that would have been taken into account when he was sentenced. That did not take place and he did not even hint at any connection with the Corby clan.'

That photograph was a pure coincidence, or rather a stroke of bad luck for Schapelle. McCauley was holidaying in Bali with friends and decided to be like thousands of others and be photographed with the famous Schapelle Corby. He joined the queue to the prison, handed over several hundred rupiah to the awaiting police, and took part in a happy snap with Schapelle, aka 'the Ganga Queen'.

How much more could Schapelle take of what was now being seen by some as a media witch-hunt? Every time I turned on the TV there was more scandal, and when the McCauley saga died down another scandal surfaced.

Lifelong friend, Jodie Power, made some startling revelations to media about the Corby family. She claimed that Schapelle smoked pot and took other illicit drugs. She said that Mercedes had asked her to take marijuana to Bali. She claimed that Mercedes smoked marijuana and took small amounts of cannabis into Bali and had been selling it there for years. But only months beforehand, Jodie Power had herself received payment for an interview stating that Schapelle was completely innocent. What had brought on this change of heart in a woman who said previously she would stop at nothing to help free Schapelle? The TV network said it was a case of a woman scorned. Another said it was done for $100,000. Whatever it was, the feud escalated, as did the innuendos. Mercedes hit back with a defamation case against the TV network that aired the comments. She engaged prominent QC Stuart Littlemore. The case featured across Australia. It was complete muck-raking in my opinion but Mercedes had no other choice.

After six hours, the jury found Channel Seven's defence of truth had failed on all but one of the defamatory imputations, namely that Mercedes Corby had possessed marijuana. Mercedes said that her drug use was limited, and her own letters referring to her drug use were written when she was 'young and immature' and trying to look 'cool'. The defamation case was settled out of court in her favour. The settlement amount was never disclosed. It was a victory for Mercedes but not for Schapelle. Each time one of these stories hit the news, it cast doubt over her innocence. Technically, it had nothing at all to do with Schapelle but for the fact that her family were now being hunted by people wanting to make some quick cash. It made for yet another sensational story.

When former *60 Minutes* staffer, Kathryn Bonella, co-authored and released Schapelle's biography in 2006, who would have thought it would cause such a stir? The Australian Federal Director of Public Prosecutions moved immediately to seize the royalties of Schapelle's book. *My Story* was Schapelle's way of telling the Australian public what life had been like for her inside Kerobokan Prison but it was never going to 'bring Schapelle home!'

What it did do was spark a reaction from the Queensland Government, Schapelle's home state. According to the Proceeds of Crime Act, no person who has been convicted of a crime is permitted to benefit commercially through the exploitation of their notoriety. This also extends to third-party benefactors. The Queensland Court of Appeal decided that the earnings from *My Story* constituted proceeds of crime. They ordered the sum of $282,750 to be seized by police. In addition, they also froze the sum of $15,000, promised to Schapelle's sister for an interview in an Australian magazine. Schapelle's publishers were under the strong impression that royalties payable to Schapelle would be used to assist her defence costs and legal challenges. The *Proceeds of a Crime Act* legislation however, does not consider this to be a valid reason to prompt any exclusion from the Act.

According to the *Proceeds of Crime Act*, people have every right to tell their story, to talk to anyone about their story, but not to profit personally from telling their story, either in Australia or abroad. They can, however, give the proceeds to charity. The legislation is quite clear, though whether it is fair has yet to be fully debated. The publisher, Pan Macmillan, and the co-author, Kathryn Bonella, were exempt from the *Proceeds of Crime Act*. Many supporters were outraged that even Schapelle's sister could not be paid for telling her side of the story. How else was she to sustain her family in Bali while fighting for her sister's freedom? Mercedes had vowed not to leave Schapelle. The cost of keeping that promise was enormous.

Just to clarify, according to the Australian Government, Mercedes Corby has the right to tell her own story and profit but the minute she relates to her sister's experience, she is then deemed to be profiting from an activity considered unlawful, of which her sister was convicted. In such circumstances, the Attorney-General's Office of Australia argues that it would be well within its rights to seize those profits. The legislation does not currently take into consideration the rights of an innocent person wrongly convicted. We all know there are numerous people throughout the world who have been wrongly convicted. Engaging legal support to fight against the system of injustice takes an incredible amount of money. How else is a person supposed to pay for top-notch lawyers to represent them, if they haven't the means of earning an income? People seldom think about such things, until, that is, it happens to someone they love.

When a person is detained in prison, they often have no control of what's going on around them and not much knowledge of what people are doing or saying on their behalf or about them. Prisoners do not lose their rights simply because they are prisoners, or at least they are not supposed to. Sadly, people tend to forget that prisoners are still human. Schapelle is still someone's daughter, sister and someone's best friend. The fact that her case was so highly publicised did, however, help to generate greater awareness in Australia about public security when travelling overseas. People started to question if they were indeed as safe as they were led to believe. People began to question their government's commitment to Australians detained abroad. Schapelle's plight has had a positive effect on her fellow Australian travellers but more awareness needs to be generated in order to ensure protection for Australians. Qantas now offers travellers departing Australian airports the full plastic wrap system for their luggage. That strongly suggests that you can't afford to have complete faith in their system.

Qantas is also the only airline to boycott advertising Schapelle's book, *My Story*. Regardless of guilt or innocence, people should be aware of her plight so that they can be reminded to take every necessary precaution to avoid ending up in a situation like Schapelle Corby's. It's no longer unreasonable or far-fetched to think that you could face a death penalty if a baggage handler allegedly puts drugs in your bags!

People should take greater care when travelling. They should lock their luggage and secure all outer pockets. They should record the baggage weight somewhere in case they retrieve their case at the other end and there's a discrepancy. Travel insurance may cover loss, theft or damage to luggage, but the airlines will not take any responsibility for what is found inside a traveller's bag even after they have carefully screened the baggage at check-in.

Even if it can be proved that the traveller had no access to their bags anytime throughout their journey, as in Schapelle's case, they may still be held liable in the event it is tampered with while in the care of the air carrier. It pays to take every precaution and nothing for granted.

Plans for a Prisoner Transfer Agreement, which would allow those jailed in Indonesia to serve part of their sentences at home, are still a long way off. The negotiations have stalled partly because the Indonesian Government stipulated that prisoners should serve at least half their sentence before applying for transfer. The Australian Government is seeking to negotiate better terms, being mindful that foreign internment also has an impact on the family. Like the costs borne by families to provide ongoing support to their loved one who has been detained, the impact of separation, travel expenses, culture, language barriers, access to medical care and, most importantly, access to offender management and rehabilitation programs.

Schapelle says she wishes to return home a free woman. Unless by some miracle someone comes forward to claim the drugs and can substantiate that claim, then her only hope of an early release is by way of a pardon or clemency. Schapelle's application for clemency was lodged in March 2010. The Australian Government publicly agreed to support it as they do in most clemency applications where Australians are detained overseas. The clemency plea was backed by reports from two psychiatrists. Schapelle's psychiatrist in Bali, Dr Denny Thong, who said that when he observed her from May 21 to 25, he was able to conclude that she suffers 'depression with psychotic symptoms'. The second report was submitted by Australian psychiatrist, Dr Jonathan Phillips, who was engaged by the Corby family. He visited Bali with the assistance of Sane Australia and financial backing from *New Idea* Magazine. He reported exclusively to *New Idea* Magazine that the best option would be to have her transferred as a prisoner to Australia and treated in a secure hospital setting.

Dr Phillips concluded by saying that Schapelle was 'hanging by a thread. She is lost in her own bewildering world where fantasy, hallucinations and bizarre ideas dominate.' *New Idea* Magazine released the story under a sensational headline: 'Bring Schapelle home or she'll die!'

Dr Thong sensibly countered this in *The Australian* when he said 'I think she is mentally disturbed. She has depression with psychotic symptoms. It's not a life and death situation. She could be dangerous to herself, but she's not hanging by a thread [as Dr Phillips claimed].'

But it had little impact in reversing the downturn in Australian public opinion which had become tired of the constant barrage of *New Idea* exclusives; 'She may be suffering from psychosis brought on by years of marijuana abuse. She may be seriously depressed by her situation' said one reader.

Kerobokan prison doctor Agung Hartawan said that Dr Phillips had seen Schapelle for only an hour. Dr. Hartawan said that her condition was treatable. He said that Schapelle exhibits no day-to-day sign of undue duress. 'Judging from her daily routine, she's fine. As of today, she's doing OK, she's socialising OK with the others. When she's stressed or depressed she will act out, but other than that, she's normal,' he said. Dr Hartawan also said that he was not consulted by Dr Phillips, nor had he seen the report.

The smart thing would have been to assemble a diplomatic task force (her lawyer, her doctors and a DFAT member) to attempt to secure a better outcome for Schapelle (treatment). The diplomatic task force could have met with their Indonesian counterparts (head of the hospital where

Schapelle had been treated, prison doctor, prisoner Governor and Indonesian psychiatrist), away from the media. They could have secured a round table discussion with all parties involved in her care and then worked through an amicable solution to best protect the integrity of her care. This is what is usually prescribed because it tends to work more effectively than the tabloid approach. It lessens the risk of offending anyone. In fact, I had been quietly working on this behind the scenes. I had both a prominent psychiatrist and a leading psychologist on standby, to fly to Bali. The psychologist was already known to the Indonesians, since he had presented expert testimony in the death row case of three Australians. Their sentences were reduced to life. I was also waiting on a meeting that following week with the then Prime Minister Kevin Rudd to let him know what we were proposing and to enlist his support. Having successfully consulted on and negotiated numerous cases prior to the Corby case, I felt quite confident that we could secure a more favourable outcome. At worst, we could have her moved from the prison to a psychiatric facility on a more permanent basis, away from the media. At best, we could achieve this and engage the Australian Government to quietly contact the Indonesian Government to seek their willingness and agreement to a diplomatic intervention. This would present an opportunity to discuss realistic options for her possible repatriation to an Australian medical prison facility based on humanitarian grounds.

It would give the Indonesians a face-saving 'out' and be rid of the circus that constantly surrounded Schapelle. It would satisfy the court ruling that she be a convicted person and that she serve the remainder of her sentence in Australia. It wasn't the ideal outcome, but at least it may have opened a more reasonable dialogue that was missing. It was a long shot but the history of these cases provided tangible evidence that the best way forward is invariably through a diplomatic solution. I was ready to put the plan into action. I was just waiting on confirmation about the logistics of who would pay for the medical team to go to Bali. The next thing I heard was that Dr Phillips was going to Bali, courtesy of *New Idea* Magazine.

I was deeply disappointed because I knew the approach would only result in more tabloid media and surely that would not do Schapelle any good? Clearly the governor of Kerobokan prison, Governor Siswanto, was offended too when the headlines broke—'Schapelle Corby Insane: could die'. It was almost as if someone was accusing the Indonesian authorities of not only being incompetent but deliberately trying to end the life of an

Australian citizen. Of course, the articles that were written were never so bold but were very much open to that interpretation. Governor Siswanto, not medically trained of course, told the media that in his opinion and from his observations, Schapelle was faking her mental illness. In his 17-page report to his superiors in October 2010, Governor Siswanto listed numerous incidents of deviant and disobedient behaviour, which he said had undermined the prison's rehabilitation program. He also said 'She should stop creating nonsense sensations because it will only hurt her case.'

His statement carried a great deal more weight than what was reported in the tabloids. This was a man of prominence and authority, used to dealing with the very worst of humankind. This was a man who had seen it all and was not easily fooled. Schapelle's people were obviously hoping that Dr Phillips' report would bring pressure to bear but clearly the strategy backfired. The Indonesian authorities were offended, the Australian Government was backed into a corner, no diplomatic task force ever went to her aid, and Schapelle was still detained in Kerobokan Prison. The Indonesian President publicly vowed never to pardon drug traffickers. Although there is a case in precedent that he has done in the past.

All went quiet again as usual. Then some months later, on national TV with a rant—'Bring our little girl home'—flamboyant Gold Coast lawyer Ms Kerry Smith-Douglas made her debut to the Australian public as the new lawyer for Schapelle Corby. Smith-Douglas was like a female version of Hotman Hutapea only with more colour and less articulate. A podium-thumping lawyer who hit the chatshow circuit with a barrage of highly emotive criticism as she proclaimed the Australian Government wasn't doing nearly enough and that they could expect 100,000 Schapelle supporters to march on Canberra any day if they didn't 'Bring Schapelle home now!'

It was more likely that a dozen supporters might march. By this stage, most people were fed up with the Schapelle Corby show. No one wanted to be associated with it. Not Get Up, Amnesty International, Fair Trials Abroad, the Innocence Project, Human Rights Watch or the Foreign Prisoner Support Service. Anyone who refused to follow the fanatical party line of the so-called official Schapelle Corby Support Group came under malicious attack. There was an endless flow of vile blogs seeking to destroy the credibility of anyone who refused to support her 'cult' following. Sadly, the only thing they ever achieved for Schapelle was to isolate her from a sympathetic audience.

In April 2011, in another twist in the ongoing story of Schapelle Corby, I stumbled across a new book by Eamonn Duff, a senior Fairfax investigative journalist, writing for Sydney's *Sun Herald*. It's titled 'The Fall Girl' and the description read:

> *When Schapelle Corby was arrested in Bali with 4.2 kilograms of cannabis in her boogie board was she an innocent dupe or the fall girl for a well-established drug running syndicate? Eamonn Duff follows new leads, and talks to family associates, police, politicians and Schapelle's lawyers to prise open surprising clues about what really happened on that fateful night and in the years that followed. A powerfully compelling and explosive work of investigative journalism, The Fall Girl provides a remarkable picture of a drug network that reached from Adelaide to Bali. It also reveals Mick Corby's involvement in the cannabis trade and how Schapelle came to be paying the ultimate price for her father's sins.*

The book was cancelled and will no longer be published.

I guess it is easy to make a case against someone who is no longer living, someone who cannot respond to the allegations. But on the occasion I met Michael Corby Snr, I certainly didn't get any impression that he was a 'Mr Big' in some kind of drug syndicate. At the end of the day, what people say back home in Australia will unlikely affect Schapelle's current situation. The judges decided long before this book was ever mentioned that 'Her defence team has not done enough to prove Schapelle Corby's innocence'. Her own lawyer, Lily Lubis admitted, 'There is no bail for drug-related offences in Indonesia, the only way to get her out is to prove she didn't do it.'

Sadly for Schapelle, they failed to do that.

Schapelle Corby was, like it or not, charged, tried in a court, and convicted pursuant to Indonesian law. Some question the fairness of the judicial process. Others believe that in Indonesian terms the sentence is not manifestly excessive; however, that does not mean that it is not harsh for comparable crimes. Regardless of whether people believe Schapelle Corby is innocent or guilty, this case highlights the pitfalls of foreign internment and how it affects prisoners and their families.

Foreign internment is a complex area. It is fraught with challenges that test the resolve of those interned to endure their destiny. If it happens to you then make sure you get a competent lawyer who won't offend the detaining party by saying their laws are ridiculous (even if you think they are); make sure they are familiar with international law, sovereignty, foreign judicial process, and be mindful of cultural sensitivities (what is and isn't offensive in that culture). Establish a good rapport with the consular officers in the field, and with your point of contact through your relevant foreign affairs department. Work with people who have proven experience to develop a sound strategic plan away from the media, using the support and advice of known professionals who have extensive knowledge and key contacts in foreign relations. Work with them to engage the foreign government with dignity and respect, after all, they are best able to make approaches without the emotional attachments that can derail negotiations early on. Understand that these processes are complex and not easily resolved. Understand the reality of what your government can and cannot do for you. Then finally remember that you attract more bees with honey than you do with vinegar.

Schapelle still sits in Kerobokan Prison, waiting to come home. Since everyone else around her has had their say, sold their story or released their films, it's perhaps fitting that Schapelle be given the final word.

> *'I long to be free and live again outside these walls ... I will never understand why this happened to me. Why my bag? Right now I'm empty, lost and numb. It's been so long since I've felt peaceful and happy. So long since I've smiled and laughed on the inside and out. I sound like a broken record but I will keep saying it: I'm innocent, I'm innocent, I'm innocent'* —Schapelle Corby, My Story

Australian Citizens
http://www.smarttraveller.gov.au

UK Citizens (Commonwealth)
http://www.fco.gov.uk

US Citizens
http://www.tnavel.state.gov

5
WHERE IS DADDY?

Jody Aggett, Thailand

Tony and Lorna Aggett are an amazing couple who live with their grandson in the small market town of Westlea, West Swindon, Wiltshire, in England.

Within their community they are seen as a loving Christian family who have boundless compassion for those in need. To each other, they are a single soul dwelling in two bodies. They believe that without faith, nothing is possible and that with faith, nothing is impossible.

Tony and Lorna are truly inspiring because they live every day without a doubt that miracles can happen. They are always positive and look for the silver lining in every cloud, even when those clouds are quite dark and ominous. They don't deserve the tragedy that has struck their lives, but they have strength and, with it, they can and will endure. Their beloved son, Jody Ryan Aggett, is currently serving a life sentence in Thailand's notorious Bangkok Hilton. Lorna explains why:

I don't know where to start, as having a child in prison is just so hard to grasp. It's so much easier to push it to the back of your mind and pretend all is well. Then every now and then reality hits home. The pain can be so bad at times that you feel as though your heart is twisting into huge knots. The fear, the feeling of helplessness, any parent would know that as a parent you protect and love your child no matter what. Now, all we can do is love Jody, be there for him, and do anything and everything in our power to help get him out of Bangkwang Prison, Thailand's notorious Bangkok Hilton.

Jody was born on 29 July 1977, according to his parents he was a beautiful baby, born along with his twin sister, Tammy. Despite being twins, as they grew, Tammy showed early signs of independence in contrast to Jody's constant demand to be cuddled and his desire to be the centre of their world. Jody loved to sit on his mother's lap where he felt safe and secure.

Jody grew up in a little village called Scottburgh on the south coast of Kwa Zulu Natal in South Africa. You couldn't ask for a better place to grow up. Scottburgh had beautiful beaches, a lovely little shopping centre and good schools.

Jody and Tammy were fiercely protective of each other and shared the same circle of friends. Tammy would organise end-of-year parties on the beach, or at one of the swimming pools. Jody was happy to just be part of these. They would go off to school in the morning, Lorna would collect them at lunch time, and as soon as all homework was done, off to the beach they went where Jody would meet up with all his friends. They'd all spend the afternoon together in one great big group. Jody's friends always felt comfortable in the Aggetts' house.

Jody loved sports and was an accomplished athlete. He played cricket and rugby, although his mum always worried about him. He was one of those tall skinny children who looked as though they would snap when tackled. But he never did. He was a good swimmer. In fact, whatever sport Jody took up he did well. Both his parents loved sport and it gave them great joy to support him. Jody was always very popular during his school years, but he loved nothing more than just being with his family. Often he would ask his mother to make up an excuse so that his friends would have to go home. There was a time when Lorna was in bed so ill that she couldn't lift her head from the pillow. Jody was the one who took Lorna her breakfast and tablets. He cleaned the house, did the washing (had to stand on a chair to hang up the clothes on the washing line), but bless him, he took care of his mother all day.

'That was just Jody for you, always willing to help in any way that he could. He was also fiercely protective of me,' says Lorna.

Jody got through his high school years and never gave his parents any problems. His mother recalls that he lost his temper about three times, but that was about it.

While in high school Jody found a little puppy which had wandered over to his house. The owner of the puppy allowed Jody to keep it. He named the dog Baron and they became inseparable. They slept, ate and played together. No one was sure who loved who more.

Jody never smoked or took drugs. He was terribly shy of girls, but later on in life enjoyed a drink or two. He loved playing pool with his Dad, Tony.

Jody's love for his Dad was always apparent. He was so delighted when Tony asked him to work alongside him in his little sales and merchandising business. Just being with his Dad was great.

Jody first met Kristin, a Thai girl living in South Africa, at a nightclub. They instantly clicked and, before long, Kristin and Jody were inseparable. Jody says it was love at first sight. Even his dog Baron was forced to take a back seat to the new love of Jody's life. Both Tony and Lorna were happy for their son. Kristin was a kind and compassionate girl. They soon grew to love her.

> *Eventually, Kristin moved in with us and became part of the family. For a year, Jody and Kristin spent every waking hour together. Jody taught her how to play pool and action cricket. We didn't know much about her other than the girl we saw before us. We simply accepted her because Jody loved her. We had no idea of her life before, or even how she came to be in South Africa. All we knew was that our son had finally found the girl of his dreams and his joy brought joy to all of us.*
>
> *If I close my eyes I can still see her dancing around the Christmas tree just after we had decorated it. She spent her first Christmas with us and was so childlike in her excitement—she even poked holes in all the presents to peep inside them.*

As the months passed, the Aggetts learned the truth. Kristin was a victim of those unscrupulous human traffickers who prey on young girls with unfulfilled promises of decent work and money. She was working in a hotel along with several other Thai girls. She had no passport, presumably because it had been confiscated by the human traffickers. Her visa had run out so the Aggetts took her to the Thai embassy to get them to issue her with a new passport. They were informed that she was required by law to return to Thailand.

It wasn't long after their trip to the embassy that Tony and Lorna began getting phone calls from people looking for Kristin.

> *They told us that they were going to report her for not having a passport and when we told them to leave her alone, they became more threatening. We sold Jody's car to pay for her air ticket home. She returned to Thailand in July 2000.*

Tony and Lorna were in the process of emigrating to the UK, where Tony was born. Tony was to go ahead on the understanding that his wife and son would remain behind until he found somewhere to live and a job. Lorna and Jody didn't have long to wait because Tony landed a job almost as soon as he landed on British soil. Not long after, Jody and his mother were winging their way to Heathrow airport.

'I knew I would miss South Africa and all my friends. But I also knew that we would build a new life and I was excited by that. We moved into a little house in Devon and it was beautiful. As the months passed, Jody continued to pine for Kristin, saying the pain in his heart was just too great and he had to be with her,' says Lorna.

It was obvious to Tony and Lorna that their son was on the brink of making his own life-changing decision. By the end of October, they waved goodbye and wished him a safe journey.

> *We later learned from Jody that Kristin had moved into an apartment leased by a Dutch-Canadian named Adrian and his Thai girlfriend, Ta, and that Kristin was expecting Jody's child. They decided to get engaged, return to the UK, have the baby and then get married. However, Kristin's doctor told her that it was too late in her pregnancy for her to travel overseas. Jody wasn't officially able to work as he didn't have a work permit, so Adrian offered them free room and board at the apartment if they would look after the garden and clean the travel agency below. The offer seemed like a godsend. It solved their immediate problems. The rest would work itself out when the baby was born, then Jody and Kristin would return to the UK. Tony and I began doing what we could to help lodge papers for Kristin's visa. We planned to visit Thailand in December 2001 for the birth of our first grandchild. But as the weeks passed, I felt something was terribly wrong —I had this heavy feeling inside of me.*

It was November 2001, when their whole world came crashing down. Tony and Lorna got up as usual and went off to work, happy to have jobs that they really enjoyed. At 12 noon, Tony rang Lorna. She sensed something had happened to Jody.

How she knew was just a mother's intuition.

'Tell me Tony … tell me what's happened!' she demanded. The three words that came next were not at all what she had expected.

'He's in jail'.

Tony and Lorna's son had been arrested in Thailand for drugs!

As I listened to my husband's voice, my heart almost stopped. The rest of the conversation became a blur. Immediately after I hung up the phone I switched on our computer and connected to the internet and started searching the newspaper reports. Suddenly, there in front of me the headline read 'South African man arrested for drugs—Jody Ryan Aggett'. I read it again and again, then shock set in. I felt numb as my eyes caught the words 'Death Penalty for Drugs'. I backed away from the computer and stood in absolute shock. What was I supposed to do? How was I going to protect my only son? I was paralysed, oblivious to everything and everyone around me. A couple of my work colleagues noticed me staring at the screen, transfixed. They called my name several times without a response. My hands shook. I felt dead inside. My fear when Jody said he was going to Thailand was that something terrible would happen. The place was a haven for drug deals and corruption. We'd seen films about foreigners having drugs planted on them. I was concerned and said as much the day that Jody left for Thailand. 'Jody, stay far away from anyone who even looks as though they may be involved with drugs—this is Thailand you are going to—be careful.

He just smiled. 'OK Mum, don't worry, you know my feelings about drugs.'

Tony collected Lorna from work after a colleague rang him and said she was in no state to work. The couple travelled home in silence. They didn't even know what to say to each other. What was there to say? Surely it must be a mistake? How could this be happening? Anyone who has lost a loved one will know exactly what Tony and Lorna must have been feeling.

Has this really happened? Why has it happened and then half expecting to see that person walk through the door … or the phone to ring to say 'It's okay, the police made a mistake'.

Tony and Lorna sat for hours in silence listening to gospel music, trying to find peace in the presence of God while they waited for news.

I knew that only God knew the truth, and so we turned to Him for our answers. Later that night, I lay in bed from sheer exhaustion, hoping to close my eyes and wish away this nightmare that had befallen us. But I tossed and turned as the images flooded my mind. I saw Jody in prison and they were dragging him down a dark corridor to a room. They placed a blindfold over his eyes, tied him to a post and executed him. The bullets pierced his heart. He quivered and slumped. My boy was dead. I screamed out Jody's name and sat bolt upright in bed. I felt sick with fear. My son, how had this happened? I lay awake

> tormented about my son's fate. When the morning finally came, Tony and I knew that now was not the time to fall apart. There would be plenty of time for that later. We started contacting our closest friends to let them know what happened. Everyone, of course, was shocked when they heard the news. They all knew there was no way Jody was guilty. I gained tremendous strength and courage from our family and friends. Without their support I doubt I would have been able to hold myself together long enough to begin making the necessary arrangements to go to Thailand. To say that Tony and I were nervous about the trip was an understatement. A foreign country with the death penalty for drugs, would we end up in prison with Jody? What would happen when we got there? My faith was strong. God would not forsake me.

Lorna remembers the first thing she saw as she entered the Don Muang Airport. It was a huge sign saying 'Don't do drugs—Death Penalty for those that do'. She says that she felt herself go numb all over. 'I imagined my boy walking this path, seeing that sign, not bothered by it, not caring because he had nothing to do with drugs. I felt a terrible sense of dread. My son's life was now in the hands of God.'

Neither Tony nor Lorna noticed the heat as they stepped from the airport into a taxi. As they passed throngs of tourists walking aimlessly along the streets, Lorna thought of all those mothers' sons, while hers sat in a prison cell with every kind of known criminal. The next morning, Tony and Lorna made their way straight to the South African embassy. Their staff had very kindly organised for the couple to visit Jody at the holding cell in the offices of the Thai Police Narcotics Suppression Unit.

> I was overwhelmed at the thought of seeing our boy in such a hideous place. Not a friendly face among all the Thai police officers who passed us by. Thailand is known as 'the land of smiles' but it could not spare one for this mother and father. The wait felt like forever before a door opened. My son walked slowly towards me. I all but broke down completely when I saw the gentle smile on his face. How brave he was.

'Hi Mum and Dad,' he said gently.

Tony and Lorna hugged their son and for a brief moment gave way to emotions they'd been holding back ever since they first heard of his arrest. The police wouldn't remove Jody's shackles despite Tony and Lorna's heartfelt pleas. The three sat talking for an hour trying to find out what had happened and why. Jody explained that Adrian had it all under control and if his parents interfered he would be hurt. Adrian would use his lawyers to help Jody and Kristin out of the mess they were in. He would defend them and would pay for everything. Kristin and Jody felt that they 'owed' Adrian for putting a roof over their heads.

'Somehow they believed that Adrian could fix everything. I was incredulous that my son couldn't see what Adrian was up to. Again, my intuition told me that it was all Adrian's fault, although I had no proof. When a lady at the South African embassy contacted us later that day, she advised us to get Jody his own lawyer. We felt helpless but we certainly weren't. One thing was sure, we wouldn't put our trust in the man who was responsible for our son being in prison,' says Lorna.

It was a frightening situation to be in. There were so many questions but so little time to ask them. Jody was convinced by Adrian that his parents should just be patient and do nothing. Tony and Lorna didn't understand it, but their son seemed certain that the matter wasn't as serious as they first thought. Lorna hugged Jody goodbye and promised that no matter how bad things got, they would always be there for him and Kristin. Tony and Lorna left the Drug Suppression Unit not knowing when or if they'd see their son again.

The whole time Tony and I remained in Thailand we were followed wherever we went. We thought it may be the police following us—or was it the other people involved in the drugs ring? Whoever it was, the feeling was unnerving and I never felt quite safe. We learned that Jody had been moved from the holding cells at the Drug Suppression Unit to a Thai prison. We weren't able to visit him for a few days. My son had been transferred to Klong Prem Remand Prison, otherwise known as The Bangkok Hilton. You could not have thought of a less appropriate name. The prison had very high white walls and the doormen at this so-called Hilton wore prison officer uniforms, no smiles and looked you up and down as if you were guilty. The prison was bordered by a stinking green cesspool of a river which was a breeding ground for insects and disease.

On the inside it was no better. The visitors' area, which ran down two sides of the interior quadrangle, was a run-down building, landscaped by a stagnant water feature and home to squadrons of hungry mosquitoes and dozens of mangy cats. The twenty-minute visit was conducted over a distance of about a metre, with both parties separated by sheets of metal into which were punched holes. There were no lights on the prisoner's side and it was difficult to see Jody without pressing my face right up to the partition. The cacophony generated by the visitors and prisoners during the visit was depressing and distracting.

A feeling of hopelessness was hammered into Tony and Lorna when Jody arrived for the visit with leg irons welded onto his legs. Although he was not yet convicted, he was seen as a highly dangerous criminal. These leg irons, or jewellery as Jody referred to them, were to stay attached for the next 18 months.

During his stay at Klong Prem, Jody was introduced to an official from the British embassy. Jody requested that she look into the possibility of obtaining him a British passport and thus his citizenship, to which he was entitled as his father was born in Britain. Jody's passport was issued in a relatively short time and he then fell under the remit of the British embassy in Bangkok in terms of his medical and consular needs.

'They have looked after Jody extremely well and have gone the extra mile in that a very strong bond now exists between Bangkok and us in Swindon,' says Lorna.

Jody's transfer to Bangkwang Prison brought with it even more fears for his parents. Bangkwang, or The Big Tiger as it is known, has a reputation for eating men alive. This was Thailand's central maximum security holding facility and was designed for holding 'lifers' and those with the death sentence. Lorna shuddered to think of her son in a place renowned as one of the most inhumane in the world. A place where prisoners are crammed into large dormitory-style cells from late afternoon until early morning. A bare light bulb shining in his face all night long, no bed, no fresh sheets or pillows and no creature comforts. Like everyone else, Jody would be sleeping on a bare concrete floor. He would be subjected to strip searches, violence and horrors neither of his parents could even imagine. He would bathe in filthy brown river water pumped into a communal trough and use an open hole in the corner of his cell as a toilet.

Every daily living requirement had a price, including food, drinking water, bedding, medicines, toiletries, stamps and envelopes, writing material, and even the bowl and spoon to eat with. There would be no three square meals a day in Bangkwang where the food is barely fit for human consumption.

His parents weren't allowed to take him any food. The daily menu, they were told, was one meal a day of red rice in a dirty-looking broth devoid of vegetables or meat. Jody said that if you were lucky, there might be a piece of fish head or some other object with the promise of nutrition. Some resorted to eating the cockroaches and rats that ran freely through the cells. Tony and Lorna wondered if their son would survive.

According to those they spoke to, there were few options for getting out of Bangkwang alive. None of them sounded appealing. You could do your time, which might still mean a 50-year stretch for most prisoners. You could be released under a prisoner transfer treaty. You might receive a Royal Pardon. These are given very occasionally and the chances of getting one are less than winning the lottery. You might get parole after two-thirds of the sentence has been served. Again, this may still equate to a decade or two behind the wire. Some prisoners have tried to escape. Most foreigners would not contemplate this, as they would have nowhere to hide once over the wall.

Their sweet boy was trapped in the Big Tiger, facing a death sentence, but there was nothing either Tony or Lorna could do. They had to return to England after 90 days because their visa had expired. They felt they had achieved very little and still didn't know why the authorities were holding their son in prison. Once back home, they learned nothing other than the consular process provided to prisoners by the British embassy. They were constantly told to be patient, to wait until things returned to normal. But one thing they knew was certain, nothing would ever be normal again.

> *I grew angry. Perhaps it was my way of venting my frustration at not being able to lay the blame at anyone else's door. Against all logic and reason, I blamed myself and Tony and questioned over and over why we hadn't been stricter with our children. Why had we allowed Jody to go to Thailand in the first place? He was innocent in the ways of the world. He had never travelled alone before. I should have protected him! Why hadn't Tony and I sent more money to Jody when he'd asked for it, before all this mess? We knew he couldn't get a work visa and Kristin couldn't fly due to her pregnancy, but we hadn't the money to spare. We'd all agreed that we'd save as much as we could to pay for Kristin to go to a good hospital for the birth of our grandchild in December. Jody and Kristin were in prison because of me, or at least, I convinced myself of that.*
>
> *'As time moved on, and with the help of a counsellor, I came to realise that to go back to Thailand was Kristin's choice and to go to Kristin was Jody's.*

Their son was caught between a rock and a hard place, accused of being a partner in an ecstasy racket. According to the Aggetts, it was ludicrous, but nothing could stop the roller-coaster they were all riding. They contacted a lawyer to represent Jody. There was no way they would allow their son to be manipulated, to take the blame for something he didn't do. But they also engaged a lawyer to help them understand the judicial process. Not that it made any sense. Prisoners are shown leniency for pleading guilty, even if they are innocent. It seemed that innocence just didn't factor into the equation as Tony and Lorna were advised. Jody was stuck behind four walls with everyone telling him 'This was the best way to go' and 'sign guilty if you want to go home'. It was a foregone conclusion that Jody would be given a harsh sentence due to the tough stand that the then Prime Minister was taking on drug-related offences. But Tony and Lorna's son wouldn't stand before a court and lie. They would make sure of that.

During the investigation of the case, the police intelligence information was based largely upon the testimony of a police informer, who spoke in detail about Adrian and his Thai girlfriend, but never once mentioned any involvement of Jody and Kristin. That same police informer did not attend the trial 17 months later. Apparently he couldn't be located. The employees of the travel agency were not detained, but they gave evidence that Jody had been waiting for a visa for Kristin and hoped to take her to the UK. They said that the couple had hardly any money and no assets. When Jody's defence lawyer asked the arresting officer why he had taken his client into custody, the officer replied: 'Because he was in the house'. When challenged as to why the employees of the travel agency, who also lived on the premises, were not equally kept on remand, the police officer had no answer.

In 2003, Jody, Kristin, Adrian and Ta were sentenced by the court and each received the death penalty plus 20 years. As the sentence was passed, it was also simultaneously commuted to life imprisonment.

Sabine Zanker, a lawyer for Fair Trials International, said: 'We believe the judgement lacks reasoning. The conviction of Jody and his girlfriend was based on evidence of a police informer who did not mention Jody or his girlfriend. There is no evidence to link Jody to the crime. He was not originally allowed access to an interpreter and in police interrogation he was forced to sign a confession. They have very harsh interrogation methods that would make me sign anything.'

At the time of the judgement, the judges were under a lot of political pressure to give harsh verdicts in drugs cases in order not to jeopardise their careers. The Thai Prime Minister had announced that Thailand would be drug free within four months. Jody's lawyer appealed on the grounds that there was no evidence to link Jody to the ecstasy-production scheme, and that he had no assets and no money, thus that there was no reason to believe that he benefited from any proceeds of the illegal drugs trade. Adrian's Thai girlfriend wrote a statement saying that Jody and Kristin had no involvement whatsoever. Jody's lawyer was unable to submit this vital evidence because of the lateness in receiving it. If the appeal ever reaches the Supreme Court, then it may be submitted, but even then, there are no guarantees that the conviction of Jody and Kristin will ever be overturned.

Kristin was sent to Lard Yao Women's Prison, one of several prisons within the Klong Prem prison system. At eight months into her pregnancy she was given no special treatment at all.

In January 2002, she gave birth to baby Ryan.

Following the birth of their grandson, Tony and Lorna travelled to Thailand and it was during a visit that Kristin begged them to take baby Ryan back to England. Lorna still remembers that day as if it were only yesterday.

> Tears were running down her face as she said to me 'Please Lorna, take my baby! Don't let my baby stay in this country. Please take my baby home with you! My son and daughter were 24 years old and I thought: 'Will I manage? Can I cope?' But when I saw that darling baby who was my grandson, we both knew there was no 'maybe' We were determined to bring him home.

Taking Ryan out of the prison and the country itself was a terrifying experience, because Kristin's parents also wanted Ryan. But Kristin had asked Tony and Lorna not to leave him in Thailand. They had to sneak him out of the country.

Kristin's parents were looking for them. An official from the British Embassy told Tony and Lorna that if Kristin's family found them and accused them of stealing Ryan, they'd be sitting in that prison with Jody and Kristin. This added to Tony and Lorna's fear and desperation.

> *While we were queuing up to hand our passports in at the airport, a woman approached us. Tony and I thought the end had come and that we were on our way to prison. However, she had just come over to assist us because we were carrying a baby. I'm sure some people might have mixed feelings about us taking a child from its homeland, language and culture, but Kristin was only ever thinking of Ryan's future when she begged us to do this.*

November 2001 seems a life time ago. It's still not any easier to come to terms with everything that has happened. All Tony and Lorna can do as parents is quietly pray that Jody and Kristin's appeals will be heard, that they will go home. Neither Tony nor Lorna can bear to think of Jody and Kristin rotting in that place. They refuse to accept that reality. Instead they cling to hope.

> *My husband has been the rock to whom I cling when the nightmare threatens to overwhelm me. When I am down and doubting my faith, Tony quietly steps in and loves me through the period of my depression. He lifts me by gently reminding me to keep my faith. When Tony is finding it hard to cope, somehow I find the strength to comfort him. It has always amazed me that as a couple, we are always able to hold each other up. It hasn't been easy. The strain of constantly holding it all together has affected our marriage, brought us closer together, but at the same time, put tremendous pressure on us both. Even making a simple phone call to Jody can be stressful because we are both so excited about hearing his voice. But we know that the arguing is part of the process and we accept it. I think both Tony and I have become much stronger as a result of all this. We have also become more aware of what is happening to other people detained in foreign prisons. Many of them are guilty, of course, but this whole experience has taught us that prisoners are still human and most of them have families waiting, just like us, wondering how long we must endure what is now our life.*

They are raising a little boy, their grandson, which at times Lorna says has been so hard. Every time they look at Ryan they are reminded of Jody and Kristin and where they are. What makes this nightmare even more difficult is when Ryan asks: 'Where is my Daddy?'

'He is such a joy to us and a true blessing in our lives, and we thank God every day that we have been allowed to raise him. But I still wish my son was home,' says Lorna.

Tony and Lorna lodged Jody's appeal in April 2006, but nobody knows what the outcome will be or when it will be. All they are told is that the prison guards will just call him out one day, take him into court, open an envelope and read him the decision.

They still question why this happened. People say things happen for a reason but Tony and Lorna Aggett can't find one. Not one that gives them any peace. How and where do they find the right path that will bring their son back home to them? Their lives are on hold. They can't make any definite plans for anything. How do they cope? A lot of the time they don't, and many times they would just love to give up so they don't have to deal with all this heartache.

My days are filled with caring for Ryan. He's the one little thing that keeps us going. When we are feeling depressed with helplessness, we only have to look at him and the reminder of whose child he is and it forces us to pick ourselves up and move forward. I guess I survive through faith. When I have no strength, I draw on God's love and it brings me through another day. I know that God walks beside me and in my heart. He is with me each and every day. He will carry my family through this terrible time and he will see us through it. I believe that the will of God will never take us where God's grace cannot keep us.

What Tony and Lorna hope for now is that they will see their son walk off the plane at Heathrow and into their arms. That is the dream they dream when sleeping and awake. They both believe in miracles. The fact that they were able to have an open visit with Kristin following her sentencing was a miracle too. No prisoner with a life sentence and an outstanding court hearing is supposed to have open visits.

Their letter of request at that time was approved immediately. There have been many little miracles in their lives. They see these as reminders that God is with them. They know that they are not alone in their fight for justice. They are sustained by the love of friends who help them in many practical ways. One friend in particular, Pete Pullen, gave them so much encouragement, love and support when they first heard the news that Jody was arrested. Pete even offered to go to Thailand with Tony and Lorna.

So many people have encouraged and loved us through this time, sometimes complete strangers. I'm grateful to them all and to Kay Danes, the author of this book. Kay has lifted Tony and me time and time again. The fact that she is reaching out to so many people, as a result of her own horrific experience, really made us want to also be in a position to help others. It was Kay who introduced us to many new supporters through the Foreign Prisoner Support Service which has helped so many thousands of prisoners. Through Kay we were put in contact with Helen Willbrink, an Australian living in Thailand. Helen became such a comfort to us over the long year of 2005. She visited Jody and Kristin every week and it made an incredible difference to us, knowing Helen was a mere stone's throw away from our son. Helen's support was a lifeline between our family and Jody. We were sad when Helen eventually left Thailand to return to Australia, but we will always be grateful that she was able to help so much in the time given to her. We have been blessed by friends who help us daily and email often, wanting news of Jody and offering their encouragement when they know we are struggling. We are surrounded by love and hope and this keeps us focused, knowing we are not alone. Our local parishioners too pray every week for Jody and Kristin, so I know that no matter what happens to me—Jody and Kristin will never be forgotten. I love my son, and even if he had done something wrong and deserved to be in prison, I would still love him with all my heart. He is a very special person and is, and always will be, my beautiful son of whom I am so proud. Everything now is in God's hands. I have faith that one day he will bring my son home!, says Lorna.

During his trial, Jody's lawyer asked Tony and Lorna what made them think that someone as young and inexperienced as their son could cope in a foreign country like Thailand. Even one of the court judges said that Jody could never be the one running the drugs as he was just too childlike.

Tony and Lorna did what they thought was best, as any parent would; they allowed their child to become a man. It's a decision they regret and one that will haunt them for the rest of their lives. But both Jody and Kristin are strong, positive young people. Kristin has just got on with it all as she said to Lorna: 'This is my life in here. I'll make the best of everything I can.'

Jody has an equally astounding resilience. 'Mum, I'm here. It's a situation I'm stuck in ... I can't change it but I'm going to make the best of everything.'

Jody now speaks the language and uses this skill to teach English to the guards. He works in the prison hospital when he can get approval. It helps time pass a little faster. He continues to hope that the pressure Fair Trials

International put on both governments will result in his immediate release, or at the very least, reduce his sentence, even grant him clemency. Jody doesn't really care now how he gets home so long as he gets home. He does have some contact with Kristin, albeit by correspondence only. But it is the little things that help him endure this journey. He says it's really difficult when his parents leave after a visit. As much as he longs to see them, he feels overwhelmed when they say goodbye. He suffers terrible depression for several months afterwards.

For a parent too it is equally difficult coping. They can't imagine how their son will find the strength to endure such horrendous conditions and self-doubt creeps in unexpectedly, not knowing how long they themselves must continue to endure their desperate situation.

Trauma can last longer than most people expect. It can take years to fully regain your equilibrium. But the healing process cannot begin until the trauma has passed, and for people like Tony and Lorna, there is no certainty about when their nightmare might end. All they can do is try to get through each day with the help and support of family and friends. They need to know that they have support for however long it takes.

Tony and Lorna may not understand from where their son derives his courage, but it is obvious to those who know this remarkable couple that their son has inherited their courage and determination. As Lorna continues to struggle with the realisation that she might never see her son again, Ryan grows up not knowing his father. He knows he has a mum and dad somewhere, but he doesn't understand why they aren't with him. At some point he will ask that question. Tony and Lorna have taken him to Thailand to see Jody and Kristin, though not as often as they all would like, given the high costs of travel and the limited visiting rights prisoners can receive. Lorna says they show Ryan pictures of his parents and share with him stories from before he was born.

Tony and Lorna took Ryan to an open day visit at the prison where families can meet in once yearly full contact visits. Young Ryan ran straight up to Jody, put his tiny hand on his father's leg and said: 'Oh Daddy, you are real!'

It was a precious moment, and Jody's heart was touched. Tony and Lorna also took Ryan to Lard Yao Women's Prison to see his mother. When the two met, Ryan just stood and gazed up at his mother without saying a word. Kristin dropped to her knees. Ryan stepped closer and then suddenly put his face up against hers and said: 'Oh Mummy, you beautiful, I love you!' Everyone cried that day and as Lorna says, 'sometimes it seems there is no end to our tears!'

Then, out of the blue the miracle came!

I received an email from Lorna sent on 4 September 2007 at 2.27 am. The subject read FANTASTIC NEWS. The email read:

Dear Kay,
Jody and Kristin have been acquitted—can you believe it? I am so excited I can't believe it has finally happened WOW.
Love Lorna

My immediate response was: 'What? You are kidding me? Send more! What's going on? Man this is a miracle if true!' Take care, Kay.

The reply came almost instantly.

Hi Kay
Yes it is true ... it is midnight here and I still can't sleep—I am just so excited!!! The embassy phoned us yesterday morning at about 10.30 to tell us that they had had a phone call from Dr Monop (he was in charge of the section that Jody was in) and he said he would be signing Jody's release forms either that evening or first thing this morning. Kate (Dufall) and the British embassy staff were almost as excited as us. Kristin is already home with her parents. We are off to London this morning to take money through to the Foreign Office to pay for Jody's flight back home. Kay, the excitement and joy in this house is HUGE! This only goes to prove that prayers do work and God listens to each and every one of them because this is just another one of God's wonderful miracles.
Love Lorna

I know that the road ahead is still going to be very hard but it is just another challenge in our lives and what a joy it is going to be having Jody home, Lorna added later.

After spending six years in a Thai jail, Jody Ryan Aggett stepped off his flight at Heathrow into a throng of waiting media. Moments later he embraced his father.

This family had endured false accusations, unlawful detainment of Jody and Kristin and injustice beyond belief, but now their freedom was restored. It was indeed a miracle.

It's not often that I get to share in such moments of joy. Too often they are marred by tragedy. Too often families wait without ever reuniting.

Life for Jody and Kristin may often seem surreal as the months flow into years. It's not easy being suddenly thrust into the 'real world', surrounded by people who have no idea what you have been through. Yes, people read books and get a general idea of what an Asian prison is like, but reading about it can never compare to breathing foul air, death or fear.

Jody may at times feel more isolated at home then when he was in Bangkwang. He may experience ill-effects that he is quite unprepared for. Sometimes when people are busy staying strong they become vulnerable when there's no longer any need to be strong. When they are thrust back into life, all the things they were switching off in order to survive, suddenly come flooding into their mind and threaten to overwhelm them.

I remember feeling like a bit of an alien in my community when I left an Asian prison to return home to Australia. I kept looking around at people moving along, caught up in their own world, worrying about everyday things that are not life threatening. Even simple things like sitting down to dinner with the family, using cutlery, sitting at a dining table, using a real toilet and not some hole in a dirty concrete floor or taking a hot shower. All these things can play havoc with your emotions because you have been denied them for so long. It's important to never lose sight of the fact that our minds need time to heal. We might think that we can put some emotional timer on and when it goes off then we will be as we were before, but that rarely ever happens.

Life can be incredibly fragile but what matters most is to eat, to sleep, to breathe, and to live.

Jody wrote to me soon after he returned to England. It seems he's discovered the internet. He seemed quite optimistic about his future. He also plans to write a book, which is tremendous, because people need to be reminded from time to time that it isn't just criminals who end up in jail.

Despite his terrible ordeal, I know he will bounce back and bring something truly positive to the rest of the world.

'I just took every day day-by-day, I just didn't let it get to me,' says Jody.

6
GONE WITHOUT A TRACE
Sheng's story, Laos

Between 1968 and 1973 the south-east Asian country of Laos became host to a secret and terrible war. Although it officially ended in Laos more than 30 years ago, for many the struggle is far from over. Sheng still waits for her husband to come home. He disappeared on 25 August 2007. Gone without a trace!

At the end of the Vietnam war, the American troops withdrew from Laos in 1975 which allowed the North Vietnamese Army to push into Laos and establish a puppet communist regime. It deposed the Royal family and sent tens of thousands of Laotians and Hmong to re-education camps scattered across the country. Including King Savang Vatthana, Queen Khamboui and Crown Prince Say Vongsavang. They, along with thousands of their loyal advisors and Royal sympathisers were imprisoned in Camp 01 at Sop Hao on the Lao-Vietnamese border. The Crown Prince died on May 2, 1978, and the King eleven days later of starvation. The queen died on December 12, 1981. All were buried in unmarked graves outside the camp's perimeter.

Royal Lao Army Hmong resistance leader, General Vang Pao, was both loyal to the King of Laos and to the Hmong people whom he championed. During the 1960s and 1970s General Vang commanded the Secret Army, a highly-effective CIA-trained and supported force that fought against the Pathet Lao and People's Army of Vietnam. General Vang Pao emigrated to the United States when the communists seized control of Laos in 1975. But he continued to fight for their freedoms in exile until his death on January 6, 2011.

Not all who initially fled to the refugee camps in Thailand had ties with the Hmong resistance. Many had remained neutral during the war. Many were farmers and their families who were in fear of starvation or in fear of ethnic persecution. From 1977 in particular, many Hmong were being rounded up ad hoc and sent to seminar camps purely for their ethnicity. It was the beginning of what would later be called the 'Hmong Genocide'. People were literally being hunted down and killed. Others starved to death. The Pathet Lao government introduced compulsory farm collectivization which left many thousands without food. Life in Laos was becoming increasingly difficult.

The refugees that fled from 1982 to 1986 were mostly by then, asylum seekers and by 1987, there were close to 80,000 refugees in the Thai camps, over 54,000 were Hmong.

In 1978, Sheng Xiong's parents made the dangerous river crossing of the Mekong River to Thailand. They found refuge at the Ban Vinai refugee camp along with hundreds of thousands of others. Being the largest camp, it held approximately 45,000 people who were forced to live on approximately 400 acres. Better to live in exile than to die in your homeland. The conditions of the camp were harsh but harsher still were the conditions of a seminar camp in Laos, so very few ever complained.

It wasn't until March 1980 that Sheng's parents and older sister were sponsored by a family in Wisconsin and, as if God was smiling on them, they finally left the refugee camp behind them and set off to a new land, a golden land with glorious white beaches and promises of peace and freedom—California, USA.

> It was difficult for my parents to leave the country of their birth and the culture and language and everything that held them to their dreams and to their ancestors. They sometimes looked back with longing, but so much bloodshed, so much suffering, clouded their vision of what used to be. Their homeland was completely unrecognisable and so they set their sights on the future with new dreams, to make a new life for their children,' says Sheng.

Two years later, Sheng was born in a small town called Merced in California's San Joaquin Valley. She was the third of six children and had a very happy childhood always surrounded by people who she knew loved her. Sheng first met Hakit in the summer of June 1996, in Merced. She was introduced to him by a friend. At the time, they saw each other as friends. It was not love at first sight. There were no fireworks going off in anyone's head. It was just a meeting and a friendship. Shortly after their meeting, Hakit left home and moved to Saint Paul, Minnesota. Sheng's family also moved to Saint Paul in August 1996 to be closer to relatives and to seek out job opportunities.

On Christmas Day 1997, Sheng was surprised to find Hakit at the home of one of her good friends. She remembers he had a big smile on his face.

I didn't think we would meet again. It was really quite funny because we found out that we lived only a few blocks away from each other. As time went by, we grew closer to one another and decided to go further with our relationship. Hakit was such an honest, caring, and loving person and he had so much love for me.

On 9 September 1998, Hakit and I got married at my parents' house. Many families and friends attended our wedding. There were tears of happiness and joy that day. I cried all the way through my wedding. Not because I wasn't happy, but because I was leaving my home and my family behind. At the same time I was very happy and excited to be starting a new life with the man I loved, Hakit. It was a memorable crazy day,' says Sheng.

Her husband, Hakit, always cared deeply about those he loved. He wasn't from a wealthy family, nor had his life been easy. Hakit Yang was born in Nam Fan, Laos in 1978. He and his family fled Laos in 1987 and, like so many, found a new temporary life in the refugee camps of Ban Vinai and Phananikhoung, Thailand. In 1989, Hakit and his family were granted entry to the United States. Unfortunately, Hakit's father never saw the land of freedom that everyone dreamed of. He passed away in 1986 in the camp.

Hakit and Sheng's marriage was always good. They worked hard together to build a good life for their children Ulond and Journie. They lived in St Paul, Minnesota. Sheng's children have never been to Laos, but on occasion they, like Sheng, wonder what life would be like there. As a child growing up, Sheng's parents often told stories from their childhood. She would sit at their knee and close her eyes and imagine the lush green rice fields where the water buffalo grazed.

Then I would become disturbed by the images of the bombs that dropped in those same fields, and killed that buffalo and caused my parents to flee the country they loved. My husband, too, would often talk with longing, sharing his quickly fading memories and experiences of growing up in Laos and his journey to the

US. It has been almost 20 years since Hakit left Laos and over the last couple of years, he often spoke about going back to visit relatives who stayed behind during those difficult years' Sheng recalls.

When the US government, under the Bush administration, announced that it would support a bill in Congress that would grant normal trade relations with the communist government of Laos, many argued against. Some however, like Hakit, became very excited. He had always wanted to return home and the US President was announcing it safe to do so.

In March 2006, Hakit and his uncle, Trillion Yunhaison, embarked on their amazing 'Reunion in Laos Adventure'. He was a little apprehensive about returning, but that was because of all the rumours about the way the Hmong were treated in Laos. Hakit tried not to worry about such things.

After all, his family were not part of any political group, nor did they get involved in those sorts of things. Hakit rang Sheng when they arrived in Laos and couldn't stop talking about how much Laos had changed. His relatives were thrilled that he and Yunhaison had returned and welcomed them warmly. They celebrated for days, and when it was time for Hakit and Yunhaison to leave Laos, his relatives begged them to return one day soon.

Hakit and Yunhaison arrived back in the US on 7 April 2006. They talked about helping the Hmong Lao and their community. Yunhaison was looking forward to starting up a small medical practice in Laos. Hmong people are always interested in natural therapies and remedies, and with Yunhaison's degree in herbal medicine, he imagined that there would be many opportunities to share everything he had learned. 'Uncle Yunhaison said that we have so much more in the US and they have so little in Laos. It would be easy for us to raise their standard of life without affecting ours too much,' said Sheng.

Hakit's relatives did not have the many advantages that he and his family in the United States took for granted and this troubled him greatly. Hakit felt a little ashamed that he had life so easy when his relatives and other Hmong in Laos were so poor. It played on his mind a lot over the coming months and he kept telling Sheng that he had to do something.

Hakit talked about the trade relations and how the US government would support him if he wanted to become an investor. He talked about buying land to either plant trees for building homes, to raise animals, or build a guest house or a restaurant. He visualised all the things that he could do and soon his mind flooded with ideas, dreams and the opportunities his education and knowledge could provide for the Hmong Lao of his homeland.

There was never any talk about uprisings or government takeovers or more killing brother against brother. Sheng's homeland had suffered more than enough. Now it was time to rebuild the dreams of their ancestors. Hakit and Sheng had been given an opportunity through their ancestors' sacrifices and had made new lives and success. Now was the time to give back, to help rebuild Laos, and to restore Lang Xang to all its former glory in co-operation with the international community and the Lao People's Democratic Republic (Lao PDR).

I was proud of my husband and his uncle and others in our family who pledged their support to help create a new dream. I wanted my husband to succeed. In doing so, it would give hope to other Hmong Lao who also dreamed of going home.

Sheng drove Hakit, his cousin Cong Shi Neng Yang and their uncle Trillion Yunhaison, to the airport on 10 July 2007. Cong Shi Neng Yang, a single father of two children, aged five and seven years, was also looking forward to visiting his brothers and sister in Laos. The group arrived at the airport in good time and chatted in the airport lounge until the passengers were called for boarding. Sheng's children kissed their father goodbye and wished him a safe journey and speedy return. Sheng waved to Hakit until he disappeared from her sight.

Hakit rang Sheng often from Laos, sometimes twice a day. He recounted all the things he saw and how much the place had changed, even since the last time he was there.

On 24 August 2007, Sheng spoke to him at around 8 am (8 pm in Laos). Hakit called from his mobile. They talked for about 20 minutes.

It was wonderful to hear his voice. He sounded very happy and tired at the same time. He had just returned from a Hmong bullfight and was getting ready to go to bed at Guest House number 5 in Xieng Khoung, Phousava. The very last words I said to my husband were: 'I'll call you Saturday night. I love you. Good night. Bye!

The morning of 26 August at about 10 am, Sheng received a phone call from Hakit's older brother, Xai Yang. He said that Yunhaison had called him to say that he, Hakit, and Cong Shi Neng Yang had been arrested and were in Lao police custody. During that brief conversation, Xai tried to find out why they had been arrested, but Yunhaison didn't know. He ended the call by asking Xai to alert the US embassy. Something was terribly wrong!

> *That was the last anyone heard of Yunhaison.*
>
> *The moment I heard the news, I couldn't believe it. My heart was pounding very fast. All I could do was cry and cry. I remember my son asking me why I was crying. I told him it was nothing and that I missed his father. I kept asking myself over and over again if Hakit would be okay and what would happen to him. All I could do was pray to hear his voice again, to say that everything will be alright'.*

Unfortunately, it was a Sunday and the US embassy in Laos was closed. Sheng waited in agony for morning to come and then dialled the number with very shaky hands.

The embassy staff in Laos were understanding and helpful. Sheng gave them all the information that she had on Hakit, Cong Shi Neng Yang and Yunhaison. The consular officer said that he was going to report the case to the Lao Ministry of Foreign Affairs immediately and that Sheng was to wait for their response.

> *I put a lot of trust in the US embassy knowing that US citizens had rights, knowing that some terrible mistake had occurred and that the embassy would sort it all out. I really didn't know what to do after that. I rang all our relatives and told them what had happened and told them that we had to wait to hear from the embassy and, hopefully, they would have good news. I didn't realise that the wait would be so long.*

U.S. Senators Norm Coleman and Amy Klobuchar said that their offices were in 'constant contact' with the U.S. embassy in Laos and state department officials in Washington.

Minnesota Legislator Cy Thao, began appealing to the international community, particularly countries who fund the Laotian government, to pressure Laos to release information about the arrest. 'Right now, no one knows whether these men have been charged for anything and, if they have, the Lao government has an obligation to the international community, and our community, and these families to let them know what they're charged with,' he said. 'If … these men have committed some crime, they need to be given a fair trial. I think that's not a lot to ask.'

It took some time for the Lao Ministry of Foreign Affairs to confirm that there were no US citizens detained at that time, and no arrests made on or around 25 August 2007. How could it be true? The fact that one of the captives had called his relative in the United States the day after his arrest cannot be discounted, or the fact that he claimed he and the other Hmong were detained and were pleading for his relative to contact the American embassy for help.

Local Lao authorities in Phonsavanh told the US embassy that they had detained the three men. This was confirmed by Kong Xue Lee, the owner and proprietor of Ber 5 Guesthouse in Phonsavanh, where the initial arrest took place. He said the three St. Paul men had been arrested, along with two others. He said the men from St. Paul checked into his guesthouse and planned to stay three nights. They rented a car for personal use and had been making trips daily, being gone all day and only returning to stay at the guesthouse at night fall. They had taken two whole-day trips and upon returning from their third one immediately notified Lee's son, Nou Cheng Lee, 18, that they wanted to pay their guesthouse bill and leave. Nou informed the men that they would have to pay the guesthouse fee for that day, as well because they had arrived after morning check-out hours. The three men agreed. They paid the fee and immediately left in their car only to be stopped by a police barricade at the entrance. The police cars were from Vientiane (Laos capital). The police stopped and arrested the men from St. Paul. Nou Cheng went outside to see what the trouble was only to be arrested by the police himself.

The other two men arrested were Vwj Yang and Yee Yang from Vientiane. They had been visiting relatives and attending a wedding. They were heading to the market when the police stopped and arrested them at the same time they arrested the Nou Cheng Lee. Vwj and Yee Yang have not been seen since.

Nou Cheng Lee was released from captivity after two days, after he and his father convinced the authorities that he had merely been working in the guesthouse that day and had only been trying to collect the guesthouse fees. He had nothing to do with the men from St. Paul or their business. (Source: *Hmong Times* Wednesday, September 12, 2007. 'Three St. Paul Hmong Men, Two Lao-Hmong Men Missing In Laos' by Elizabeth Thao)

On September 6, 2007 The Lao government denied reports that authorities had arrested three US citizens of Hmong decent Laos. They later informed the US embassy, that the three men left Laos on August 29, 2007 via the Lao-Thai Friendship Bridge between Vientiane and Nong Khai province.

The Lao Immigration said that their records showed a man with a similar name, Mr Halhit Yang, born on June 15, 1978, entered Laos through Wattay International Airport on July 12 this year (2007), left Laos on August 29, 2007 via the Lao-Thai Friendship Bridge between Vientiane and Nong Khai province. They found a similar name for that of Mr Cong Shi Neng Yang, born on June 15, 1976. An investigation found no date of entry to Laos, which might be due to incomplete information in the immigration record system, but the authorities did uncover a record of Mr Cong Shi Neng Yang having left the country, also on August 29, 2007 through the Lao-Thai Friendship Bridge. For Mr Trillion Yunhaison, the authorities found that a Mr Trillion Yunhaison, born on May 8, 1966, arrived at Wattay International Airport on August 3, 2007 and left the country on August 29, 2007 via the Lao-Thai Friendship Bridge .

At no time, however, did the Lao Authorities produce any Lao departure cards to authenticate their claim. They did produce arrival cards to Thailand, but there is no way of authenticating these. Thai immigration officials confirmed that there was no record of the St. Paul men being registered at any hotels on the Thai border as claimed by the Lao government. The American Citizen Services unit in Bangkok contacted many hotels in Thailand in search of the three missing Hmong, but there was no record of them.

Through my sources in Laos, I was able to provide essential 'proof of life' information to the families of the missing Hmong men, and to various foreign officials investigating their confirmed disappearance. I provided the names of the three St. Paul men, their families details, their hobbies and details of their detainment.

As I told the US embassy, there was no way I could have known that these men had travelled to Laos or where they had been detained. But everything I provided proved accurate.

Lao authorities deny that these men were detained and said that they departed Laos via the Lao–Thai border and disappeared en route back to the US. But nothing can change the fact that eye-witness reports substantiated that the men passed through Phonthong Prison on 26 August 2007 and were removed from there on 28 August 2007. A Lao policeman that I knew previously from when I lived in Laos, rang me. He told me the men were loaded into a truck, secured in wooden leg blocks, blindfolded and gagged, under a tarpaulin with several other Hmong prisoners detained for political reasons. They were transported to an unknown destination. This was also later confirmed by a UK prisoner who was detained in Phonthong Prison at that time.

Most likely, the St. Paul men were taken to the seminar camps in Phonsali in the far north of Laos. No one can check because no one is permitted to investigate or monitor the many camps operating in Laos today.

A Lao policeman rang me and confirmed, though not officially, that the St. Paul men were alive and that the authorities believed they were part of General Vang Pao's freedom fighters. He said that they would remain alive in the camps for so long as they could survive. He said that they had been mistreated during interrogation but that the matter was settled and they would simply disappear like everyone else who had been arrested in secret. I knew this Lao policeman quite well and he was not prone to lying. In fact, he sympathised with the St. Paul men and their families but he could do nothing. I asked him to meet with a US embassy staff member to give them a statement but he was too afraid. He drew me a map instead. He told me to tell the families to move forward with their lives as these men will never leave the camps. Part of me knows this is true but I still hope that more Lao authorities like my Lao policeman friend might find a way to somehow help these men secure their freedom. From my own experiences in a Lao prison camp, I know that nothing is ever impossible.

As of early 2008 there is still no official word about the disappearance of Hakit, Yunhaison or Cong Shi Neng Yang. Since they disappeared, since the shadow fell over Sheng's life, she has not been herself. She has lost more than six kilograms (15 pounds) and worries that maybe one day her family will look for her and she too will have disappeared. 'Maybe I will fade away like an old memory and no one will be able to find me' says Sheng.

As hard as she tries, she finds herself always sinking into some dark sea of depression. She seems to have lost all motivation to function in this world. Sheng doesn't want to cook or clean. She doesn't have the energy to do these things today or tomorrow. She tosses and turns in bed thinking about Hakit. She dreams that her husband has safely returned home and she is standing with their children, holding flowers of purple and orange. Her face is smiling because she is so happy.

> *Then I wake up and life is not the life I want to be part of. Our son, Ulond, also dreams of his father. But his dreams are not happy ones. His dreams show Hakit with steel locks around his neck, arms, and legs. He dreams his father is dead. Ulond was only eight years old when his father disappeared. He cries softly and tells me how much he misses and loves his father. He looks at his picture every day and every night before he goes to sleep. All I can do is hold our son for both of us and tell him not to worry, that everything will be fine, and it's just a bad dream. Our daughter, Journie, is only five. She doesn't understand much at this age but she misses Hakit. 'Where is Daddy?' she cries. 'Daddy come home!*

The arrest of Hakit has had an effect on everyone in his family: his friends are devastated and worry that there is no news from Laos. His family's lives are on hold. None of them can imagine that this will be forever. Surely it cannot be?

The days and weeks are passing and there is nothing that Sheng can cling to. She still cannot convince the US embassy to post a missing persons' link on their website. It is like her husband, his uncle Yunhaison and cousin Cong Shi Neng Yang did not exist at all. Can she help but think that if they were middle-class white Americans who just upped and disappeared, that the people in Congress might take some greater interest? Is it wrong for her to think like that?

> *I try to wake each morning with hope in my heart. I try to tell myself that I have children to cook for and a home to keep clean for when the nightmare is over. I look in the mirror and see the face looking back at me and have no words of comfort for that woman, even though I know that woman is me. I have my family and friends. I have my children to comfort me through this difficult time. Without them, I don't know what I would do. Who does Hakit have, wherever*

he is? Who does he have to help him get through his difficult days? I can almost feel him thinking of me, willing me to know he is still alive. Will he ever come home? I ask myself this question every day, not wanting to think about other Hmong Lao who have disappeared over the years. I don't want my husband to be like them. I don't want my family to be like those families who always have an empty space at their table'.

She is hurt when some people say that Hakit went to Laos for the wrong reasons. They say he went back to make a problem for the Lao government but it just isn't true. Sheng's husband was an ordinary man to most people, but to Sheng and their children, he was a great man who had hopes and dreams, and none of these were ever destined to hurt anyone. Sheng prays that the Laos authorities will investigate this matter and regardless of what has been done or what has been said, that they will find a way to reunite her family.

In the meantime, they will continue to hope that this nightmare will end. Somehow Sheng will find the strength to become a stronger person, to endure, but she must know what happened to her husband. She deserves to know. Her children deserve to know why their father disappeared. Other US citizens deserve to be protected when their governments sign agreements, as the US government signed with Laos, to normalise trade relations. Sheng waits. She hopes. She prays.

The following is an excerpt from the *Star Tribune* newspaper written by Chao Xiong, on 9 September 2007.

> Sheng Xiong clutched a bouquet of purple and orange flowers at the Minneapolis-St. Paul International Airport on Sunday afternoon, her ninth wedding anniversary, patiently waiting for her husband to return home from a trip to his native Laos. The slight Xiong watched for an hour and a half as the waves of travellers passing through the international arrivals gate dwindled to a trickle, hoping Hakit Yang would disembark from Northwest Airlines Flight 20 from Tokyo, greet their two children at the baggage claim and head home for a large family gathering. But in her heart, she knew: Her husband and his two travelling companions, Cong Shi Neng Yang and Trillion Yunhaison, were probably still being held in a Lao jail since their reported arrest August 25. They were all scheduled to arrive on the flight that landed at 11:50 a.m. 'I guess they're not coming,' Xiong said.

Around the same time that Hakit, Yunhaison and Cong Shi Neng Yang disappeared, I was alerted to yet another disappearance in Laos. A friend of mine, Joe Davy, who tirelessly works to secure the freedoms of the thousands of Hmong persecuted by the Lao government, wrote to inform me that another Hmong man had been arrested in Laos. He was arrested in the region of Vientiane in late August 2007. His family said that the Lao police went to the village elders and asked them to call the Hmong man to their office. They gave no reason for his detention. His family started to worry when he didn't return home that night. They had no idea what happened to him or why he had been detained. He had led a peaceful and lawful existence. The detained man's cousin told Joe that it wasn't until three days later, on 28 August 2007, that the Lao police called the family to the station and informed them that the Hmong man, their loved one, was dead. They claimed it was suicide.

His family said nothing, but they did not believe the police. They said that he had no reason to commit suicide. They collected his body, which had been tightly wrapped at the police station and took it home, as is usual in Laos. When they got home, they unwrapped the body to prepare it for burial. They could see that their loved one had been badly beaten. His skull had been bashed in and all of the bones in his head were broken. His face was badly bruised. Dried blood covered his ears and nose.

Although no official reason was given for his arrest, the family believe he was killed because of his connection to the United States. His father was a former soldier who had fought on the side of the United States in the Vietnam War, as did his brothers, who escaped into the jungle. They lived in the jungle for many years after the war to hide from the communist Lao government. They currently reside in the United States.

It sounds incredible, but the authorities in Laos watched the Hmong man, now deceased. No one knows for sure why they were suspicious of him. Perhaps it had something to do with his brother who had fled to Thailand in 1990. As most people who are familiar with the ongoing persecution of the Hmong in Laos know, it doesn't take much for a Hmong to be accused of rebel activity. Their ethnicity alone singles them out for harassment. The deceased's cousin, who alerted Joe Davy, said it was an unfortunate incident, but hardly surprising. Any Hmong who is suspected or thought to have any connection to former freedom fighters allied to the United States will fall foul of the law eventually. Perhaps disappear without a trace.

Finally in late 2008, the US embassy listed Sheng's husband and his companions on the US embassy website. They did not provide details of their disappearance or their arrest, not even a date. They merely posted a photograph of each of the men with a message:

If you see these American Citizens, please contact the American Embassy in Vientiane at : +856-21-267-241, or email: conslao@state.gov

It is now April 2011 and three years and seven months has gone by and still not a single word from Hakit, my husband. Not a word of his whereabouts or situation since the arrest and detainment by security forces on August 26th, 2007 in Phonsavanh, Laos. To this day, my children and I are still waiting and praying, hoping that today would be the day that we'll receive a call from Hakit or someone telling us that he is well and alive and is coming home. Life has been a roller coaster ride for us and our lives have not gotten any better.

Every night, my children and I say our good nights and prayers for Hakit's safe return. We long for him to be reunited with us again. Raising my children as a single parent has been difficult and challenging. Making sure that they are well taken care of has rested heavily on my shoulders. The hardest thing that I have had to overcome is being both parents to these two young children, who need a lot of attention and comforts. Most of the time, I feel really heartbroken for not being able to provide them the things they need or asked for, but I am grateful that they do try to understand why some things are impossible. I'm still struggling, trying to meet month ends but I have learned to accept the fact that I have to be strong and do the best I can. If I am not strong then I will not be able to overcome the sadness and sorrow that has taken over me, for the sake of my children.

Ulond, my oldest son, is now twelve years old and has grown very well, looking a lot like his father. He is very interested in the outdoor activities that his father used to do when he was home. Ulond somewhat understands his father's situation and keeps most of his feelings to himself, which is also very much like his dad. When Ulond can't hide his feelings anymore, he will burst into tears and say how much he misses his father. He has become very sensitive and emotional since his father's disappearance. He finds it quite difficult to speak to anyone about his father, or to express his feelings. Sometimes when Ulond feels sad or angry, he will say, 'Mom, when I'm a grown man, I will travel to Laos to find my dad and bring him home, despite the dangerous situation I might face'. Hearing this always breaks my heart because I can't lose another loved one. I can't let that happen! Sometimes, I feel so hopeless because I cannot take away his pain and anger and shield him, so that he will never know those feelings. He even saved a piece of cake from his birthday and put it in the freezer for his dad. He did this so Hakit would not miss his birthday.

Journie, our daughter, is now 8 years old and still remembers the day her father disappeared as if it were just yesterday. She asks about him every day and all I can say is for her not to worry because her father is doing well and will be home soon. Even though, deep down inside my heart, Journie may never be in her father's arms again. Every year, when it is Journie's birthday, she asks me, 'Mom will daddy be home for my birthday this year to celebrate with us?'

I reply to her, 'Maybe not this year but even though your daddy is not here, he will always remember your birthday and wishes he can be here. Don't be sad.' What else can I say to such an innocent young girl who loves her father so dearly and waits patiently every day to have her prayers answered?

Often times when Journie is alone, she'll write letters to her father and draw pictures of the family living together or the places and things that she had gone to and shared with her father. She even made him a Valentine's card on Valentine's Day. But these are the things he may never see.

There are times we talk about the good memories that we have of Hakit. We laugh about it when it's funny. We watch old videos over and over and keep trying to remember as much as we can. I have to limit it down to how much we watch old movies of Hakit because sometimes we get too emotional and end up crying. Every day, I wish that life can be brighter and that my children and I will be happier. No matter what, I fear that a part of us will always be missing. It's like a puzzle that cannot be completed if a piece is missing and we are incomplete because we are missing Hakit.

I am very grateful to have such wonderful friends and families who care and love my family so dearly. Without them, I don't know where I would be right now. They gave me the courage and strength to live every day and this hardship and trouble times will only make me stronger and become a better person.

Too many years have gone by without a trace of where Hakit might be or if he's still alive. It's like he just vanished from earth but in my heart I know he's still alive. Friends and family would encourage me to move on to try to find happiness again for myself and my children. They want me to be happy and not waste anymore time waiting. They want me to live again, to feel love and comfort that I once had, but how can I move on right now when all I have in my heart is

Hakit? My love is still too strong to let him go or to forget about him. I want to know if he's okay or if he's thinking of us. I always say to myself, 'I know Hakit is alive and I must wait for him no matter how long it will take for us to be with each other again.' I know I still have a long life ahead of me and can never tell what's in front of me, but whatever road I may take, Hakit will always be the one that I love and cherish the most and will always remain in my heart and soul.

I have not for a second forgotten him and never will because he is the father of my children and the love of my life forever. I just pray he comes home. I don't care about anything else beyond that.

Today is a another new day among so many now, and still I wait.

On April 23, 2011, a coalition of Laotian and Hmong non-governmental organizations (NGOs), and the Center for Public Policy Analysis (CPPA), joined the families of three missing St. Paul men, in issuing an international appeal for the release of the men who have been imprisoned in Laos for four years now. The appeal requests that the Lao government, and US President Barack Obama, work at a higher diplomatic level, with urgent priority, to release the three Hmong-American citizens.

The Center for Public Policy Analysis (CPPA) is a Washington, D.C.-based research organisation and think-tank focused on foreign policy, national security, human rights, refugee and other policy issues of concern to the public and international policymakers. It's President, Mr. Phillip Smith, has worked with the Lao and Hmong community on refugee, human rights and veterans issues for more than 20 years. I know Phillip personally and I know he'll never give up on fighting for the rights and freedoms of those oppressed people in Laos, and in other parts of the world. He is a good man and a great support to Sheng Xiong and the families of the missing St. Paul men.

'We would like to ask the President, Barack Obama, and the U.S. Government, to please seriously help to press the Lao military and government to cooperate in telling the truth about the arrest and imprisonment of our families in Laos so that they can be released and come home to their loved ones, including their wives and children,' Mrs Sheng Xiong said.

In May 2011, I received an email from a friend in the United States, the brother of a political prisoner who had been detained in Laos for over two decades. Like Hakit, Cong Shi Neng Yang and Yunhaison, his brother had disappeared without a trace. I met his brother in Phonthong Prison when Kerry and I were illegally detained in 2000. Mr Joy, as we called him, because he always wore a smile, had once been a young man with a passion for democracy. Though perhaps in his youth he did not appreciate the sacrifice that wanting such things would mean. To live a life without family, friends, or familiar places, to exist only in someone's memory as a child and to become an old man, withered from malnutrition.

Mr Joy always told me that one day I would be free. We just had to be patient. He taught me 'Never give up your hope' and even during our darkest moments, his smile would radiate to warm the coldest moment. He had endured unimaginable ordeals and must have witnessed untold injustice over the years.

In Phonthong, Mr Joy would often ask me to sing one song that he remembered from his youth. A song so beautiful that held the essence, he said, of all things good. A song he had longed to hear. It was John Denver's Annie's Song and I sang it every day for my dear friend, to the tune of an old, red, wooden banged-up guitar.

Two long decades passed and I had long since returned home, as had so many other prisoners of the communist state. The long awaited email from Mr Joy's brother was to inform me that Mr Joy was now a free man. I could hardly believe it until he sent the photo as proof. There he was, smiling that old familiar smile and reminding me, 'Never give up your hope!'

This was another miracle. It says to me that there too is hope for Hakit Yang, Cong Shi Neng Yang and Trillion Yunhaison.

Hmong International Human Rights Watch
www.hmongihrw.org

Hmong Lao Human Rights Council
www.laohumanrightscouncil.org

Fact Finding Commission
www.factfinding.org

7
DICING WITH THE DEATH PENALTY
Australians in Bali

> *Criminals no doubt deserve to be punished, and punished with severity appropriate to their culpability and the harm they have caused to the innocent. But severity of punishment has its limits—imposed both by justice and our common human dignity. Governments that respect these limits do not use premeditated, violent homicide as an instrument of social policy.*
> —Hugo Adam Bedau, Professor of Philosophy at Tufts University.

There is a consistent trend towards abolishing the death penalty worldwide. Since 1977, 16 countries have become abolitionist. This figure has since risen to 133. Among those countries that still retain the death penalty, Bangladesh, Iran, Iraq, Nigeria and Saudi Arabia apply capital punishment to persons under 18 years of age. In Iran, for example; the minimum age for execution is 15 years for males and nine years for females (Iranian civil code, Article 1210). Although there is no record of girls that young being executed, the fact that the law enables this speaks clearly about what kind of regime Iran is.

The United States reinstated the use of the death penalty in 1976 and, since then, there have been over one thousand executions as of October 2007. According to the Death Penalty Information Centre, there were 53 executions in 2006 alone. The minimum age at the time of the crime to be subject to the death penalty in the United States is now 18.

The list of crimes that can lead to the death penalty is long. Capital offences throughout the world vary on where a person is detained. Execution may be imposed for murder, rape, armed robbery, blasphemy, serious drug trafficking, repeated sodomy, adultery, prostitution, treason or espionage. Mosleh Zamani, a 17-year-old teenager, has been sentenced to death after serving four years of imprisonment for having a sexual relationship with his girlfriend.

In some countries mandatory sentencing exists, like in Singapore and Malaysia, where a mandatory death sentence is given for drug trafficking. These countries' judiciaries believe that mandatory sentencing reduces crime and ensures uniformity in sentencing. They believe that the death penalty is and should be the strongest deterrent. Sadly it isn't.

The Australian government recognises the death penalty as an inhumane form of punishment which violates the most fundamental human right: the right to life. On 2 October 1990, it signed the Second Optional Protocol to the International Covenant on Civil and Political Rights aimed at the abolition of the death penalty, an obligation recognised by the UN Human Rights Committee.

In 2007, before the newly elected government came to office, it was suggested by many civil libertarians that the Australian Federal Police (AFP) appeared to be in direct conflict with the leadership's policy on the death penalty. This view was supported, particularly by the families of an Australian group dubbed the Bali Nine. The Bali Nine, were arrested in Bali, Indonesia, on 17 April 2005 and convicted of drug trafficking 8.3 kilograms of heroin. Six of them are now facing execution by firing squad.

On 25 April 2005, the AFP Commissioner, Mick Keelty, told the nation that the AFP would hand over all evidence it obtained to the Indonesian authorities detaining the Australians known as the Bali Nine. This was done despite the fact that most of them faced the death penalty if convicted.

The Commissioner said that the AFP was not under any obligation to hand over evidence, but argued that it didn't really matter because the Australians had been caught red-handed. In his words, 'any information offered in this case will not influence the fate of the accused Australians.'

Mick Keelty says that as a practising Christian, he is personally opposed to the death penalty, but that he has a duty to fulfil as AFP Commissioner and his personal beliefs about the death penalty don't matter.

President of the NSW Council for Civil Liberties, Cameron Murphy, believes that Commissioner Keelty's comments pre-judged the Australians. He condemned the AFP's actions.

'According to media reports, these Australians were either about to board a plane for Australia or were due to do so within 24 hours. The Australian Federal Police should have arranged for the suspects to be arrested in

Australia—where they would not face the barbaric death penalty,' Mr Murphy said.

'The Justice Minister is wrong to say that these matters are solely Indonesian matters and that Australia cannot get involved. Australia is already involved—the AFP worked closely with Indonesian police to secure the arrests of these nine suspects. It's too late to say that Australia cannot get involved. If these Australians are put before a firing squad, it will be because the AFP helped to put them there. It is not appropriate for Australian taxpayers' money to be used to put people in front of firing squads,' Mr. Murphy continued.

A number of Australians feel that if people are going to break the law then they deserve the consequences, though many oppose the death penalty in principle. Law enforcement officers join the force to uphold the law and they risk their lives every day. Those in the narcotics departments make no secret of the fact that their job is primarily to prevent drugs from ending up on Australian streets. They expect society to understand that swallowing packages of cocaine, heroin or other illicit drugs for the purpose of smuggling, strapping drugs to your body, concealing them in your clothing or luggage are all very serious criminal offences, with tough penalties.

On 13 February 2006, the sentencing of the 'Bali Nine' got under way. Martin Stephens (aged 29), who had given evidence against his co-accused, was sentenced to life in prison, as was the only female of the group, Renae Lawrence (aged 27). An appeal by Renae's lawyer was lodged which saw her original life sentence reduced to 20 years.

Scott Rush (aged 19) was sentenced to life imprisonment, but appealed his sentence. On 6 September 2006, his sentence was upgraded to the death penalty. His family was understandably shocked by the news.

'We were quite dumbfounded. It came totally out of the blue. We did not expect this decision at all,' said Scott's father, Lee Rush, to the media.

On 14 February 2006, 24-year-old Myuran Sukumaran was sentenced to death by firing squad, as was 21-year-old Andrew Chan. They were labelled the 'king pins' of the operation. In reality, the king pins were probably sitting comfortably somewhere in their penthouse apartments watching the case unfold on their widescreen plasma televisions.

Michael Czugaj (aged 19) was sentenced to life in prison. His mother, Vicki, was devastated but at the same time relieved that her son would not face a firing squad for his stupidity.

Matthew Norman (at 18 the youngest of the group), 20-year-old Si Yi Chen and 23-year-old Tan Duc Thanh Nguyen were dubbed the 'Melasti Three', having been arrested together at the Melasti Beach Bungalows with a suitcase containing 350 grams of heroin. They were each sentenced to life but upon appeal their sentences were reduced to 20 years, then later upgraded to the death penalty.

International law experts said that the decision to upgrade the sentences to death was surprising because the original prosecutors had requested the sentencing be upgraded to life imprisonment. The judges were not convinced when some of the Australians declared in their defence that they were simply young and vulnerable to threats against them. One of them had even reportedly committed numerous crimes prior to his arrest, all stemming from an addiction to illicit and prescription drugs. What was missing in each of their court statements was a genuine plea for forgiveness. Had they admitted their guilt and shown remorse, then it is more likely that the judges would not have come down so hard on them.

They gambled and lost.

One family was forced to listen as their loved one publicly announced that he had turned to illicit drug use at an early age because he felt unable to live up to his parents' perceived expectations.

With strong assurances that 'everything was taken care of', 'everyone's been paid off', the nine Australians entertained no thoughts of actually getting caught. It just seemed like easy money.

None of them anticipated the level of skill, thorough and incorruptible narcotic interception operations in both countries. Nor did any of them envisage such heavy sentences, or entertain the 'impossible' outcome of being caught. Certainly, none of them expected to have their sentences upgraded to the death penalty.

While their plight generated a good deal of media coverage in Australia it wasn't anywhere near the level of interest—or general sympathy—generated at the onset of the Schapelle Corby case, that is, before it derailed.

The case of the Bali Nine, however, generated a more consistent negative reaction from the start. Most agreed that the Bali Nine knew full well what they were getting into. The message was clear. The message was tough: Death to all drug traffickers

The Indonesian court wasn't concerned about the circumstances that led these Australians to attempt to traffic narcotics through Bali. Their interest was in the consequences, had the drugs they were carrying ended up on Indonesian streets. They believe, and rightly so, that drugs destroy lives and communities, no matter what country they are transported to or from. Street and misused prescription drugs undermine sustainable human development and generate crime. Indonesia takes a tough stand on drug trafficking in an effort to protect its young people. This is why the penalties are so high. However, it is an unfortunate reality that the war on drugs will not be won or lost by the execution of a few drug mules.

The Bali Nine are small fry in the grand scheme of things. On the other hand, take someone like Antonios Sajih 'Tony' Mokbel, also a convicted drug trafficker, an Australian currently detained in Greece, pending extradition. He is alleged to be the mastermind behind the Melbourne drug trade. He's been linked to all sorts of nasty business, and accused of having some involvement with the killing of several victims of the Melbourne gangland war. Mokbel was convicted in absentia and was sentenced to 12 years in jail.

Meanwhile, in an unrelated case, six young Australian drug mules were given the death penalty.

With such inconsistencies in sentencing for drug-related offences, the general public cannot gauge for themselves the possible consequences for drug trafficking. Is it any wonder that some people feel the war on drugs is one that can never be won?

I've had communications with all of the six Australian men on death row in Bali, either directly, or indirectly through their families, consular and legal advisors. I see them as young men who made terrible, stupid and dangerous choices. Such horrendous errors in judgement have a far-reaching ripple effect and touch not only themselves but their families, friends, their community and, ultimately, their country.

It is unfortunate but true that mistakes made by these six people in particular, will not be the last mistakes of their kind. The AFP has delivered up these boys to Indonesia for them to be marched out to a firing squad, but as we have seen time and time again, the death penalty does very little to deter people from drug trafficking. The war on drugs cannot be fought and won by burying our heads in the sand and thinking that this problem won't touch our lives in some way. We have to generate greater awareness that drugs ruin lives and kill. We have to try to learn from all this something positive to teach our children and our communities, to save them from this continuing cycle.

People make wrong choices. Sometimes desperation overrides logic and common sense. One thing leads to another. Drug recruiters come along at the right time and offer what seems like a cushy deal to the right audience. The potential 'mules' ask no questions. The rest is history.

Someone wading in economic despair wants a way out. Add to that their own possible drug addiction and they will most likely be prepared to do anything to feed their habit. There are other addictions as well, such as gambling, that can drain already dwindling resources and this can drive one to desperation. They slide further and further downward until they finally hit rock bottom and become even more desperate to get out of the rut they're in. They take huge risks.

On the other hand, some people have all the opportunities in the world, come from wealthy families and still get mixed up in the seedy world of drugs. Some are looking for a way to relieve their boredom, while others are curious. Some want to rebel against authority because they've been living under someone's domination for so long. They throw all care to the wind, just to break free. Some like to live on the edge. Most are convinced that they will never get caught. Some are just plain greedy. There are countless reasons why a person may turn to crime and just as many reasons why people don't.

Crime is unacceptable. Full stop. As citizens we all have a responsibility to abide by the law. It doesn't mean, however, that we cannot feel empathy for those whose lives are destroyed by the drug trade, while the 'Mr Bigs' profit from the human misery and destruction.

Matthew James Norman was born on 17 September 1986 in Brisbane, Australia. He was 21 years old when he wrote on death row in the Republic of Indonesia.

> *I want to personally express my deep remorse for my actions that were wrong and violated the laws of Indonesia. I wish to appeal for mercy.*
>
> *I fully accept the Indonesian authorities have every right to punish me because I broke the law and in doing so, I have brought shame on my country, my family and upon myself. Since I have been on death row, I have learned a great deal*

about myself. I realise now that my actions don't just affect me. I realise that I was foolish and did not really think about the consequences that I would face. Admittedly, I was stupid to believe that I wouldn't get caught breaking the law but at the time, I was at a point in my life where I didn't care too much about myself or anything else. I must however, take responsibility for my actions but I hope that the Indonesian authorities will give me a chance to turn my life around.

I want to thank the Indonesian prison guards at Kerobokan for caring about me and helping me to become a better person. I have learned many things from them that I took for granted before, like my freedom and what I might have achieved in my life had I made different choices. Even if I am executed, I am still grateful that they treated me with human kindness.

I wish to ask, most respectfully, that you accept this personal expression of profound remorse, and allow my life to be spared so that I might have an opportunity to one day return to Australia where I can be closer to my family and where I can participate in rehabilitation programs to help me become a better person and an example to other young people, to deter them from making the same mistakes I've made.

I am deeply, deeply sorry to the Indonesian people and hope that they might forgive me of my foolishness.'

—Matthew James Norman, Death Row Tower, Bali, Indonesia.

This was part of Matthew's appeal to the Indonesian court in 2007. He now admits that what he did was really stupid. He didn't think that he'd get caught. He thought that things like that happen to other people. It couldn't happen to him.

Matthew was a cute baby, smiling, happy, with a possibly bright future ahead of him. When he was very young he wanted to be a 'Power Ranger'—a long-running American children's television series whose characters defended the world against tyranny and evil. As he grew older he wanted to become a fire fighter. At school he was well liked and loved sports, particularly rugby union. He represented his local football club and was always joking around with his many friends. Yes, Matthew was exposed to drugs in his teenage years, but that didn't cause him to develop a pro-drug or pro-crime attitude. To the contrary, it made him aware just how harmful drugs could be. Most of his friends had a general awareness of drugs. They knew drugs were illegal and didn't present any worthwhile career opportunities. They knew that drug dealing might seem a lucrative business to the guy at the top not taking any of the risks, but it was a dangerous business for a young would-be drug mule.

Matthew graduated in Year Ten and like every other teenager in the world, he had dreams. But he fell in with the wrong crowd. He got caught in a rut. He was depressed. His parents divorced. His life had no real purpose. He felt trapped between a rock and a hard place.

How then did Matthew get from Year Ten to an Indonesian prison? I'm sure every parent would love the answer to that question so they can prevent their child from falling into the same trap.

Who is to blame for Matthew ending up on death row for drug trafficking? Is it his parents who split up when he was only a child? Can a divorce really have such a devastating effect? Was the difficulty of coping with the disintegration of his family reason enough to turn him from a lost boy to a criminal? Or was it his new circle of friends, his fellow employees and now fellow convicted accomplices, Renae Lawrence, Martin Stephens and Michael Chan, who were responsible?

Matthew's parents' divorce wasn't the cause of his transgression, although it may have affected his emotional outlook to some degree. Matthew knew the difference between right and wrong. His parents raised him well. There are no excuses or justifications for breaking the law and Matthew knows this. He knew it before he broke the law. He just didn't think he'd get caught.

The truth is that not one event or person or experience can be blamed for Matthew or the other Australians ending up on death row. Any young person can become involved with alcohol or drugs, regardless of ethnic, economic or educational background, and not turn to a life of crime. They are on death row because they did what they did. They became desensitised to the drug scene and allowed themselves to be fooled by others in the business. They believed the lies so often told to ensnare those most vulnerable. Of course, they knew that drugs destroyed lives. They made mistakes and now they have to face the consequences.

What would you do if someone came to you with an offer of the opportunity of a lifetime? What advice would you give your friend if they were about to do something you knew was really stupid but they either couldn't see it was stupid or just didn't want to? How would you react if someone you knew was going to accept a free holiday abroad and all they had to do was bring back a little tiny package for the guy paying their fare?

Would you inform the authorities? Would you try to stop them leaving the country? What if they just refused to listen?

There is a very strong possibility that the six young Australians on death row will be taken to a deserted plot in Bali and shot through the heart repeatedly by a military firing squad. Whilst we can hope that it doesn't happen, if worst comes to worst, I hope they each find the strength to be brave. I hope that peace will surround them in their final moments.

> *'My name is Si Ye Chen and I am currently on death row in Bali, Indonesia. I have thought a lot about the choices I made since I have been here. I want to say that I deeply regret my actions. I did not mean to hurt others, especially my family. I am so sorry! I hope that if nothing else, some young person might see what has happened to me and make better choices for themselves. It's not worth the risk!'*

It certainly isn't.

Sometimes we have to hit rock bottom before we learn from our mistakes. But what if we aren't given an opportunity to make amends? What if our mistake is so significant that we end up paying the ultimate price with our life?

Regardless of whether or not these Australians are executed, we must hope that something good will come from this whole ordeal. We must hope that other young people will learn that sometimes the offer of a fabulous deal—a free trip to an island resort, all expenses paid and the promise of having the time of your life—is too good to be true. We must hope they ask, 'what is the catch?'

Many people make good choices and many go on to lead very successful lives, but there are countless people who get sidetracked. They become overwhelmed by seemingly simple choices and before they even know it, they're often in trouble way over their head. Some are at risk of falling through the cracks very early on because they have low self-esteem, they are easily led, and they haven't developed strong enough convictions to resist temptations they clearly know they should. Some fail to recognise the value of good role models. Sometimes there is an accumulation of events that mess with young minds, cloud their judgement and lead to disastrous choices. It's difficult to back peddle and make things right when you take a wrong turn. Sometimes there is no going back.

Prisons around the world are filled with stupid people. They always think they won't get caught and, if they do, that the salesman who sold them on the idea in the first place will take care of everything. Will shooting six young Australians deter other young people from taking those same risks? No definitive study has ever proven that the death penalty is effective as a deterrent. Some might learn from their mistakes while others won't even care. There will always be those who continue to think they are just that little bit smarter or little bit luckier. There will always be those who think what happened to the Bali Six could never happen to them.

On 20 August 2007, Matthew Norman, Si Yi Chen and Tan Duc Thanh Nguyen wrote me this note:

Dear Kay,
On behalf of the boys, I would like to say thank you for your ongoing support and efforts for us. We are eternally grateful for everything you have done for us. We also know that you're not going to give up on us and will fight for us until the end. We haven't given up hope yet. We would like to say that your support has touched us in ways we didn't know existed. Thanks again for the unlimited support and help that you have given us.
Sincerely,
The Hotel Boys

I have been campaigning for these three young men in particular, because I believe they are capable of rehabilitation. I have have known others who have been involved in the drug trade and they have turned their lives around for good. Some have gone on to do the most amazing things for humanity.

I have talked with these boys on death row extensively and they do seem genuinely remorseful. They accept that every country has the right to enforce its own laws. They have learnt a valuable lesson. Whether or not they are given a second chance remains to be seen. What is important to them now is to maintain some dignity for the sake of their families. They have no intention now or in the future of insulting the Indonesian government or its judiciary; they just want to live. It doesn't get simpler than that.

In May 2007, I arranged for an Australian Professor of forensic psychology from Monash University to assess Matthew, Si Yi and Tan Nguyen. Professor James Ogloff did so and then testified to the Indonesian Supreme Court that the boys were not serious criminals. They were simple and easily led.

'I was quite touched by the fact that none of them complained about their conditions. They were concerned primarily about their family and lack of ability to give their apologies for what they've done. It would be inhumane and ineffective to execute them ... They're not hardened criminals.'

The time may come when the families of these boys will be called to embrace them for one last time. Perhaps the boys will then walk to their death. They will fear. They will cry and no loving arms will comfort them in their final hour. If their families are lucky, they'll have their son's' bodies returned to them. Meanwhile, some other foolish kid is contemplating a similar journey that could ultimately lead to a similar fate.

Chavoret Jaruboon, a Thai prison guard, was the last person in Thailand to execute criminals by firing squad. Now it is done by lethal injection. Chavoret shot 55 men and women throughout his career. He says that he is not afraid of being haunted by dead convicts, but rather, his wife. On a more serious note, he says that being an executioner is difficult.

'We are not proud to be involved in the ending of someone's life—it is simply part of our job.'

Chavoret believes in an eye for an eye. He believes that there are some people who will never see the error of their ways; who will not benefit from years in prison and who will go back into the world and kill again, or traffic drugs to kill others. He believes that the death penalty is not the perfect solution but he cannot think of a perfect alternative. *The Last Executioner* by Chavoret Jaruboon was published by Maverick House. It is confronting and I guess people will always be passionately divided in their views on the death penalty. Many will argue that it is the ultimate denial of human rights. Equally, others will argue that there are some people who have earned the ultimate punishment. Either way, whether you are for or against capital punishment, it won't undo that which has been done. It won't bring that loved one back who was the victim of a crime, murdered, raped or peddled narcotics to others for money or to feed their own addiction. It's all so senseless.

On 6 March 2008, I was informed that the Indonesian authorities overturned the death penalty of Matthew Norman, Si Yi Chen and Tan Nguyen.

It brought us nearer to the end of an emotional campaign. Prior to the decision they were facing a deadline for a firing squad. Now they face a timeline to rehabilitation and we have been given time to help these boys find a new path and to use their lives in more meaningful ways.

Myself, Tony Fox, Martin Hodgson, the Indonesian legal team, the boy's families, a handful of Australian supporters and Sian Powell, a reporter with *The Australian*, adopted an approach that was respectful to the Indonesian authorities and the judicial process of Indonesia. It was paramount to our campaign; after all, no one can deny that these boys broke the law. We just didn't want to see them executed for making the wrong choices in life.

Despite the fact that they were given life sentences, it didn't mean that they would have to just sit idly by and wait for the minutes to pass. They could still provide a valuable contribution by setting an example for others to follow. We are grateful to the Indonesian government and authorities for their compassion, consideration and mostly for their willingness to give these boys a second chance. In due course, we hope they will have an opportunity to transfer home under a prisoner transfer agreement, yet to be finalised. We hope that the agreement will include appropriate parole conditions. For now, we are simply relieved by the outcome of this decision.

Drug trafficking is a very serious business that destroys lives and whole communities. While debate continues on whether or not the death penalty is a deterrent, I am just grateful that these boys' lives have been spared. Most people in their position don't get a second chance—they are put to death and their death is gruesome. It's never quick or painless and families are left with nothing but despair for the rest of their lives.

It's now 2011 and the final three of the Bali 9 on death row, Andrew Chan, Myuran Sukumaran and Scott Rush, await the outcome of their final appeals. If their appeals fail, then the three will need to directly appeal to the Indonesian President for clemency. Their situation has improved remarkably, although there is no guarantee that their lives will be spared. According to the *Daily Telegraph*, Scott Rush's bid to beat the death penalty has been boosted by a panel of Indonesian judges labelling his sentence 'incorrect and inappropriate'. He was, after all, a minor player.

> *I pray that I may be given a chance to show my remorse and to give back to the community in a practical way. I would like to be an ambassador against drugs … I am a living example of how drugs can destroy lives and do cause family and friends so much unnecessary pain and distress.*

Those closest to Scott know that his plea is genuine. He has spent the last six years thinking about the choices he made at 19. 'I have only hope that I can be forgiven,' says Scott.

May 10, 2011 and the headlines announce: 'Bali Nine's Scott Rush avoids death penalty'. The Indonesian Supreme Court voted two to one in favour of a life sentence. His parents, Lee and Christine, who have been incredibly strong throughout the last five years and a half years, told the reporters they were hoping for a lighter sentence but they're definitely relieved he's off death row. 'The sentence was far too harsh from the beginning for the crime that he committed. We must continue to get Scott and the other Australians back home where they belong' said Lee Rush, following the news of his son's appeal

As for Chan and Sukumaran, their rehabilitation was endorsed earlier this year by testimony from the governor of Bali's Kerobokan prison, Siswanto. He submitted to the court his personal desire that their lives be spared. He also praised them for organising art, computer, graphic design and other classes for Indonesian inmates at Kerobokan. The panel of three judges also submitted a written declaration to the Supreme Court, that the right to life must not be ignored, reduced or taken away by anyone. They may be convinced that the young Australians deserve a second chance but the Prosecutors continue to call on the Supreme Court to uphold their death sentences. They are adamant that death by firing squad is an appropriate punishment for those who traffic drugs, and is a deterrent for others. The families of these young men would undoubtedly disagree.

Australians Against Capital Punishment
http://aacp.wordpress.com/

8
Shirley's anguish
Alan Hodgson, Ghana

Shirley Ann Morris should have been enjoying her retirement in Turkey where she lives with partner, Yusaf. Instead, she received a most disturbing telephone call at 11 am on 8 January 2004.

Her son, Alan Hodgson, had been arrested the day before in Ghana in West Africa, and was accused of being part of an international cocaine syndicate. Shirley has not seen her son since his arrest, but spends every waking moment campaigning for his release.

It was 8 January 2004 when Theresa, Alan's wife, rang Shirley.

'Have you heard?', she said.

'Heard what?' Shirley asked, feeling her heart skip a beat.

'Has Nina been in touch?'

Nina was Shirley's daughter. Something was wrong. She could sense it. Had something happened to Nina?

Suddenly Theresa burst into tears and hit Shirley with the news that Alan had been arrested in Ghana. Shirley started shaking all over. She couldn't hear herself saying anything, but her partner, Yusaf, entered the room, saw her distress and asked why she was crying. Shirley didn't realise she was. Her head and her heart felt like they were going to explode.

Theresa explained that Alan had gone to Ghana to see Shirley's brother Kevin who had married and moved to Ghana in 1974. Alan had agreed to take Kevin his diuretics from their family GP for his prostate cancer. The same general practice that Shirley herself had worked for many years ago during her nursing days. She was horrified when Theresa began describing the events that followed.

Incredibly, while Theresa was receiving the news on the telephone from the UK Foreign & Commonwealth Office (FCO), officials from UK Customs burst into her house without warning. They tore the place apart, pulled up the floorboards and even took Shirley's grandson's personal computer. They confiscated bank statements and address books and had a drug sniffer dog go over their belongings. Shirley sat imagining the horror and humiliation Theresa and her son, Dean, who was 17 at the time, had endured in the normally sleepy Welsh village where they lived, where Shirley once lived too.

'Theresa and Dean kept in touch with me by telephone, but I felt the distance between us a real hindrance. The days following these events are still very much a blur for me, but I recall that I was constantly on the telephone trying to get answers, trying to get updates, trying to understand what on earth was happening and who was looking out for my son, apart from his wife. I spent each day trapped in some strange sense of unreality. It was like being in a dream. I would wake each morning and realise the dream was a nightmare, only it was real,' Shirley says.

After a few numbing days of mindless shock, Shirley went onto the internet and looked for humanitarian agencies that might give her some advice. She was better at that sort of thing than Alan's wife because she ran an online forum called Turkish Living Forum where she gave Turkish lessons to English-speaking people.

Theresa had enough to deal with, and the shock of having her life and home turned upside down was overwhelming her. It seemed they were all in a state of shock, but somehow they had to manage. Shirley stumbled across an organisation in the UK called Prisoners Abroad and rang them straight away. They said that they often assisted UK citizens detained overseas and this gave her some relief. That was until they said that as Theresa was Alan's immediate next of kin, they had to deal with her and not with Shirley.

UK Prisoners Abroad emailed Theresa some leaflets, but, according to Shirley, Theresa was in no fit state to follow up on these. From their website Shirley found a link to another organisation called Fair Trials International. They were also based in the UK. Their website stated that they worked to ensure that those accused of a crime in a country other than their own, would receive a just and fair trial. It seemed exactly what Shirley was looking for, only they too told her that they would only deal with Theresa because she had been nominated as the immediate next of kin. Shirley contacted the FCO, but they just told her to get in touch with her son's next of kin. She phoned the Ghana desk at the FCO and the girl was not at all sympathetic. In that call and in subsequent emails, Shirley felt belittled. She felt like she was being treated like an interfering old so and so with no rights at all, even though it was her son sitting in that foreign prison.

'I have to admit that even though I now understand why these processes are necessary, at the time, I felt completely frustrated by them. I felt that time itself was against us and the time wasted jumping through everyone's hoops was time my son didn't have. I felt I was being kept in the dark. I felt that as a mother I wasn't as important as a spouse and it hurt to be excluded from helping my son, from knowing what was going on behind the scenes. The process was impenetrably difficult for me to comprehend. I assumed that I would have automatic rights to know what was being done for my son, but as the FCO informed me, it was protocol that 'the prisoner' would have to actually name me and give them permission under the Data Protection Act to let me know any changes in his circumstances. It took some time, but Alan eventually got the message and with that he told them to keep me informed,' says Shirley.

The morning after Alan arrived in Ghana (7 January 2004) police raided Shirley's brother Kevin's home and found 650 kilograms of cocaine. Upon hearing this news, you could have knocked Shirley over with a feather! She says that it is absolutely absurd to suggest that her brother could be a drug dealer.

'Granted Kevin is no saint, but neither is he a criminal,' says Shirley.

Surely this was a mistake? In all his life Alan had never been in trouble with any authorities. He had neither the wit nor the wherewithal to be a drug smuggler. It was preposterous.

'My son, Alan, was described in the news as a grandmaster in the drug business. Obviously, the media had Alan confused with someone else. Unfortunately, I learned from the FCO that it wasn't a mistake. They confirmed the news reports,' says Shirley.

Her son and her brother had both been arrested along with Mohammed Ibrahim Kamil from Ghana, Sven Herb from Germany, David J. Logan and Frank D. Lavenck from the UK. The authorities stated that all six men were charged with two counts of engaging in criminal conspiracy to commit an offence relating to narcotic drugs and possessing 650 kilograms of narcotic drugs (cocaine), worth an estimated US$145 million, without licence from the Ministry of Health. At the time the security officers arrested them, Craig Alexander Pinnick, from the UK, escaped arrest but was later detained by Interpol in Burkina Faso and handed over to Ghanaian security agencies.

Bail was set at 300 million cedi each (£157 million) but granting bail sparked a public outcry. The state appealed that the Regional Tribunal erred in not taking into consideration the gravity of the alleged offences before granting bail. The Tribunal argued that the law allowed bail to be granted to narcotic suspects. The Court of Appeal, however, after hearing the matter, quashed the bail to satisfy the public outcry.

It was weeks after the arrests that Shirley finally got to speak to her son. He was terrified and had no idea what to expect. He told Shirley that the reports were completely untrue and begged for her help. Alan was sitting in some African hellhole, a long way from his home in Carway, Carmarthenshire, where he worked as a carpenter for Carmarthenshire Council before illness forced him to give it up.

It was six months before Shirley heard his voice again and only because a kind prison guard sent her a text message to say that he was detained in Nsawam medium security prison in Accra awaiting sentencing. This prison held 2300 prisoners—three times the number of inmates it was built to hold in 1960.

Shirley's son shared a cell with 14 other men. He described it as a tiny, airless, hot, windowless space where they were locked in at 6 pm until the following morning. The open toilet in the corner of the cell made perfect breeding conditions for any and everything crawling, he said. Some of the men kept cats which Alan thought was rather odd, until he discovered that they weren't pets but to eat in the event the food ran out. There were no beds to speak of in each cell. Inmates slept on the floor, covered by mosquito nets. Alan at least was able to buy a roll-up mattress and mosquito net, but unfortunately, he contracted malaria.

Tuberculosis, dysentery and malaria are rife in that prison, and Alan was hospitalised twice, once with malaria and once with a blood infection.

Shirley worried mostly about the violence and brutality that she imagined he would face, but Alan always assured her the Ghanaians were not like that. He said they were more inclined to be soft natured and, of course, that was exactly what she wanted to hear.

It's hard for people to imagine what it is like to be in a situation like this and perhaps people don't care what Shirley's son is going through. But when you are faced with this sort of situation, how he got there is less important than the fact that he is there.

Some days I sit alone and just wonder if my son will survive. On the rare occasions I get to speak to Alan, he simply says 'I love you Mam ... love you Mam'. Then he usually breaks down and cries. The telephone calls are frightfully expensive and distressingly brief.

When Alan was first detained, Shirley wrote a tonne of letters to as many people as she could think of. She wrote to Members of Parliament, judges, lawyers and anyone who would listen. She couldn't believe that Alan would be sentenced, especially when he continued to claim innocence. The writing helped. She felt that she was doing something useful and if she stopped, she would feel desolate, like she was abandoning him.

One of the worst aspects of this entire ordeal is trying to fathom the legal process. The lawyer representing her son failed to lodge his appeal. Yet he lodged the appeals for two of his co-accused, David Logan and Frank Lavenck (released in February 2007). Was it the rumoured payment of £200,000 that enabled that pair to walk free? Shirley complained to the FCO and to the lawyer himself, to no avail. It all seemed so hopeless. She didn't have that sort of money to buy her son's freedom.

In October 2004, the case was brought to trial. Shirley's brother, Kevin, admitted that he had taken money from his co-accused but denied any knowledge of cocaine. The court, however, heard that the police had found the cocaine stash at his home and that this was part of an ongoing two-year investigation. The judge described Shirley's brother as the 'centre of the wheel around which everything evolved' and said that the others, including her son, were leaders or grandmasters in the distribution of narcotic drugs in Ghana and elsewhere.

'It was horribly disturbing for me to think about these statements rationally and the allegations were incomprehensible as I sat in my home trying to absorb the enormity of what was taking place in Ghana. My brother had admitted that he accepted £50,000 to look after the bales that had been dropped in the sea, but denied knowing what was in them. Did that make his actions any less criminal? I couldn't determine,' Shirley recalls.

During the trial, a policeman identified her son as having been on a beach in Accra when the cocaine was brought ashore in the bales. His passport, however, showed that Alan was not even in Ghana at the time. The court said that her son made the cupboard where the drugs were stored at her brother's house and that was evidence of his involvement. Alan's GP wrote a report at the trial to say that Alan wasn't physically capable of constructing this storage place due to the extensive work involved. He suffered from severe spinal arthritis and this was the reason he had retired from his work with the council. The court ignored the GP's testimony.

Shirley's brother blamed himself for Alan's predicament and, in a way, Shirley did too, but laying blame wouldn't change anything.

All six men were eventually taken to court and found guilty of illegally importing cocaine and possession of illegal drugs. Each one was sentenced to 20 years' hard labour and was detained separately in prisons throughout Ghana.

It is now 2008 and, at 69 years old, Shirley sits waiting for her son to return home. She says she feels as if she has been pedalling uphill in the dark for far too long. Her appeals to Tony Blair and Jack Straw went unanswered, but Sabine Zanker of Fair Trials International told her that she has expressed concerns to the FCO and perhaps that might help. Sabine said that she believed Alan has a very good case for appeal. The maid who gave conflicting evidence said she saw Alan coming back from the beach when the drugs had been dropped, but he wasn't in Ghana at that time, and the stamp in his passport proves that. He arrived a few days later. The housemaid's evidence saying he made the safe in the house could hardly be trusted either, especially when Shirley's brother readily admitted that it was he who collected the bales of cocaine and not Alan.

> *I believe there was a lot of politics at the time to get as many men convicted as possible, and three of the six men were in the wrong place at the wrong time. We are considering flying over to Ghana to look at the appeal of the other two, and I hope we'll be able to speak to Alan too, as his appeal will be launched once theirs is over,'* said Sabine Zanker.

Sabine has encouraged Shirley on so many occasions to stay strong when she could have easily fallen into a great heap. Shirley has a good deal of faith in Sabine's kindness and her abilities as a lawyer.

> *I guess I am fortunate in some ways that I don't still live in that small Welsh village where people get their facts from papers and television. These are generally not very thought-provoking, nor do they promote any compassion for families*

facing ordeals similar to ours. But there have been some wonderful people who have stood beside me to make this journey less lonely, says Shirley.

Iris Baker, another UK mother, whose son Nick is detained in Japan, has assisted Shirley tremendously. It was Iris who first referred Shirley to Sabine when she was at her lowest ebb. Shirley had a long phone call with Iris one night and Iris invited Shirley to look at her website and write about Alan. It was like lighting a tiny candle of hope in what had been a very dark place. Shirley says that she's learnt a great deal from Iris and others in the time that's passed.

> 'For one thing, I feel very strongly that governments, and maybe even the United Nations, do not do enough for people detained away from their own country. Prison in your own country would be hard enough to handle, especially the effects on the family, but to be far away in a foreign land where you can't speak the language or follow the customs, and where you have no family visits or regular contact, seems to me like a double torment. I feel consumed by a terrible depression most days that I find difficult to shake off. I have become somewhat of a recluse lately and find it hard to enjoy the simple pleasures of life as before. I feel guilty for any happiness I have with Yusaf, knowing my son is still trapped in a nightmare of someone else's doing.

Depression can also be a shield that people like Shirley hide behind when they don't wish to face the world. It helps them to avoid social occasions, trivial chats with others which they might ordinarily enjoy. Shirley can only hope that she can keep going until Alan comes home, but even she admits that at her age, time is against her.

> *I agonise with each day that passes, not knowing how many more days I have on this earth. This experience has been dreadful and has had an awful effect on my daughter-in-law in particular. At the moment, she has had enough of it, although she sends money every month for Alan's upkeep through a friend's housekeeper. At least that way my son will be assured of getting clean food and drinking water. I'm so grateful to her for that.*

On one visit, the housekeeper tried to give Alan some writing paper, but the authorities wouldn't allow it. Alan asked for a packet of playing cards after that, but the governor of the prison said that would only corrupt the other male prisoners. If Alan didn't have anyone to help him, then Shirley thinks he would just rot in that prison. She doesn't think he can handle the conditions. In fact, she doubts many foreigners could.

Shirley says that Alan became suicidal when he was sentenced, particularly after they moved him far away from the capital to Central Kumasi Prison in the Ashanti Region of Ghana. The city is home to the former Secretar-General of the United Nations, Kofi Annan, but that is the only remarkable thing about Kumasi. It is a typical third-world African environment with a population of over 1,517,000 people. Kumasi is commonly known as the 'Garden City', but all the aerial photographs show nothing but hundreds of cars crammed along dirty and dusty streets, with masses of Africans going every which way. Somewhere amongst all that chaos is Shirley's son!

> *My brother, Kevin, was taken to hospital in Accra and is now completely bedridden with prostate cancer. The day that Alan was sentenced, Theresa's father had a stroke and has since died. She told me last year when I was crying, that we've cried enough and we shouldn't cry anymore. I can't seem to stop crying.*
>
> *My grandson, Dean, had a promising career in football and was attending an academy, but since his father's arrest and imprisonment, Dean hasn't played a game. Neither does he mention his father. Alan finds this hard to handle. He has only spoken to him once in three and a half years. My daughter's husband was killed in an arson attack. Shamefully, I didn't go home for his funeral. I couldn't afford it. I never told my family that my small restaurant in Alanya went bust or that I had hit rock bottom. I felt that with everything else going on, my own despair and financial ruin was too much to bear let alone disclose to others. I was drowning in debt and my meagre pension wouldn't allow me a trip home. I felt desolate. One thing seemed to pile on top of the other and I felt like I was losing my grip on reality. I was so emotional that I felt I wouldn't have done anybody any good. I hope to go back home some day. I hope that my family will understand that I handled things the only way I knew how.*

Is there light at the end of the tunnel?
At the moment Shirley can't see any, but perhaps one day there will be a faint glimmer to give her hope.

Now all that she can do is hold on to memories of Alan as a young boy growing up in the Welsh village in the Gwendraeth Valley community of Carway, where he sat on the sports club's committee and helped organise local community events. Where he encouraged his son, Dean, to follow his dreams of becoming a footballer and where he once told jokes with his brother, Michael, and old friends, over a pint of beer and raved about how great Manchester United was. Shirley says that she will remember him as others do and not as the media portray him. She says that Alan always believed in an honest day's work for an honest day's pay. He was a great gardener and loved the outdoors and his dog called Patch, a Jack Russell, whom he misses terribly.

'I will continue to look for people in the same predicament, people like Iris Baker who also longs for her son's return. I will draw on their strength and take some reassurance knowing that I'm not going through this alone. I will try to stay active and constructive and continue to write to the MPs, hoping that they will write back.

'I've found it useful to share Alan's plight with others and the internet has been particularly helpful. I've had some great support as a result, and so has Alan. A simple thing such as a postcard from a stranger, half a world away can seem like a ray of sunshine to a person locked away from the world. We all want to feel cared for. I always try to remember that there are many more good people in the world than there are bad people, and I'm learning that it's okay to show our vulnerabilities. I try not to bottle my emotions up so much and do my best to accept that I need support to get through this very painful time. Often I am exhausted from staying strong and wonder how much longer this will go on,' says Shirley.

Nothing lasts forever and one day, one way or another, all this will be behind Shirley and her family. She remains grateful that she has friends who will stand by her no matter what and don't judge her for what others might have done or through mistakes they might have made.

'People like Sabine Zanker, Iris Baker, James Mooney, Garry Lowes and the members of Carway Sports Club, Kay Danes and the Foreign Prisoner Support Service for creating Alan's campaign on their website, and a lovely lady from Holland called Yvonne, who has supported Alan immensely and done wonders for his morale. It helps knowing you are not alone, but it doesn't make it any less painful,' says Shirley.

Shirley wants to see her son home. She wants to see her family healed.

She wants to put this behind her and have peace of mind. She wants to be free of worrying about her son's health, her brother's prostate cancer and her own life and the limited time she too has left on this earth. She hangs on as best she can and tries to remain grateful for small mercies.

Her son, Alan, is alive for now, although his health is of critical concern. He was transferred in April 2007 to the hospital in Accra after he collapsed. He lost the use of his arms, and Shirley says that his legs are now weakened to the point where he can no longer walk. He has lost almost 31 kilograms in weight since his detainment. He used to be a stocky 95 kilograms. He continues to deteriorate with severe arthritis of the spine and the nerve endings are under so much pressure that he is riddled with numbness and pain. The British consul visited him in June 2007 and reported that he was very frail. It's now 2008 and Shirley doesn't know if her son will survive much longer. She knows the conditions in the hospital are at least better than the prison, but he still has to sleep on the floor and he cannot get the proper medical care that she knows he would get back in the UK. His only luxury is a single oscillating fan in the corner of his room.

The irony of it all is that Alan is in hospital alongside Shirley's brother.

August 21, 2010 and Alan Hodgson is finally back in the UK. He was transferred to Wandsworth prison in London under a prisoner transfer agreement and will serve another three to five years. His mum Shirley went to visit him and said that she was shocked at first by his appearance. She wasn't expecting to see him so thin.

'I went to see him in Wandsworth the week after he was repatriated. I didn't recognise him. I saw this old man with a stick and a neck brace and a face and scalp full of sores. It was his eyes smiling at me that made me realise it was my son.

It's now 2011, Alan has been transferred to Rye Hill which is a contracted out prison in the Midlands. He is doing much better though he has an extensive skin cancer burrowed deep into his basal cell. They says it's non-invasive but destructive to other tissues. He had another on his face and neck but they have been treated. He also had three tumours excised from his chest wall. Alan's legal aid solicitor is trying to get a judicial review to hear his appeal for an early release based on compassionate grounds. But for now, Alan and his mum Shirley are just so relieved that he's back home on UK soil.

Alan Hodgson
http://www.usp.com.au/fpss/case-alan-hodgson.html

9
Proof of life
Mohamed Abbass, Egypt

By the end of 2005, there were 109,531 active missing person records held by the US Department of Justice. Each year throughout Australia, approximately 30,000 people are reported missing—one every 18 minutes. The impact of having a loved one suddenly disappear can be, and usually is, devastating.

People go missing for many reasons. They may have chosen to go missing to escape conflict, domestic violence, financial entanglements. Or they have been abducted. Some are missing for a day, some for a week, while others go missing for years. Some are found and some are never found. Those they leave behind often have to deal with the trauma of never knowing what happened to their loved one. They are left suspended in a state of bewildered bereavement.

Mohamed Abbass used to live in Sydney, Australia, with his wife, Seham Abbass, and their three children, Jasmine, Sara and Ahmed. That was until the 64-year-old Telstra senior technical engineer took annual leave in January 1999 to travel to his native Egypt for a family visit. There was nothing unusual about this, or any other trip he had taken over the last 20 years since migrating to Australia.

On the morning of his departure, he went through all the usual processes pending an international flight. He checked that his passport and travel documents were all in order and made a final check on his bags. He had breakfast with his family. He boarded a plane with Egypt Air at Sydney Airport never suspecting that it may be his final moments ever on Australian soil.

Mohamed's wife, Seham, spoke to her husband briefly on the telephone while he was still in Egypt. Mohamed mentioned that he was going to take an impromptu couple of weeks sightseeing in neighbouring Turkey prior to returning home to Sydney on 13 February 1999. That was the last she heard from him.

Seham waited at home for her husband to return. He never appeared. Had he missed the flight in Egypt? Was he on the next one?

Flight records did not show any record of Mohamed Abbass on any returning flight, or any subsequent flights.

Concerned that something terrible had happened, Seham contacted her relatives in Egypt. Her brother confirmed that he had seen Mohamed off at Cairo Airport and that was the last time anyone in Egypt saw him.

The Australian embassy in Ataturk and Istanbul (Turkey) were notified, as was the Department of Foreign Affairs & Trade (DFAT) in Canberra. Mohamed's disappearance was reported to local police authorities in his home suburb of Flemington. Subsequent reports were made by his family to the Australian Federal Police Missing Persons Unit.

Almost a whole year went by and still no one heard anything from Mohamed. Then in December 1999, an electrical fault sparked a fire that caused major damage to Mohamed's home in Sydney. Fortunately, Seham and their three children were unharmed, but the property was damaged extensively. The State Emergency Service assisted with a tarpaulin where the roof no longer existed. Imagine their despair at having to deal with this on their own and then to find out that only Mohamed could make a claim because the house and insurance policy were in his name alone! It was a nightmare for Mohamed's family to lose treasured memories that they would never be able to replace.

The family wrote often to the Australian Foreign Minister, Alexander Downer, hoping he would be able to bring them some relief from the agony they were enduring. Warren Macilwain, then Director of Consular Operations, responded on behalf of Mr Downer, explaining that the family's concerns were being taken very seriously by DFAT, the AFP and Interpol. Mr Macilwain assured the family that all possible steps were being taken to locate Mohamed.

The AFP and Interpol learned that Mohamed had entered Turkey in February 1999, but no one was able to provide any information beyond that. There were no records of where Mohamed might have gone, who he met, if he had booked into any hotels, if he had rented a car or gone on any sightseeing tours. In fact, no one could provide any further information.

Behind the scenes, DFAT was investigating to establish the exact whereabouts of Mohamed Abbass. They pursued the case through the Egyptian authorities, who were adamant they didn't have Mr Abbass. The Australian government had no idea where he was.

'The reports are that the last concrete evidence we have is that he was in Turkey' said the then Parliamentary Secretary, Mr Bruce Billson. This, of course, confirmed earlier AFP and Interpol reports, but the family was convinced that Mohamed was still in Egypt.

'In terms of flight movements through the airline he was using, travel plans, immigration checks and not only our own federal police but Interpol both in Turkey and also in Egypt, that seems to be the only concrete basis we have to work from,' said Bruce Billson.

Mr Abbass wasn't a wealthy man, he was a family man with no dark secrets and no connection to terrorism. They could find no motive to warrant his disappearance. The Australian intelligence agencies confirmed this was the case.

According to Mohamed Gharib Abdel Aziz, the family's Egyptian lawyer, there was an explanation of sorts as to why the airline and immigration records might show Mohamed Abbass departing for Turkey. He believes that Mohamed may have been detained after checking in and going through immigration at Cairo airport. If this was the case, it would look as though he'd left the country when in fact he hadn't. Mr Aziz said that this sort of thing had happened before, even to him. Fortunately however, he was released after questioning.

No one can explain why Mohamed Abbass would have been detained. There are no allegations of his being involved in any criminal or even questionable activity. According to police, he's never been charged with anything in any country and never been suspected of anything. Was he mistaken for an Islamic fundamentalist?

It is possible that someone of a Middle Eastern appearance could be mistaken for an Islamic fundamentalist, but Mohamed Abbass wasn't one. He had absolutely no interest in politics and no contact with any Islamic groups. It's more probable that he was a victim of foul play. Egypt has quite a long history of arbitrary arrests, detention and disappearances.

Seham sought and engaged legal representation from an Egyptian-based solicitor, to mediate searches for Mohamed from Egypt. Another two years passed.

The only 'information' Seham had received was the unsubstantiated rumour that Mohamed was being held in unofficial detention in Egypt. Without any other information or possibilities to go on, Seham decided to return to Egypt, with the children.

On their arrival, Seham and Mohamed's son, Ahmed (aged 10) was held by Egyptian airport security authorities. Seham's screams for help and her subsequent vigorous protests resulted in her son being released by the authorities.

Seham paid an 'Egyptian mediator' an agreed $2000 to be driven, blindfolded, to a secure prison in an unknown location, to meet her husband. Inside a tiny room, inside a prison, she sat staring at her husband's gaunt features. Seham's gut feeling to chase down a rumour had paid off. He was alive! Seham reports that Mohamed did not understand why he was being held and begged her to get help. 'Please, I am an Australian citizen. Ask our government to help me!' Mohamed pleaded so formally to the woman he knew so intimately. 'He was sad and deeply psychologically stressed. I couldn't say things to him that would upset him too much, so I didn't tell him our house had burnt down'.

Following this heartrending, brief encounter, Seham was blindfolded and driven back. She had done well to get this far. She had not only located but personally contacted her husband.

Seham was told by the 'Egyptian mediator' that if she wanted to see her husband again, then it would cost money. He told her that she should not report any of what had just occurred to the authorities because someone would be watching her and there would be repercussions for her husband, for her and her children. Seham was terrified, but she managed to convince the 'Egyptian mediator' that she didn't have the sort of money he was asking for, and, therefore, she would have to return to Australia to raise it. He agreed.

When Seham was safely back in Australia, she contacted DFAT and told them everything that had occurred in Egypt, which even to her sounded incredibly fanciful—only it was disturbingly true.

'I thought that when I informed them here, they'd help me. But they didn't care about anything at all' she reported sadly.

The 'Egyptian mediator' in Egypt continued to demand money in return for Mohamed's release, US$200,000 in fact. It was impossible to raise that sort of money without selling their family home, but that too was impossible since the property was in Mohamed's name only. Seham could only sit in despair and wonder what to do next. She had sat with her husband in a prison in Egypt, and there he had begged her for help. What on earth could she do?

In another astounding twist in this story, it came to light that someone else had seen Mohamed in the Egyptian Al Masre. Ex-Guantanamo Bay detainee, Mamdouh Habib, claims he saw Mohamed Abbass in that prison where he was detained for six months from late 2001 to early 2002, after being sent there by the US.

Habib claims that Mohamed Abbass, whose face he knew from Sydney, was paraded before him by interrogators. Habib's captors used this to reinforce their point that they could, if they wanted to, make people disappear any time, any place. In fact they fulfilled that promise by illegally handing Habib over to US government authorities. He was later transported by US armed forces, under forced detention, to the US military base in Guantanamo Bay, Cuba. Habib was released after three years of detainment. He was not the terrorist the US claimed him to be.

Despite both eyewitness testimonies, the Australian government said that it couldn't do anything more than it had done. The Abbass family's Australian lawyer, Stephen Kenny, vehemently argued that the Australian government wasn't doing nearly enough to protect the rights of one of its citizens.

Mr Kenny said that there was enough evidence to prompt the Australian government to demand from the Egyptian government an explanation and insist they conduct a proper and thorough investigation.

'Time is running out for Mohamed Abbass,' said Stephen Kenny. 'I have very grave concerns about his welfare and safety, to be honest.'

The facts of this case are that two eyewitnesses have verified that Mohamed Abbass was in an Egyptian jail. There have been demands from Egypt over the last six years for his family to pay money in return for his release. What can and should the Australian government do in this situation?

The 'Egyptian mediator,' gave Seham his bank account details with instructions on how to deposit the so-called ransom for her husband's release. 'Your husband's held unofficially. How will you get him out officially?' he told her.

Seham provided five proof-of-life questions to the embassy to provide to the 'Egyptian mediator' as a test of the credibility of the information.

Proof-of-life questions are personal questions to which only the prisoner would know the answers.

On 27 March a breakthrough occurred. The embassy reported that the 'Egyptian mediator' contacted them, and during this conversation they learned that a prison guard at the Al-Masre prison camp in Cairo had given him answers to two proof of life questions.

This was an encouraging development and proved officially that Mohamed Abbass was still alive and, importantly, alive in Egypt. Armed with this information, the Australian government had something substantial with which to confront the Egyptian authorities. However, again they didn't. Instead, they decided to wait for the 'Egyptian mediator' to work through his unofficial channels, thinking it would be more worthwhile to allow the process to unfold.

In 2006 the Australian embassy in Cairo issued a new passport for Mohamed Abbass. They just had to wait for him to turn up. But after months of waiting there was no sign of him. The Australian Ambassador in Cairo contacted the Egyptian Foreign Minister and suggested to him that his country might be detaining an Australian in a case of mistaken identity.

The Australian embassy wrote to the family: 'We are hopeful that by offering the Egyptian government a face-saving solution, they might be more likely to confirm that Mr Abbass is in detention. However, I should stress that there is no guarantee the Egyptian government will provide a positive response, and there is a small risk that Mr Abbass might be relocated to prevent his discovery.' However, the Egyptian authorities denied holding Mohamed Abbass and insisted he had travelled on to Turkey.

The Egyptian community rallied in support of the family and offered to assist in negotiations with the 'Egyptian mediator', but unfortunately, time had well and truly run out. The 'Egyptian mediator' said it had become too dangerous to continue negotiations and that he himself had left the country and was in Germany.

'I am in a dangerous position and I cannot do any more. You have to forget about this deal,' he concluded.

Seham Abbass placed her hopes back in the hands of the Australian government. Together with her lawyer, Stephen Kenny, and a senior advocate of the Foreign Prisoner Support Service, Martin Hodgson, Seham travelled to Canberra for a scheduled meeting at Parliament House.

DFAT spokesman, Greg Hunt, said that the 'Egyptian mediator' had '… denied having encountered Mr Abbass, he denied any information as to where Mr Abbass might actually be, and he denied having made requests for money from Mrs Abbass.'

In an appeal to the 'Egyptian mediator', Seham Abbass pleaded on SBS television for the 'Egyptian mediator' to contact her.

'I want to tell him please, please help us. Help my children, help us. You know the situation inside out. So, please help my children because they're upset and sad. Nothing can make them happy except the return of their father. Please, help me to let my children smile again.'

It is now eight years since Mohamed Abbass went missing in Egypt. There seems to be very little anyone can do.

'What the Australian government can do, and has done, and will continue to do, is canvass every avenue to try and establish where Mr Abbass is. If there can be some evidence … We've had people working on this for many years trying to establish actually where he is, not simply assert where he is. What we're missing here is some concrete evidence to challenge the very clear and repeated assertion by the Egyptian authorities that Mr Abbass is not in Egypt,' says Bruce Billson.

It now seems to be a case of what is fact and what is asserted as fact. The Egyptian government says that Mohamed Abbass left for Turkey, but no one can locate him. The family says he is in Egypt and no one can locate him. It looks like an impasse.

'The Australian government needs to speak out very strongly and insistently to the Egyptian government to insist that he be released and sent back to Australia on whatever terms and conditions,' says Stephen Kenny.

Seham Abbass still firmly believes that her husband is alive. Yet her husband has disappeared and no one can say where he is, or why he vanished. He is essentially lost between countries, metaphorically fallen into a chasm somewhere between Australia, Egypt and Turkey.

For eight years, the international community, the AFP and Mohamed's loved ones have searched for him, to no avail. No one (officially, at least) knows where he is or whether he is even alive. His family grieves his daily absence in their lives. They cannot give up hope, they cannot give up on him, and the hope that one day they will be together again.

This is an uncomfortable, half-lived life for his loved ones of looking back, unable to move forward, missing the man who means so much to them.

One person who has vowed to keep searching for Mohamed Abbass is Martin Hodgson from the Foreign Prisoner Support Service. He continues to investigate the Sydney man's disappearance and the plight of numerous other Australians jailed overseas. Martin thinks it's not impossible that Mohamed Abbass could be secretly detained for this long.

'There have been plenty of cases of people going beyond the 10-year mark and being released after this time. I have the names of 50 people who have been gone more then five years with no contact from anyone and then they have been released. I'll just keep searching and hopefully one day this family will be reunited or, at the very least, get the answers they so desperately need!' says Martin.

Foreign Prisoner Support Service
http://www.usp.com.au/fpss/campaign-mohamed-abbass-petition.html

Cage Prisoners Campaign
http://www.cageprisoners.com/prisoners.php?id=1850

Stephen Kenny
Case Lawyer
http://www.camattalempens.com.au

Kay and Kerry Danes are taken before the Lao court on 28 June 2001 after six months of wrongful detainment. They were told beforehand that no one had ever been acquitted once charged.

Kay Danes thanks Foreign Minister Alexander Downer (right) for reuniting her family in October 2007 after such a terrible ordeal. Two of the Danes children are pictured in the background (Jessica and Nathan), along with Federal MP Andrew Laming (front left).

The Danes receive an historic Presidential Pardon in November 2001, as part of diplomatic negotiations by the Australian Government and Ambassador Jonathan Thwaites (centre), that secured their freedom.

Kay Danes with Terry Hicks on 9 December 2006 at Adelaide Rally calling to bring David Hicks home from Guantanamo Military Prison, Cuba.

David Hicks

Gilbert Mwamba and his children, 2007.

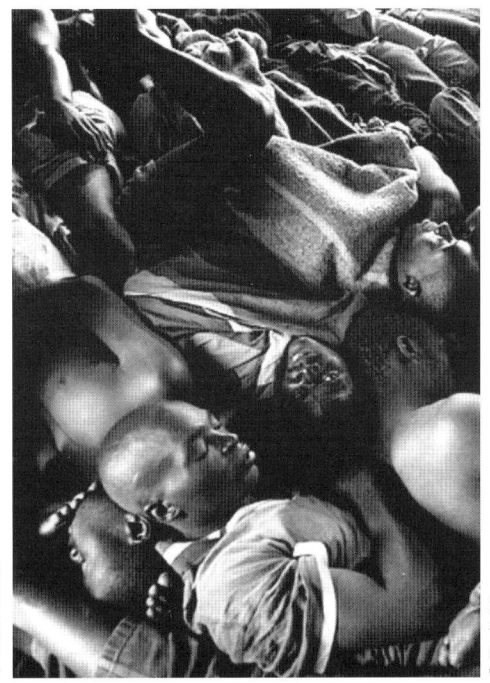
Prisoners in Zambia (2007) endure horrendous conditions.

Orphan children in Gilbert Mwamba's care in 2007. Fathers are all on death row.

Julie-Anne Peake with her brother Brad before he went to jail.

Scott Hurford meets his nephew Archie for the very first time on the day he is sentenced, 1 March 2006.

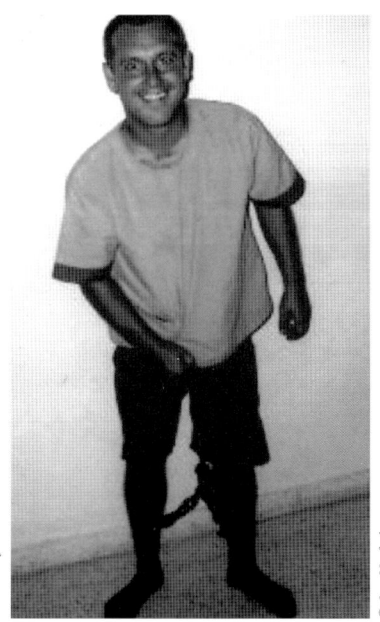

Scott Hurford puts on a brave face for his family, despite the heavy elephant leg chains he must wear to court on 1 Mar 2006.

Harry Bout is given some encouragment from a long time Dutch supporter, Sandra Kroep, co-founder of the Free Harry Bout Campaign.

Harry Bout before prison—20 years ago.

Jody Aggett and girlfriend Kristen before their lives took a turn for the worst.

Hakit Yang (left), his daughter Journie, his son Ulond and Sheng (right) two weeks before he left for Laos in 2007.

Michael Connell smiles from his Bangkok prison cell. His 99-year sentence was reduced to 30 years.

Si Yi Chen contemplates the poor choices he made which landed him on death row in Bali.

Eugene Henry Debruin at University in 1960.

Rickey Johnson (2007) endures 26 long years of wrongful incarceration.

Rickey Johnson finally released from Angola prison on 12 January 2008 after DNA testing cleared him of a 1983 rape conviction.

10
NO TIME FOR SECOND CHANCES

Michael Connell, Thailand

'Nothing could ever change the fact that he is my boy, and despite everything that's happened, I'll love him no less' Derek Connell.

Derek, the father of Michael Connell, was at work driving his taxi around the quiet streets of London when he got the call. It was around 7.30 am on the 11th day of the 11th month—Remembrance Day 2003—when his wife Joan, anxiously informed him that she'd been contacted by Derek's former wife, who'd heard on Bury FM radio that their son Michael was in trouble. Derek tuned into the radio just in time to hear the tail end of the report.

> *… following a tip-off from within Thailand, Michael Connell, 19 years old, from Bury, Greater Manchester, has been arrested at Bangkok airport in possession of 3400 ecstasy tablets.*
>
> *To say that my blood ran cold would be an understatement. My hands gripped the steering wheel, my knuckles white as I turned my taxi round and headed straight home. I was oblivious to everything around me as my mind went numb. Joan waited by the gate as I pulled into the drive half an hour later. The look of worry and concern written all over her face mirrored the shock and apprehension obvious on mine. It hadn't been a mistake after all, as Joan re-confirmed everything at my insistence.*
>
> *I'd always believed that I was able to cope with any pressures that came my way. I now know that this is not the case. The radio program had stated that my son was facing the death penalty, death by firing squad. The shock of it disorientated me to the point where I couldn't piece together a single thought other than visualising my boy tied to a pole with a gun pointed at his chest. I felt useless,'* says Derek.

Within a short space of time after Derek arrived home, there were cars and vans screeching to a halt outside his house. Flashbulbs of hungry photojournalists recorded his every movement. The media circus had come to town and Derek, it seemed, was its main attraction.

The doorbell rang constantly. Derek and Joan despised their intrusion into the time they needed to come to grips with what was happening. To her credit, Joan remained calm. She peered outside and recognised Stuart Flinders of the BBC. 'The only way we'll get rid of all these people is to talk to Stuart Flinders' she said.

So Derek ventured outside, motioned Mr Flinders to his car and quietly reversed into the street, heading off back down the road, leaving the circus far behind them. Despite the fact that his head was swimming from the day's events, and Derek couldn't remember much of what he'd said in that interview with Stuart, he does recall that he was very compassionate and seemed to have a great deal of understanding of the crisis facing Derek and Joan. He told Derek that the BBC would contact him shortly with a proposal to go to Thailand and cover the story. Derek kept himself hidden in the house as much as possible and the more the doorbell rang, the more he wanted to hide. He says he felt like a coward as his mind raced in every direction. He says he didn't know how to act. He didn't know what to say. He could barely comprehend that his son was facing execution. How does a father get his head around something like that?

Michael Allen Connell was born on 8 April 1984 in Bury, Greater Manchester. Derek proudly watched him grow into a very caring, inquisitive child who loved to learn. Michael did quite well in his first reception year of primary school, but when he moved into the first year it became apparent that he couldn't keep up with the other children. He became very angry and upset as learning became a constant struggle, and his primary teacher would massage his temples to soothe him. His very first teacher adored Michael and he adored her, but other teachers weren't as understanding or patient. When Michael went to high school, his learning difficulties became a real frustration to him. Michael was born deaf in one ear and sometimes sat in a desk with his unhearing ear to the class, and was then accused of not listening. Michael began to lose his confidence and learned to hate school.

It was a constant struggle to keep Michael at school. His self-esteem was low. Finally, he was sent to an adult learning centre for 12 hours a week, which was a disgrace. He was not given the chance to progress and get the education he needed to fulfil his ambitions.

When Michael left school, he worked in a number of factories but was not happy. Just before he left for Thailand, he was unemployed and very down. No one even knew that he was going to Thailand.

The BBC news reported that Michael had been arrested and this came as a complete shock to his father. Derek Connell told the BBC: 'I didn't even know he'd gone to Thailand—the first I knew about it was on the news. He has no money, so how the hell he has managed to get over there is beyond me.'

Derek thought his son, who was unemployed, might have been set up.

'He doesn't go out, he doesn't drink, he hasn't really got any friends, so how has he managed to end up with those kinds of people? He will be petrified—I don't know if he's going to cope with it. It's hit me like a bombshell,' said Derek.

His head began to pound as he tried to piece together everything going on around him. 'Joan was a rock—bless her. She was the one who deserves all the credit for holding things together', says Derek. She stayed up until the early hours of the morning, emailing the embassy in Bangkok and sorting things out. She spent hours researching Thailand and finding the right contacts to help young Michael.

'One night we saw Michael on the news. He was being led away by the Thai police. The horror of that image is something that all of us who love Michael will never forget. He was shouting: 'Family I love you all. I am more worried about you than myself'. It broke my heart to see my son so distressed. And then he was gone!' says Derek.

They needed answers, but neither of them had ever had any dealings with the embassy. Joan quickly established contact with them and though she didn't really find out much, they were helpful in sharing what they did know. Derek was somewhat disappointed with them. He expected more than carefully worded reassurances.

He felt totally useless being 6000 miles away from his son.

'If he needed me, I couldn't just pop round and comfort him, but I was more fortunate than most people in that the BBC wanted to do a documentary about Michael. They said they'd pay for me to go over to Thailand with a member

of their staff to do some filming. Sally Williams contacted me a few days later. She would accompany me to visit Michael and help me engage a Thai lawyer to represent him. In Thailand you can only use a Thai lawyer and I had no idea where to begin looking for one. I was grateful to the BBC for their tremendous support and assistance, but disappointed they wouldn't pay for Joan to go with us. We had to scrape together money from our meagre savings to cover her costs. Just as well Joan did come, because I lost my temper through endless frustrations and may well have ended up in the same cell as my son.

They met their embassy who recommended a lawyer who was apparently the best English-speaking lawyer in Thailand. His fees were £3000, provided Michael pleaded guilty. Derek couldn't believe the authorities would want his son to plead guilty. Was he guilty? Did he know about the drugs? Then Derek read a story in the news:

Mr (Michael) Connell told the Times newspaper correspondent, Andrew Drummond, that the tablets had been found in two tubs of body cream he had bought at a supermarket in Greater Manchester.

He said: 'I still have the receipt. Somehow when the tubs were opened by customs in Bangkok, the pills were inside'.

'I do not know how they got there or how this could have happened. When I arrived in Bangkok, my suitcase did not come off the conveyor belt. I was taken to one side where they said they were X-raying my luggage. They said they had an informer. The tubs did not look like the same ones I packed.'

He added: 'I spoke to my parents last night. They were very upset. Tell my mum and dad that I love them and not to worry about me. I'm more worried about them than they should be about me.'

He said: 'I'm innocent, but I have been told if I do not explain the whole story I will be found guilty and get the death sentence. So I am pleading guilty to save my life.'

Thailand has now changed its execution method from firing squad to lethal injection.

On the embassy's recommendation, Derek hired the local lawyer for Michael and paid his fee. The lawyer explained to Derek and Joan that the mandatory sentence for possession of ecstasy was the death penalty. However, he also advised that if a prisoner confesses to a crime, then their sentence is halved. It seemed he thought Michael was guilty. Derek didn't know what to think. He was told so many different things that it was difficult to know what was true and what wasn't. He couldn't believe any of it was actually happening.

> *It was insane. But even more insane was knowing that my son was a prisoner of the Bangkok Hilton, regardless of whether he deserved to be there. I'd heard rumours of the prison and how bad the conditions and overcrowding were, but it didn't hit me until the day I stepped into that world. I felt the life drain out of me when I realised just how hopeless my son's situation was. If Michael survived the trial, would he survive that horrifying place filled with murderers, rapists and paedophiles? I felt like we were on our own. Up the river without a paddle. It seemed Michael's fate was in someone else's hands, and all we could do was sit on the sidelines and wait for it all to unfold.*

The embassy staff were good at the beginning, which was a great relief to Derek. They sent someone to visit Michael every week, but as time went on, this dropped back to fortnightly and after a while, monthly visits.

> *I suppose they had limited resources and other prisoners in a similar predicament, but it was hard waiting for each week to pass for some news. I've since learned that most UK prisoners are only granted visits once a month. We heard of the bullying and intimidation that goes on in prisons all around the world. I worried a great deal about how my son would cope. He wasn't a big lad. In fact, there wasn't much of him at all. I asked the embassy to make sure Michael was being treated okay. They said he was, but it didn't stop me from worrying, or wondering if they were merely sparing me the truth. Eventually, I started getting letters from Michael. He said he was okay and told me not to worry. I suppose I was a little foolish in doubting what the embassy had been telling me, but in my own defence I put it down to the tremendous stress we were living under.*

On 24 March 2004, Michael went to court. His father waited anxiously back home in the UK because he couldn't afford to even be there. Derek prayed they'd not give him the death penalty. The defence lawyer, Prutti Kuranon, assured them that if Michael confessed to the crime then he would escape the death penalty. He also said that he'd probably be given a 50-year sentence and even maybe a 25-year one because of his young age and because he had cooperated fully with the authorities.

That didn't happen. Michael admitted to smuggling 3400 ecstasy tablets into Thailand, and the Thai Justice Department hit him with the full 99 years. Although Derek and Joan were thankful beyond belief that Michael's life had been spared, they were still devastated by such a harsh sentence. They would appeal the decision, of course, but that was about all they could do.

As time passed, Michael admitted to them that all was not exactly how he had described when he was first arrested. He was scared, he said. He was young and naïve. While it didn't take an Einstein to figure out that he deserved to be punished, he was still Derek's son and he loved him dearly. Michael pleaded for a second chance. Obviously, he'd made a decision with fatal consequences. He'll never have another shot at life if he is to serve the full 99-year sentence.

The years passed.

On 27 April 2006, Michael went to the Criminal Court in Thailand and the judgement of the Appeals Court was read to him. The court reduced his sentence from life imprisonment to 30 years. He will be due for release in 2038 when he is 54 years old. By that time, his father will most likely have died of old age.

> *I suppose Michael could apply for a transfer in 2008 when he becomes eligible under the Prisoner Transfer Agreement that the UK has with Thailand, but from what I've read about it, it isn't such a good thing. Before Michael seriously considers it, I'd like to see the UK government try and cut a better deal for all its citizens. If Michael was granted a transfer under the present arrangements, then he'd still have to serve at least half of his sentence in a UK prison. Given these circumstances, many say it's better he stays where he is and hopes for a King's Pardon, given annually to the lucky ones.*

He's not sure what the answer is, and says that it's up to Michael. In actual fact, Derek thinks his son is more frightened of being transferred back to a UK prison than he is of staying in Thailand. In a UK prison, he'd be locked in a cell for up to 23 hours a day with hardened criminals. He'd get very little time outside in an exercise yard and even though Derek and Joan would be able to visit more often, Michael would still be locked in a cell for all that time regardless. At least in the Thai prison, he can go outdoors into the sunshine, play football and not be beaten up every moment of the day and night by older prisoners trying to get at him. While the conditions are most likely more horrendous, Michael is doing his best to stay positive. For now it's a safer option for him than exchanging life for the unknown.

> *I've never been an optimist. I always believe that life will kick you in the teeth given the opportunity. I've always thought the glass was half empty, not half full. But I hope Michael will get his chance. I pray he'll come home. But until he's on British soil, I will worry every day that the Thai authorities will cancel the transfer agreement or that he will die thousands of miles from home and those who love him. Joan and I do the best we can, but it's good to know we're not alone in this and we are thankful to all the hundreds of people who have offered their support to us over the years. We've been overwhelmed by the compassion of others who don't even know us, yet they write letters and send cards which gives us great encouragement. We've also had such good support from the UK Prisoners Abroad group and the Australian-based Foreign Prisoner Support Service. Between them, they've continued to help Michael financially, emotionally, practically and spiritually. They're a lifeline for those poor sods detained overseas and their families. I also don't know what we would have done without the support of Bev Saunders and Gale Bailey who made weekly visits to Michael in Bangkwang. They helped him a great deal when things were really uncertain and I know he's eternally grateful for their support, the food and treats. Joanne Burns, Michael's primary school teacher, did lots of work on Michael's behalf, on her own initiative, when Michael was first arrested. Alistair Burt, the member of parliament for North East Bedfordshire, gave us tremendous encouragement. I sit here waiting for my son to come home. There's not much more I can do but wait.*

Joan and Derek pay money into Michael's prison account. The embassy distributes to him the £25 a week from the account that Prisoners Abroad provide him and the little his family can scrape together. This has to buy everything he needs like food, toiletries, cigarettes, stationery and stamps.

Michael says they feed prisoners one bowl of rice a day, plus a bowl of what Michael calls fish head soup. He says that it looks like muddy water with fish heads floating on the top. He doesn't eat it because with the little money his family sends, he can buy food from the prison shop.

> *He was 19 when I last saw him, a teenager with a teenage take on life. Now he has become a man. He turned 21 in that prison and has lost his youth forever. Looking back now, I think that Michael's learning problems may have made him an easy target. Now he's paying a terrible price. What he did was wrong, but even so, I still think that someone out there is responsible for what's happened to my son. Of course, Michael must take some of the blame for his part, but not all the blame surely? I believe he was used by some smooth-talking con artist who promised him easy money. They put him on a plane and then phoned the Thai authorities and told them his name, the flight he was on, the clothes he was wearing and the drugs he was carrying. They did this because they obviously had someone else on the plane carrying far more drugs. I'm told this is what happens. So while my son was being arrested by Thai police, someone else on that flight walked straight through customs undetected.*

Derek believes that his son is a genuinely good person. He is missed and loved by family and friends. He's not a hardened criminal. Some might say he is easily led, but he's always been the first to stand up and look after the younger ones in his family. He had never been in trouble with the police in the UK and the trip to Thailand was his first time away on his own.

Derek wishes he could afford to travel to see him again but the costs are totally beyond him and Joan. They barely scrape by as it is. So they just keep their fingers crossed that nothing goes wrong with Michael's forthcoming repatriation or his health.

> *'When I think of Michael in Bangkwang Prison, I try not to imagine the worst. I try not to think about the prison's nickname 'The Big Tiger' or its meaning 'The place that eats men alive'. I try to block out the images of my son crammed into a cell with 25 others for 15 hours a day. Instead, I picture my boy running onto a field, granted far from the fields of Manchester United, but wearing his footy boots and Man United jersey, with the sun on his face and a smile in his eye. I'm just thankful he's still alive and in that he can take hope. I am surprised at how well he has managed to cope with the situation and how he has remained so positive in*

his thinking. I know that I would not have been able to do that.

I kept thinking my boy was doing okay and then my world was rocked in June 2007, when I was told that he had just finished his third week in the hospital wing of Klong Prem Prison. He was transferred there after feeling unwell in Bangkwang. They discovered he had pneumonia and acute anaemia. Tests showed that he also had a ruptured stomach ulcer, probably from all the worry about whether or not he'll survive. They say he'll be patched up and sent back to Bangkwang when he's feeling better. It is cold comfort to me sitting here.

Sadly, Michael's grandad passed away. They had shared a very special bond and Derek worried how Michael would take the news of his passing. He struggled to make a decision about what to say, but eventually he told him that his grandfather was in hospital, not in any pain, but that his heart was failing and there was nothing that could be done to save him. He was 85 years old and dying of old age. It was a terribly sad time for the Connell family, but each of us has our time. Michael's grandad had already been dead three days when Derek told Michael, which in some ways had given him a little time to grieve before listening to his son's grief. When Michael phoned the following week, he took the news reasonably well, but was deeply troubled that he could not attend his grandfather's funeral. Derek thinks Michael felt he'd let the old boy down. But that was never the case.

My boy may have lost his way, but nothing will ever change the fact that he is my boy, and despite everything that's happened, I'll love him no less. If people want to write letters to help us campaign for Michael's return then this would be most appreciated. Details can be found at the following websites. Thank you to those who continue to stand by Joan and me, but most importantly, to those who continue to support Michael.'

As of 2011, Michael Connell has at least 23 to 24 years left to serve but he holds onto the hope that he may be shown mercy, after all, even in Bangkwang, miracles do happen!

Foreign Prisoner Support Service
http://www.usp.com.au/fpss/case-michael_connell.html

Prisoners Abroad (UK)—Caring for Britons held overseas
http://www.prisonersabroad.org.uk/index.html

11
Do you know where your kids are?

Rachel, Hong Kong

Only first names in this chapter have been used to protect the identities of the prisoners and families.

Rachel is a young 17-year-old girl from Sydney who left Australia on 5 April 2005. The trainee hairdresser told her mother she was sleeping over at a friend's house, but instead she flew to Hong Kong with two other Australians, Chris (15 years) and Tran (21 years), to play her part in a $1 million heroin racket, or so the media reported. In actual fact, the street value was $242,000.

On 12 April 2006, police raided the low-budget hotel room in the Tsim Sha Tsui district. They discovered the drug in 114 condoms and several glove fingers that, they say, the two teenagers , Rachel and Chris, were to swallow before boarding a flight to Sydney. Hong Kong prosecutors said Rachel and Chris had been promised $200 by a drug syndicate for each 5-centimetre packet of heroin they swallowed. Their arrest was part of a joint police operation to stop the use of drug mules smuggling drugs between the two countries.

Public debate in Australia questioned whether the Australian authorities should have prevented these teenagers from leaving Australia, given that they were minors. In fact, Julian Wagner, a former Commonwealth prosecutor and currently a barrister in Queensland, has stated his intentions to call for a Royal Commission or Open Review into the matter.

It is possible for the Australian authorities to legally detain people on Australian soil before they embark on a journey to a country where the death penalty may be mandatory. Rachel's parents believe that if the Australian police were aware of their daughter's involvement in something that might result in a crime, then they should have been told of her activities, so that appropriate action could have been taken. They believe that the police should have prevented her from travelling. They believe that the police could have detained their daughter on Australian soil and investigated her involvement through an Australian court. If the Australian authorities believed that Rachel was involved somehow in a crime syndicate, then surely they could have, and should have, detained her in accordance with legislation relating to conspiracy to import narcotics.

Some might say that kids like Rachel don't deserve any leniency, but others would argue that many kids are prone to making mistakes.

Rachel's father, Ferdie, received a late-night call from the Australian Department of Foreign Affairs and Trade (DFAT). He was told that his daughter had been detained by authorities in a foreign country. The family did not even know that Rachel was travelling abroad. They thought she was at a friend's house. Rachel had simply asked for her passport so that she could get her learner's permit to sit her driving test.

Rachel's father flew immediately to Hong Kong with only $150 dollars in his wallet. He took the fast train to a city in the area of Tsim Sa Tsui, hoping his journey would lead him to his young daughter. There he met the Australian consular officer who explained the seriousness of Rachel's dilemma.

'The DFAT officer called the prison for me to ask for a visit. We then went to the prison that day. The consul took me up to the gate and also bought me a train pass with HK$100 credit. He was very helpful and understood my position,' says Ferdie.

It was an emotionally charged reunion between Rachel and her father.

'My eyes were full of tears. I couldn't believe that I was seeing my daughter behind bars and could not even touch or hug her. We could only talk on the speakerphone with a glass window between us. I was so helpless at that time. There was nothing I could do. The meeting lasted for just 15 minutes with both of us crying our hearts out. Afterwards I went straight to a nearby church and prayed all day,' Ferdie recounts.

A missionary group gave shelter to Ferdie over the coming weeks. If not for them, Ferdie says that he would have ended up in serious trouble, since he did not know that his initial lodgings were in a dangerous part of town.

On 12 August 2005, the Hong Kong government provided a legal aid solicitor from the firm Boase, Cohen & Collins to represent Rachel. Mr Melville Boase's firm was established in 1985, boasting 15 lawyers plus a list of paralegals, trainees and supporting staff. Three of his partners had over 60 years' experience between them practising in Hong Kong.

Rachel's barrister pleaded for mercy from the judge, saying that although Rachel came from a supportive family, she'd already had several setbacks in life. She had been indecently assaulted when she was five years old and raped when she was 12. He said she had been 'scared' of the syndicate and was assured she did not have to swallow the drug and only needed to accompany the younger boy, Chris, on the trip.

According to news reports, Tran, a Vietnamese-Australian, was recruited by the crime syndicate in Sydney after losing his money playing poker machines at a casino. It was alleged that he had recruited Chris and Rachel to act as drug couriers and would supply the heroin for them to swallow. His lawyer described Tran, Chris and Rachel as three individuals from good families who had ended up as 'down-and-outs'.

Tran was the first among the three Australians to plead guilty. The barrister for the youngest defendant, Chris, who was only 15, pleaded for a lenient sentence due to his client's 'extremely young' age. The media described Chris as a schoolboy brought up by a single mother. A young man who displayed all the stereotypical teenage behaviour by falling in with the wrong crowd. When he was 13 or 14, he lost interest in school and fell in with an older group who, his lawyer told the court; 'got him into the horrendous trouble he is in now'. Obviously, those older people didn't tell him that there can be serious negative consequences for every negative action. Or did they just say that things are morally okay as long as you don't get caught?

No one expected these young teenagers to get the usual 20-year sentence, but the judge said that while courts were naturally reluctant to sentence young people to jail, the gravity of some offences made substantial terms inevitable to deter others from following their example.

In April 2006, Rachel was sentenced to serve 10 years and 8 months for her involvement in the syndicate and was transferred to a maximum security prison in Hong Kong. Chris received nine years and Tran, 13 years.

As at October 2007, their appeals were still pending.

Before this nightmare started, what were the most difficult things these kids had to deal with? Did they ever think for a moment in high school that they might end up convicted as international drug couriers and sentenced to do time in a foreign jail?

Research shows that to some extent parents are role models for their children. They way in which they live their lives and the behaviours they display will have some influence on their children. However, the blame for one person's actions cannot be laid entirely at the door of another. We all have choices and sometimes we don't make the right choice.

Rachel's parents wonder when they will ever see their daughter again. Rachel wonders the same thing of her parents as she sits in a prison cell thousands of miles from home. She is isolated in a country where she can't even understand the language. She is alone with her thoughts and constantly reminded of the poor choices she made. Gone are the days when she would 'hang out' with friends, go to the mall with her mother or spoil her two brothers. Gone is her youthful ignorance. She's had to grow up quickly.

Rachel says that she was only going to Hong Kong because someone else offered to pay for her holiday and, while there, she could get hair and eyelash extensions. She didn't question her friend's motives for offering the free trip. Why would she? How else would she ever be able to afford such an extravagance herself? It was an opportunity of a lifetime, or so she thought.

But what about her parents? Rachel was only 17. Didn't she think her parents would find out? Obviously not. Her mother, Agnes, was hospitalised at the time with a pulmonary embolism. Her father was struggling to hold down his job, take care of her brothers, visit his sick wife and keep the household running alone. No one was watching Rachel for those early warning signs that she was in any trouble.

Rachel herself didn't think that a free trip would have such consequences. She thought that she could fly over to Hong Kong, have a great time and no one would be any the wiser. How many teenagers think before acting? How many young people get caught up in the false promises of others seeking to take advantage of their vulnerabilities?

I have had several letters from Rachel and I know that she is genuinely sorry for the trouble she's caused her family.

'I love my family and I'm so sorry for all the hurt I've put them through. I want to be the best daughter I can possibly be to make up for everything,' says Rachel.

For the first time in a long time, she's opening up to her parents. In fact, Ferdie says that this experience has brought them closer together. But it's been a life-changing experience for all of them.

This was very challenging in the beginning for Ferdie and his family. He says that he felt like he'd lost his senses completely and was beyond thinking straight. Life became very difficult. The company he worked for looked at him as a number and not a human being. Their shareholders were only interested in profits. Ferdie says that his boss knew that his family was struggling with the situation with Rachel, but it didn't appear to affect him at all. Ferdie says that he was forced to resign from his job a week before Christmas and he says he did not get any separation pay.

> *How do you explain to your children that Christmas will have to wait because we don't have enough money even for food? I just kept telling myself that things would get better and prayed every day that a miracle would come into our lives. We survived on noodles and prayer. Then our apartment was broken into, our belongings stolen and because we didn't have any money to pay bills, our credit rating was ruined. Half a dozen creditors were sending me threatening legal letters. They didn't care that we were living in a garage the size of a small tool shed. My wife developed depression and her blood pressure became very high. None of us could get anything that resembled normal sleep. I had a tendency to wake up during the night thinking of my daughter. We just took each day as it came, hoping that it would soon be over. Whenever we felt despair, we would try to think of all those happy moments we had together as a family.*
>
> *Nowadays, whenever I see a family together, wearing a smile and sharing laughter, I always look elsewhere. I cannot bear to be reminded that my family has been torn apart. I question myself at other times, I blame myself for the decision I made to migrate to Australia. Would we have been better off had we remained in poverty in our little Philippine village? I don't know. We had a simple life and ate noodles and now, we have a complicated life and eat noodles.*

Ferdie and Agnes both agree that they are fortunate that they have made many new friends throughout their ordeal. The Filipino Women's Migrant Organization in Hong Kong opened their arms and never denied them the support they needed, when they needed it. This organisation was not established to help people like them. They help Filipino citizen workers in Hong Kong, but they understood the difficulties of Ferdie and his wife going to a strange land, without any understanding of the culture or language.

> *'Kay Danes and Martin Hodgson from the Foreign Prisoner Support Group have always been there for us and given us their unbiased support. I cannot count the times that I have relied on them as a shoulder to lean on when things have been at their most bleak.*
>
> *We have many friends and family members in the Philippines, including my sister and eldest brother. At such times, it's important to remember that we are not alone and that our family, no matter where they are, will always be there for us. That in itself is a tremendous blessing and comfort. I can only hope that after all these trials and tribulations my daughter will now listen when her mother and father speak. I hope that she will stay with us for the remainder of our lives. That somehow she will find a way to rebuild her own life and somehow she will find a way to put all the hurt behind her. I only hope that she remembers how much we love her and how much we are willing to go through for her. All the suffering we endure now is not for any other reason but to bring our daughter, our beloved Rachel, back into our lives.*

If he could share a message for other families with children, then he would say:

> *Take advantage of the time while your kids are young, show them how much you love them and how much you would care and support them no matter what. There is only a small window of opportunity to show how much you care and love your kids. Once they reach a certain age they tend to drift away. They want to mingle with different types of people and friends. Some are lucky to have a real good friend who is a good role model for them. But sometimes, like what happened to our daughter, she was a good girl who fell in with the wrong crowd. Do not stop telling your kids you love them and always hug them and kiss them good bye and greet them with warm hugs and kisses when they come home. Just do the best you can do and pray that it all turns out the right way! And to those young teenagers who might be reading this story, please do not make the same*

mistakes Rachel made. It may sound like a good offer, but it may also be one you will regret for the rest of your life.

Thousands of teenagers risk their lives every day throughout the world. Many of them know the risks, but we know that teenagers don't necessarily think through the risks as a clear-thinking adult would. Some teenagers currently on death row have told me that they never believed that they'd get the death penalty if caught. Despite all the warning signs at airports that clearly state 'the penalty for drug trafficking is death', they thought that they wouldn't get caught.

Could it be that in our society we are failing to get the right messages out to our youth? Have our values deteriorated to the extent that we no longer fear things our parents would have feared 20 or 30 years ago? Could it be that instead of teaching French or German, say, in high school that we should be focusing more on a holistic approach to education by developing positive peer culture, self discipline and cognitive self change. Should we be teaching our children how to cope with challenges and stress and how to make the right choices in life?

Maybe if teenagers were taught more life-training skills they wouldn't resort to the behaviours that some of them are resorting to now. Usually when a teenager has suffered some form of emotional turmoil, physical or mental abuse, they turn inwards. The door closes and the earphones get put on. They shut everything and everyone out. They may lose their ability to feel for a situation, rationalise it, analyse the consequences. After a period of time, they don't even recognise themselves.

For teenagers like Rachel, who are able to recognise their mistakes and accept that they do need support to get their lives back on the right track, there is hope, provided there is also opportunity. Sometimes people are arrested overseas and are unable to get home because there are no mechanisms in place for that. For example, an international transfer of prisoners scheme allows people imprisoned in one country to apply to transfer to another country to serve the balance of their sentence. Sometimes the agreements are not formalised between states and they have to go through the very long and drawn-out process of implementation.

In 2003, another young Australian woman was sentenced in Thailand to 31 years' jail for attempting to smuggle heroin and possession of heroin. She had been arrested three years earlier trying to send an envelope containing 10.4 grams of pure heroin from the Bangkok Central Post Office to Australia.

In November 2006, the Australian and Thai governments agreed that the young woman was eligible for repatriation under the existing treaty on prisoner exchange. Her application was rejected at her home state level by the Minister for Corrective Services, claiming that she was not suitable for transfer due to her lack of family support, her past prison record and the recidivist nature of her offending. The young woman had made some dreadful choices in the past, but she no longer had a drug habit. She also proved to the Thai authorities that she was willing to take responsibility for her actions.

As a result of lobbying by human rights groups and individuals close to the case, the Minister eventually agreed to a federal government proposal for this woman's repatriation on medical grounds.

In an astonishing turnaround decision, the minister stated:

> *Her health condition is sufficiently serious that we believe her health would be compromised were she to continue to be in a Thai prison. She will serve five years in prison, which means that (her) total term of imprisonment will be over 12 years. She will then be subject to a further five years' parole supervision. I think that's long enough for anyone to reflect on what they have done—and a deterrent to anyone who is minded to go to overseas countries and commit serious drug offences'*

Prisoner transfers are not 'get out of jail free cards'. Prisoners are treated as any other federal prisoners. The sentence imposed by the detaining state does not change. Just as a lesser sentence cannot be imposed by the receiving state, so too a harsher sentence cannot be imposed. The principle of these transfer agreements is to allow the foreign sentence to be served in the prisoner's own country, and not replace or substitute the existing sentence with a new one.

Of course, parole conditions and remissions can still be obtained, but the conditions are set by the detaining foreign state and these cannot be interfered with.

Such agreements are important for social rehabilitation, which is more likely to occur in the prisoner's home country, where the prisoner is able to be closer to family and within their own culture. The benefits of transferring to a modern, Western facility usually mean that prisoners have access to rehabilitation and custodial programs, educational and employment opportunities, more hygienic living conditions and a cultural and linguistic environment that is familiar.

Medical care and mental health services are also beneficial to prisoners and factor high on a prisoner's priorities, particularly when you consider that a simple toothache left unattended in an Asian prison can result in extreme pain and additional complications.

There are also many financial benefits for taxpayers who will no longer pay the ongoing costs of a prisoner's incarceration in a foreign jail. For example, on average, it costs $250 per day to maintain a foreign national in an Australian prison. Australian authorities are currently processing approximately 75 applications for transfer out of Australian prisons. This would result in a saving to Australian tax payers of $7 million over one year.

Transferring prisoners from overseas also reduces the demand on assistance provided by consular posts to citizens. Some prisoners are detained in isolated locations and the costs of travel to and from these locations are high. And of course, as I've mentioned in previous chapters, there are tremendous financial savings to families who often struggle with costs of travelling for visits, and maintaining basic food and medical supplies for their loved one detained abroad.

Prisoners do not have an automatic right to make application for transfer when detained overseas. If a prisoner makes application, either state can refuse their request without giving any reasons. International transfer applications can take a long time to achieve. Some prisoners have submitted applications and are still waiting 12 to 18 months later. Some prisoner transfer agreements require prisoners to serve one-third or one half of their sentence before they are allowed to make an application. Transfers are almost always consensual, requiring the agreement of the transferring country, the receiving country and the prisoner. Deciding who pays and who doesn't or who is deported and who is expelled are all issues that must be addressed.

Social rehabilitation is not the sole purpose of incarceration and so it cannot be the sole consideration for determining prisoner transfers. Research has shown that prisoners who maintain contact with their family and/or solid networks of positive support, are less likely to re-offend. Reintegration is difficult and sadly a number of people do re-offend, but with proper rehabilitation and access to offender management programs, access to support networks and a little understanding, there is always a good chance that a prisoner will find a better path in life.

In March 2008, Rachel was granted a sentence reduction of two years as a result of her good behaviour and cooperation with authorities. All that is left to do now is for her and her family to wait patiently. Rachel said, 'I've learnt a very big lesson. I'll do my best to make it up to my family. I'm so sorry!'

Rachel has been released from prison and has reunited with family. Her father says 'We're all doing fine. Life has returned to some normality at last!'

12
Morocco madness

Kelly's brother, Morocco

Only first names have been used in this chapter to protect the identities of the prisoners and families.

It took about a month for Kelly to get the news that her brother had been imprisoned in Morocco in North Africa in May 1999. Kelly was at home when she received the phone call from the American consulate. It is difficult to explain the sheer shock and terror she felt upon hearing the news of her brother's arrest in a foreign country, and particularly when they told her he was detained on drug-related charges. All Kelly knew of imprisonment in a foreign country she had learned from movies.

Kelly called her husband at work and told him of the situation. He came home immediately. This, of course, was only the beginning of a long, ugly nightmare. Next, Kelly looked on the internet for resources and can sadly say she did not receive many responses, and those she did receive were of no help. All suggestions were for arrests that happened in the US. Kelly then started calling Congress members and other such officials. The only one she received any help from, albeit limited, was Dunkin Hunter. Kelly says that he will receive her vote for the upcoming presidential elections. Sadly, she says that the American consulate provided the least help.

Kelly sent money to the American consulate for food. They said that it was a long drive to the prison and that they did not have the time to do this for one person more than a few times a year. Knowing this, she would ask them to take certain foods, ones she knew her brother liked and ones she knew would last.

This did not matter, they would bring whatever they decided to bring. Many items went bad within the first couple of weeks, or immediately. There was no refrigeration for prisoners. Kelly complained over and over about his not receiving his mail and asked if she could send it to the consulate so they could take it to him. Again, this was too much of a problem for them.

As time went on, Kelly learned through trial and error. She was unhappy with the lack of support from the embassy and the authorities. Dealing with them was extremely frustrating, she says. Kelly failed at every attempt to hire a lawyer. Her brother sent her phone numbers of lawyers in Morocco. She called all of them, and got nowhere. Not one could speak English. Kelly's brother was losing his mind each time she had to tell him she was unable to hire representation, and why. Kelly agonised. She could hear his complete frustration. This broke her heart.

Kelly persevered and tried talking to many attorneys in the US. Not one was interested in getting involved in a case abroad, even to suggest what could be done. Throughout all the years her brother was incarcerated, she was never able to retain an attorney.

She tried to imagine where her brother was, the conditions he faced and the treatment he endured. She had horrendous nightmares. Her nightmares did not do justice to the true horrors her brother was going through. He did everything to shield her from knowing what he was enduring, but in the end it was he who needed shielding. Their father died of a heart attack about three years after her brother's imprisonment. The war broke out in the Middle East and Kelly's brother was beaten up because he was the only American citizen in the prison. He had to be taken to hospital for a period of time. Five years into his incarceration, their only sibling, their sister, committed suicide, and this triggered a mental breakdown for Kelly's brother.

He lived crammed into a 14 foot by 16 foot (four metres by four and a half metres) cell, caged with 30 to 35 other prisoners, locked up for 21 hours of each day. He described the conditions as appalling, and said they slept on a dirty cement floor. Others were lucky enough to have had a family member bring them an air mattress, sleeping bag and blankets. There was no toilet in the cell, only a hole in the middle of the room. There wasn't even a wall to separate it from the sleeping quarters. Kelly's brother wrote to say that their human waste went into the floor below their cell and the stench of it was overwhelming. Many died of infection, beatings or starvation and their bodies were left in the cells for days prior to removal.

Kelly's brother, as well as others, found themselves degraded to the point of eating cockroaches for nourishment. He said he was always hungry and described the food provided by the prison as unfit for human consumption, but they ate it all the same. It was either that or starve, he said.

> *My brother told me some were selling their bodies for small amounts of food. Every night the screams of prisoners filled the prison compound. Prisoners were beaten repeatedly, including my brother. At night, while sleeping, the guards would take their turns beating the soles of the prisoners' feet,* says Kelly.

One of the most alarming aspects of the report coming out of Morocco deals with evidence that children as young as 12 are being kept in the prisons and are regularly falling victim to sexual abuse including rape, even though legally nobody under 16 years old is allowed to be in prison.

Kelly felt helpless, so far away from her brother, trapped in a place where all kinds of madness reigned. The distance between them made things worse. Kelly knew he was not telling her the truth about the extreme abuse to which he was subjected. Even if she were able to make the trip, which she wasn't, her brother was only allowed a person to visit for 30 minutes a couple of times a week. Kelly wrote often, but the mail did not arrive at either end. Once she understood the tricks being played by the guards, more of her brother's mail reached him. She sent what funds she could to the American consulate for phone cards, and her brother was able to call for very limited amounts of time. The calls were heartbreaking.

> *I could hear prisoners screaming in pain. The calls were limited to a few minutes as there were so many waiting for the few phones used by inmates. In order to stay sane, I wrote letters and made phone calls hoping for assistance. Mostly I prayed. I was put on stress medication due to heightened blood pressure, sleeplessness and general anxiety. My fear of what he was going through and the possibility of never seeing him again terrified me on a daily basis. His incarceration deeply affected all areas of my life, financially, emotionally and in my ability to do my job.*

Her neverending involvement placed huge stress on her marriage. Kelly's husband worried about her health. He tried to understand her frustration in not getting anywhere in her attempts to obtain help for her brother. Kelly herself cut out friends and other relationships during this time. She was unable to find time for others and her anxiety was so high most people did not want to be around her.

> *I know my friends tried to understand, but how could they? I do not think anyone could understand unless they were put in this nightmare. There were times when I felt complete and utter despair and the only thing that got me through was prayer. I had no idea what the best course of action was for my brother. I only knew that he needed my help. By researching Moroccan law on the internet, I found out that the only approved pardon would be from the King. I began a letter campaign to the King's sister, who was in charge of his correspondence. I made form letters addressed to the King for people to sign. Unfortunately, the majority of people seemed more concerned about what others might think or say if they found out they had signed such a letter. It might appear that they were somehow involved in the drug smuggling.*

In 2005, a miracle happened. A prison guard went to Kelly's brother's cell and told him he was free. Her brother assumed this was another form of mental torture. He had endured so much mental and physical torture by this point that he did not believe it and did not bother to stand up. Hearing the commotion from the other cells, Kelly's brother realised the news was true. He ran out of the prison. Just like that, his ordeal was over!

Kelly received a phone call from her brother saying: 'I am having a steak and a glass of wine'. She was so shocked that she stood rooted to the floor, open-mouthed, the phone dangling from her hand, as he explained what had happened.

His original 10-year sentence was quashed when the King of Morocco died. All foreign inmates had their sentences reduced when the King died. Then all foreign prisoners had their sentences reduced again when the new King married. When the King had a son, all foreign prisoners, except one, were released.

Kelly's brother believes that the overwhelming amount of letters sent to the King on his behalf were the main reason for his pardon. When she thinks back to those dark days, she wonders how they ever got through.

> *I thought the pain would never end. But despite everything, there was light at the end of the tunnel. Nowadays, I am overjoyed that my brother is back home with his family, his children who love him dearly and friends who never gave up on him.*

There is so much more to tell, but it is just too painful to recall every memory. I'm told by others who have endured their own horrific ordeals that it's good to talk about these things. In some ways I do feel less burdened emotionally. I know I will never heal completely and nor will I ever forget. Nowadays I look at my brother and see that hunted look on his face. Everyday he remembers and every day I worry that those memories will push him over the edge. I really can't think of too many positives from this ordeal, other than my brother making it out alive and being home with his family. I know he will never be the same and nor will I.

In a final thought, I will add one positive thing that has resulted from this terrible ordeal and that is that I have had the opportunity to make a good friend. He is a gentleman who was imprisoned with my brother and became a great friend of his while there and has also become a good friend of mine. He is still there in prison. He was imprisoned for something that he did not do. I know that most prisoners say this, but he truly is an innocent and was sentenced to 10 years because of racial bias. His release date is coming up this coming year (2007). His health is poor, but I am praying he will make his way out just as my brother did. He has a strong belief in God and I am sure this is how he has lasted so long.

If I could offer advice to other families who are going through a similar situation, then I would simply say: I know what great difficulties you are facing. Please do not give up. I know many times you will hit dead ends and feel that you are running in circles. Again, please do not give up. I know letters help to keep you going, whether coming from you or others you get involved in your loved one's situation. If people are able to send funds to a prisoner detained in a foreign prison, then this helps enormously. Depending on where they are incarcerated, money can be all that will keep them alive. For instance, in Morocco, one cup of broth is all a prisoner receives each day. Most inmates are from the area and are kept alive by the food brought to the prison by friends and family. It is hugely important to find out exactly what is provided in the prison in which your loved one is incarcerated. Sometimes we take things for granted.'

What does Kelly hope for now that the nightmare is over? There is no simple answer, she says.

I would like to see our government take more of an interest in their citizens overseas. Their refrain seems to be, 'we have so many other issues to deal with, we just do not have the time'. I would like to see this issue brought to public attention. I believe most citizens have no idea what happens when one is in trouble while travelling abroad. I worry about others who are in this situation. I was one of those people who did not think about something like this happening. I realise there are many right now going through hell with so little help to be had. For now, I will just continue to have faith and pray that our ordeal might prove positive in helping someone else who feels beyond despair. We won't give up. We know the road ahead is still a little rocky, but at least we are together and we pray that will be enough to get us to a place of peace.

13
Death for 250 grams

Scott, Thailand

> *I took drugs across the Thai/Cambodia border to pay off a £600 gambling debt. The bloke that gave me the 250 pills then informed the police that I was coming across the border into Thailand from Cambodia, where I was living. I know that many people will not believe that I was so stupid, but we all make mistakes! Mine is costing me 30 years.*
> —Scott Hurford, Thailand

Lee was driving from the seaside resort town of Skegness to Boston in Lincolnshire, UK, home of the Boston Stump, the biggest parish church in England. It was ten o'clock in the morning. His mobile phone rang. He noticed it was a London number as he pulled to the kerb. The voice on the other end sounded official.

'Yes that's me,' Lee responded.

The British Foreign Office staffer explained he had bad news concerning Lee's brother, Scott. Lee's first question was if Scott was alive. The official confirmed he was. What he told Lee next caught him way off guard. Lee's brother had been arrested and was currently sitting in a prison cell on the Thailand–Cambodia border.

Being a former Royal Marine, Lee Hurford was accustomed to dealing with the unexpected challenges life often brought. He had spent a decade in service to Her Majesty and was often faced with the test of human endurance, both physical and mental. This was different. This was personal. This was his brother.

After the initial shock had begun to set in, Lee felt disoriented and confused. He searched to understand what had happened. He questioned the embassy as to how it had happened, but they had very little information to share. Was Scott being treated well or beaten like a prisoner of war? Lee had no idea and for the very first time in his life he felt at a complete loss. He debated with himself on what to do first. Should he fly 13 hours to Thailand or tell their mother and then fly to Thailand?

In the end, he decided against telling his parents, at least until he could verify the situation and put himself in a better position to lessen their shock. He knew it would break their hearts thinking about their son sitting in a prison. It would devastate them.

Lee's first contact with the UK embassy in Bangkok was with a consular officer by the name of Jeff Mitchell. He was quite compassionate and seemed to understand Lee's dilemma. Little did Lee know that Jeff Mitchell had, over the course of his many years as a diplomat, assisted families in a similar predicament. Too many families in fact.

At the time of Scott's arrest, 19 March 2005, more than 160,000 prisoners were being detained by the Thai Department of Corrections, guarded only by 11,451 prison officers. In 2002, it had peaked at 245,801. The majority of arrests were for drugs. As at 2007, there were 130 UK prisoners detained in Thailand.

Jeff Mitchell explained by phone to Lee the grim reality of his brother's situation. By the end of their conversation, Lee realised that there wasn't much anyone in the embassy could do, other than accessing Scott and providing him with consular support. Lee felt helpless.

Lee mustered the courage a few days later to tell his parents of Scott's fate. As he expected, they both took the news hard. His mother cried so much she couldn't stop. Lee felt as if he and his family were caught in a nightmare, but no one would wake them up. What made things even worse was that Scott was to be the best man at Lee's wedding in a few short weeks. Their mother had been so looking forward to the wedding and Scott's return. Her joy suddenly turned to anguish.

There wasn't anything that could be done to change the situation. Legal matters and judicial processes in Thailand move at an incredibly slow pace. Nothing could be achieved by postponing Lee's wedding or by putting all their lives on hold. It was a heartbreaking dilemma but the family were resolute that they would tackle one day at a time.

Lee finally saw his brother while honeymooning with his wife, Clare, coincidently in Thailand.

The image of his brother, detained at the provincial Sa-Kaeo Prison on the Cambodian border has never left him. Scott looked like a frightened animal backed into a corner. Lee unashamedly cried his heart out at the end of their visit. Little did he know the horrors his brother had seen and the conditions he had to endure.

Scott shared a cell with 30 to 40 other men. He paid 2000 Thai Baht for his tiny sleeping space to avoid sleeping in the corner of the cell where those without money literally slept on top of each other. With the money Lee gave him, Scott was able to purchase some essential basic supplies: food, water, a bowl and spoon, a mug to drink from, a blanket and some soap. But Lee couldn't protect him from the horrors of a Thai prison. Scott was haunted by the treatment he saw of some of the young Cambodian inmates. He was helpless to stop the beastly violations of young boys who were put together with older Thais and used for sex. They were turned into slaves. They would wash clothes, fetch and carry for their masters and, in return, were fed and watered and left alone by everyone else—meaning they would not be raped. They were nothing and had no means of support. Most of them had crossed the border into Thailand looking for work. Most of them had no way of letting their families know where they were or what had happened to them. They simply existed the only way they could and did whatever it takes to be able to eat and survive.

Scott told his brother none of this. He kept trying to reassure Lee that things were not so grim, but both men knew Scott wasn't fooling anyone.

Lee came away from the visit with the weight of the world on his shoulders. He phoned their mother to explain that even though it would be difficult for her to see Scott in his present state, she ought to make the trip.

Scott's mother got on the very next available flight to Bangkok. His family were forced to face the harsh reality of Scott's situation and the consequences that might result in him spending the rest of his life behind bars. It was a daunting prospect that none of them really wanted to think much about, least of all Scott. They couldn't turn back the hands of time. Scott was in serious trouble and his boyish good looks would be absolutely no help to him now.

Lee kept thinking that no matter what happened, his brother would know that he could count on his family for however long it took to get him out of the situation. Their presence in Thailand seemed to calm him down considerably. They continued their visits as frequently as time would allow. It was extremely difficult and it took most of their energy, Lee says, to wear a smile and tell Scott that things would be okay. They were never sure that they would be, but it was easier to fool each other with the fantasy that by the end of the week, or the next week, Scott would be home. Lee hugged his mother after every visit and told her it would be okay.

The first year passed by like a dream. Lee says that it was hard to come to terms with the fact that he was still fighting for Scott's release a whole year later. At first, he'd had great difficulty communicating with the guards at the prison because none of them spoke English. Luckily however, Scott had by now learned a great deal of Thai language. Though it certainly made communicating easier, it didn't make the whole experience any less traumatic. Lee says that his brother had lost his freedom and this affected not only his life, but the lives of everyone around him.

For the entire evening before the trial, Scott Hurford chain smoked cigarette after cigarette. He contemplated many things—his life up to that present moment, just how long is 25 years, what would his family think, would he ever get married, would he ever have children, would he ever see the night sky again?

When the rest of the Thai prison population woke up at 5.30 am, Scott was still wide awake.

At 6.30 am he was given a brown prison uniform to wear and was told he had 20 short minutes to shower, shave and eat. Afterwards, he would be taken to a room where heavy iron chains would be fitted to his legs. These were no ordinary chains. These were the type they frequently fitted to elephants to prevent them from running away. Scott Hurford was nowhere near the size of an elephant. The locking pin was hammered in place by a 12-pound sledge hammer. One slip and Scott would be maimed for life. He says the experience in itself is enough to make an atheist pray to God that the guy doing the hammering doesn't miss.

One of the hardest days of Scott's life was arriving at the court and seeing his mum and his stepfather, John, waiting to support him. His heart raced. His girlfriend, Urai, and his brother, Lee, stood beside them with an Australian named Glen who lived in Sa Kaeo and had been visiting Scott in prison.

All of them watched anxiously as Scott shuffled off the bus in heavy chains. They clinked when he passed by, on his way with an armed escort to the holding cells. Once inside, Scott's family was allowed to talk to him through thick wire and a 2-metre gap. The wire was so thick they could barely see him. They shouted reassurance to him until they were told that he was about to be taken for sentencing 10 minutes later.

On 1 March 2006, Scott and his family waited quietly inside the Thai courtroom. They didn't have long to wait. The judge entered and Scott stood to his feet. The judge spoke rapidly for 10 minutes then left the room.

Scott's Thai girlfriend struggled as the tears filled her eyes. Scott was found guilty of importing narcotics into the Kingdom of Thailand, 250 methamphetamine pills worth £130.

The judge had sentenced him to death, though since Scott had pleaded guilty, his sentence was reduced. His mother and brother cried at the thought of Scott spending the next 30 years behind bars. He would be eligible for release in 2035. He would be 62 years old.

It was more than any of his family could bear. The news broke his mother's heart. She felt consumed with guilt that she hadn't been able to protect him from his fate. When the police guards prepared to take him back on the bus, Lee felt the bottom fall out of his own world. The image of Scott with chains around his ankles and a look of desperation in his once clear blue eyes is the only image that Lee Hurford remembers whenever he thinks of his brother.

At 5 pm, Scott Hurford was loaded onto the bus, with his girlfriend and family looking on helplessly. His mother could no longer hold back her tears. His brother, Lee, did his best to comfort her, and Scott's resolve not to cry in front of them completely disappeared.

Everyone on the bus waved as it pulled away.

'The sight of the people I love in tears because of my actions shot me through the heart,' says Scott.

Because Scott had been given a sentence of 30 years, the chains had to stay in place, something which he wasn't expecting. He was taken to his cell and left to ponder once again what a 30-year sentence meant to a guy who had yet to fully live.

In October 2006, the Thai authorities transferred him to Bangkwang Prison in Bangkok. He'd requested the move because he said that his chances of survival would be much better. Lee couldn't see how this was true since Bangkwang was known as a living hell. But then Lee didn't know the true reality of Scott's existence in Sa Kaeo.

Despite the fact that Scott will spend the best years of his life in jail, his family still hold on to hope that one day he may come home. Lee refuses to believe that his brother will die in that place, even though the sad reality is that he may.

Many people have come to know Scott's plight through word of mouth and quiet campaigning. Most of them are kind and sympathetic to the family's situation. However there are still many who look upon Lee's brother as the worst kind of evil, a drug dealer who deserves all he gets. Lee can't see his brother in that same light. He says he's no angel and he's made some terrible choices, but at the end of the day, he's Lee's flesh and blood and he's still a human being after all.

'I've learned many valuable lessons from my brother's detainment, all of which have made me grateful for my freedom and thankful that I've made the right choices in my life. I sometimes think that one wrong turn could have resulted in me being in his shoes. I think that we all make mistakes in our lives, but that some fare better than others. I appreciate the support we have. Not all prisoners are lucky to have family that stand by them. Some, as we have learned, do not even have enough money to buy a bottle of clean drinking water. So it can make a world of difference when someone comes forward and offers a hand of friendship or a word of compassion,' says Lee.

As a parent, Lee is more aware now of the importance of a good education. Not that his brother didn't have one. Lee just wants to make sure his children are educated on real life so they will learn from Scott's dilemma and be more aware about the dangers of drugs. He has seen his mother's pain and anguish, what she has had to endure and the patience she has shown. She is an incredible woman who will now face years of suffering and that is something no mother should ever have to face. Lee often questions himself if he would have been as understanding, unbelievably strong and supportive as his mother, if it were his own child in his brother's dilemma? He hopes he never has to find out. He is very anti-drugs, more so than ever before. He is a firm believer that we have a society that accepts them too easily, yet Thailand sets the sentences so high that it's impossible for anyone to make any second mistakes. If only there was a compromise between the two extremes.

Lee does not advocate that his brother shouldn't be punished. He simply thinks the punishment should be more comparable to the crime. In a Thai jail, the punishment for Scott's offence is far greater than if he had killed a dozen people in the UK. Scott is no hardened criminal. He's just a lad who made a bad decision. And for that he is paying dearly. All his family can do now is hope that the Thai authorities will have mercy on him sometime in the future and grant a Royal Pardon that will enable him to return home. This ordeal has been enormously painful and continues to present constant challenges, but Lee wishes to acknowledge the support to Scott and his family from the Foreign Prisoner Support Services, Prisoners Abroad, Consul Officer Jeff Mitchell at the British embassy in Bangkok, Jules from the Hand of Friendship website and Gail and Katherine.

I am so grateful to so many people who continue to stand by Scott through this terrible ordeal. My sincerest appreciation must be given to Scott's girlfriend, Urai, who has supported my brother from the day this nightmare began. Her support has been a great comfort to him and to us. I wish to thank also, Rowland and Gav in Pattaya, Thailand, for everything they do and everyone who writes and sends parcels to Scott. This really does make an incredible difference to his quality of life. My family is completely humbled that there are people who look beyond the surface and understand our plight, says Lee.

He is not usually emotional, but gets upset when he thinks of his brother languishing in a Thai prison. Scott is now the uncle of Lee's 16-month-old son and four-month-old daughter. Yet he will most likely miss their entire lives.

When I lay my head down to sleep, I think of my brother and imagine him at the end of yet another day. It's quiet as he lies down on his thin blanket that covers a dirty concrete floor. He stares at the cobwebs on the ceiling of his overcrowded cell and contemplates both the past and the future. His thoughts are always troubled, wondering how long he can endure. He thinks and thinks until his head hurts, and then he tells himself to stop and think no more.

Scott's terrible predicament has made us all take a closer look at ourselves. I truly believe that despite everything, we have a lot to be grateful for and together, as a family, we can get through this. I only hope that we all don't have to spend the rest of our lives doing so.

On 11 December 2007, Scott Hurford was informed that after months of speculation and rumour, he has been included in the King's 80th Birthday Amnesty. He received a three-and-a-half year reduction and now has $26^{1}/_{2}$ years to serve. He said the light at the end of the tunnel just got a little brighter.

> *I've done wrong. I don't complain about my life in here, which anyone with half a brain would know is not too good. I'll keep smiling and be as happy as my life will let me, for the sake of myself, my family and my friends,* says Scott.

On 11th November 2009, Scott Hurford was escorted by UK prison staff back to London after spending four years and eight months in Bangkwang. He will still have to conclude his sentence but the first major step is over – he's out of Bangkwang Prison and home to where his family can access him.

Scott's release date is scheduled for 8th August 2020. He still finds it difficult to come to terms with the fact that he's serving a 30-year sentence for possession of £130 pounds worth of drugs. He appealed to the UK Government, not for a pardon, but to have his sentence bought into line with the maximum which could have been given had the crime been committed in the UK. (14 years). The High Court in London declined his request. Scott does not dispute the fact that he broke the law and deserves to be punished but he says it's difficult to accept the terms of the treaty when the UK Government can apply the same treaty differently to others. Libya called for the release of Abdelbaset al-Megrahi, otherwise known as the 'Lockerbie Bomber'. He was responsible for the death of 270 victims of the Pan Am terrorist attack in 1988. The same British Transfer Treaty that applies to Scott Hurford applies to the Lockerbie Bomber and yet he was released early on compassionate grounds. It would suggest that his transfer was worth billions in oil and contracts and enabled the wording of the British Transfer Treaty to be over looked or interpreted in a different way.

Scott's Website
www.scottsbangkwangtime.net

Foreign Prisoner Support Service
http://www.usp.com.au/fpss/case-scott-hurford.html

Prisoners Abroad (UK)—Caring for Britons held overseas
http://www.prisonersabroad.org.uk/index.html

14
MADAM GIN GIN

Mrs Outachin, Laos

> *During my unlawful detention in Phonthong Prison (Pon Tong) Laos, I met an elderly Chinese woman. Her name was Outachin, but we called her Madam Gin Gin. Her brown skin was wrinkled from age and from too many hours in the sun. Her tawny brown hair with the occasional grey strand hung in a long plait all the way down her back.*

No one knew how old she was, but some guessed she was around 60 years old. She was slim and would have been very attractive in her day. She wore long, faded blue prison pants with a thick white stripe running up the outside of each leg. Her favourite shirt was green.

Madam Gin Gin stood 165 centimetres, about the same height as me, and like me she was locked in a cell, 3 metres by 4 metres. But unlike me, she was all alone in her cell, whereas I had five other women in mine. We slept head to toe, shoulder to shoulder. We had each other to comfort us whenever we cried, thinking of our children and loved ones so far away.

Madam Gin Gin had nothing but the isolation she endured in the rear cells, where all the male prisoners were detained. It must have been terrible for her to be the only woman back there. We weren't even allowed to visit her. The rear cells were forbidden.

All through the day, she was tormented by the male prisoners passing by. It was rumoured she'd been raped. The police said Madam Gin Gin stayed on her own because she couldn't get along with anyone. They said that once she was put in with the Thai women, but they got too angry with her.

Gin Gin washed her clothes in the water trough and contaminated what little water the cell bathroom provided. Other prisoners said she was ka moi (a thief) and when they'd go outside their cells, she would try to steal their things.

Madam Gin Gin had a photo in her small bag of belongings—a scarf she wrapped her bits and bobs in and kept hidden under her blanket. No one knew who was in the photo. She never let anyone near it, but most people suspected it was her daughter. Many were curious about Madam Gin Gin. What secrets did she hold in her faded and tattered scarf?

Many times she would fly off the handle and rant and rave in her strange mountain dialect. She waved her arms and pointed to police, then pointed to the black door to freedom, pointed to herself and stomped her foot. She was never violent, just angry, and I suppose quite frustrated that no one could understand her.

In early 2001, the police moved all the prisoners into different cells. Madam Gin Gin moved to the front cells where we were detained. She seemed much happier and for many days she sat gazing out through the bars of her cell window watching the daily life inside Phonthong. No longer did she scream at night. But some nights we heard her groaning and mumbling. No one could understand exactly what she said, but another Chinese woman in one of the front cells said some of the words spoken sounded very much like, 'nobody cares about me anymore'. Of course, Madam Gin Gin just wanted to go home like everyone else. I found myself chanting along with her at times, wondering if I would ever see my children again.

Then one week Madam Gin Gin decided she'd had enough and she stopped eating and drinking water. She lay in her cell burning with fever, and the prison police didn't care. They said that she had the right to die. I begged them to let her outside the cell where I could care for her but they refused.

When Major Suvany came on duty, he told them to open her door and they brought her out and laid her down on the dirty concrete floor. I immediately administered first aid, keeping her cool with an old dirty rag dipped in some unfiltered tap water. She groaned and tried to wave me away, but she was too weak. I suspected she had malaria. 'Please don't give up Gin Gin', I begged quietly as I sat for hours watching over her.

Human life was worth nothing in Phonthong Prison—we were only prisoners. It didn't matter that most of the detainees hadn't committed any crime, other than that they once wanted democracy and freedom for all.

Our lives became a constant struggle. We had already witnessed the death of two prisoners in the space of a few short months, the torture of countless others, and now my old Chinese friend, who spoke not a word of English, lay weakened on the dirty concrete floor waiting for death to claim her.

'Stay strong Gin Gin', I pleaded.

By the end of that week, she started to improve. I managed to sit her up and continued with small sips of water. I knew Madam Gin Gin appreciated what I was doing, because she faintly smiled at me one day. From that day on, I pretended to be her daughter. When she had regained her strength, we walked hand in hand around the perimeter of the prison. It was something I had never done, because the women weren't allowed to walk near the kitchen or in front of the men's blocks. My husband, Kerry, got to see me. Madam Gin Gin waved to him in his cell. She rattled on in her strange dialect and I nodded my head and copied her language. She laughed and I'm sure she thought that I was the crazy one who needed her protection.

I took care of Madam Gin Gin, and in the mornings I hung out her washing. One time I draped her green shirt and blue pants on a garden hedge not far from the cell blocks. She got angry and started yelling at me and pointing 'away away'. I quickly moved her clothes and draped them over a tree branch and she said 'er er' and nodded her head approvingly.

Major Suvany laughed, and all the prisoners joined in, making gentle fun of me. They explained that she didn't want her clothes on the hedge because the leaves would make her skin itch.

Another time I was being quite cheeky to her and she chased me round the prison grounds with a straw broom. When she caught me, she slapped me hard on the back of the legs and hurled abuse at me. Again, everyone laughed and Major Suvany said that she thought she could beat me now because I told everyone I was her daughter! I laughed too because I knew that Madam Gin Gin would never actually hurt me. She did have quite a temper though, as the Muslim David discovered when he chased her round the prison grounds after she interrupted his prayer session. He was ranting something about her defiling his prayer area, a tiny concrete patch near the steps of the rear cell block. She argued that he was just a crazy African who was as stupid as he was half blind, and if he wanted to pray, then why pray so close to the sewage pit.

Madam Gin Gin was truly entertaining on occasions, particularly when she'd had enough of being treated like an animal. One day she got really angry when the prison guard refused to let her out of the room. He ordered all the shutters to be locked so she would have to sit for days in complete darkness, isolated from everyone. Whenever we walked by her cell she would throw buckets and buckets of unfiltered water through the cracks of the shutters and through the tiny vents at the top of her cell. We worked out that we could coordinate her water-throwing fits to coincide with the routine patrol of a particular guard whose heart was as black as coal. When he came up the concrete steps we all gathered round and pretended that we were happy to see him. One of the prisoners walked by Madam Gin Gin's cell as planned, and as he did, he banged on the shutters and kept moving along. Within seconds, Madam Gin Gin was throwing buckets of unfiltered water, all of which ended up on that guard. It was hilarious and he got really angry until we calmed him down by saying how handsome he looked all wet.

When almost a year had passed, it came time to say goodbye to Madam Gin Gin. Our government had secured our freedom. Although I was happy to be leaving Phonthong, I felt really sad to be leaving my friend.

I wished in that moment that I had added Chinese to the other languages I had learnt in Phonthong. I wished that I could tell her that I would always think of her. I worried that no one would take care of her the way I did. Her life would be difficult again, and lonely. The little happiness we'd shared would disappear and she would be left to sit by the window gazing at the black door and wanting to go home. How appalling for a woman her age to be doomed to such an existence. How horrible for anyone to be treated with so little dignity.

It was Sunday 4 October 2001 and the next day my husband and I would be leaving Phonthong forever. I stood at Madam Gin Gin's cell window just as I did every morning and we talked. Then the most amazing thing happened. Madam Gin Gin gave me her favourite green army hat, minus the red star of communism that is usually found on the centre front band above the brim. I'd been asking her for it for the last 10 months but she always said no. I couldn't believe it. Did she know I was leaving? Did she understand? She laughed at the look of shock on my face and smiled, waving me away, talking in her thick dialect. She sat at her window and watched me as I proudly paraded my hat to the other prisoners. Some of them clapped and some got upset with me for being proud to wear a hat that symbolised communism. To me it was just a hat that my friend had given me. Major Suvany said that I would have good luck because Madam Gin Gin never gave anything away.

When I returned to her cell, I heard her whisper 'beautiful' in Chinese. My husband and I left the prison that day, but I never forgot Madam Gin Gin or the many others I left behind. They are always on my mind.

In 2003, I received information from the embassy that Madam Gin Gin and the other Chinese prisoners had been released and returned to China. I have no way of knowing if this is true. I can only hope it is. I hope Madam Gin Gin found her way back home to her daughter and that she remembers me as I will always remember her!

In September 2007, I went to China with my neighbour, Alyson. We only went for a holiday and shopping, but during the times when I walked those city streets or sat in a rickshaw cutting across town, I couldn't help but think of Madam Gin Gin. Wouldn't it have been wonderful to have seen her just one more time? Sadly, that just wasn't meant to be. But it didn't stop me looking for her, on occasion, in the sea of a thousand oriental faces.

I included her story because, after all, I was once her daughter.

15
TRADING LIVES
David Hicks, Guantanamo

People's lives are traded by governments every day. Sometimes political solutions favour the prisoner and most times they don't. Real-life diplomatic negotiations are usually quite different to the expectations of a family with a loved one detained in a foreign prison.

People usually expect that their government, if it agrees, will establish diplomatic dialogue and bring their loved one home in the shortest amount of time possible. Sometimes the strategies differ, depending on each individual case. Sometimes a solution may be heavily influenced by hard power, a term used in international relations. It is a theory that describes using military and economic means to influence the behaviour or interests of other political bodies. It is used in contrast to soft power, which refers to power that comes from diplomacy, culture and history.

Historically, most states have a general acceptance of official and unofficial protocol in dealing with political resolutions. Sometimes it becomes necessary to resort to international arbitration, while at other times, matters can usually be resolved by states abiding by general principles and protocols related to international law and justice. Other times, international law and justice itself become victims of abuse, and when that happens, then it's anybody's guess what the outcome of a particular case will be.

David Matthew Hicks is an Australian who was born on 7 August 1975. He is from a working-class family who lived in the northern suburbs of Adelaide, South Australia. I don't know David Hicks personally, but I came to know his story through his father, Terry, a man for whom I have come to have enormous respect.

According to Terry Hicks, his son David was sitting at a taxi stand in Baghlan, Afghanistan, waiting to leave the country, when he was arrested by the invading Northern Alliance and sold to the Americans for US$1000. Many have speculated on the treatment that he and other detainees were subjected to at the hands of their captors. Hicks claimed that he and other detainees were made to lie face down in the mud while US soldiers walked across their backs.

> *We were roped together, biceps to biceps. I was taken from the group and led to a shed and stripped naked. In the shed, pictures were taken of me naked. My head, armpits and crotch were shaved. I was photographed naked and a white piece of plastic was forcibly inserted in my rectum. Some of the staff joked about this procedure. The US personnel made remarks such as, 'extra-ribbed for your pleasure' (like a condom) as the item was stuck in my rectum.*

In another statement, Hicks said that he was bundled into a plane, handcuffed and strapped to his seat, wearing goggles, earmuffs and a face mask, for the flight to Guantanamo Bay, Cuba.

Whatever happened to David Hicks in Afghanistan is not something that affected him alone. Since US President George Bush declared the 'War on Terror' following the September 11 attacks against the US, hundreds of detainees from the Middle East, in particular Afghanistan, were illegally transported to Guantanamo Bay, to the US military base, now known throughout the world as 'Camp Xray'. Among them was David Hicks.

At 9 pm on a Tuesday evening on 11 December 2001, officers from the Australian Security Intelligence Organisation (ASIO) informed Terry Hicks and his wife, Bev, that David was okay, but that he had been arrested in Afghanistan as a suspected terrorist.

Imagine their shock.

By the end of the evening, ASIO had raided the homes of everyone in David's family and some of his friends' homes too.

A photograph of David Hicks brandishing a rocket launcher while training in Albania, prior to the US–NATO liberation of Kosovo, appeared on television screens and newspapers round the world. It immediately branded him a terrorist and he was immediately guilty in the eyes of the world.

The wheels of the propaganda machine for the War on Terror began to turn in earnest. Most people I knew didn't question the position of either the US or the Australian government on Hicks or any of the others rounded up and taken to Guantanamo Bay. Most people chose to believe that the government had every right to do whatever it liked to terrorists, so that we could all feel safe. That may or may not be true, but at this stage, no one knew if David Hicks was a terrorist or just someone who had been caught in the wrong place at the wrong time. Hundreds of tourists flock to places like Afghanistan every year, for a variety of reasons, despite there being an ongoing conflict they're still there.

In our society, it's almost impossible to conceive that children as young as 13 are terrorists, but in the military base, Guantanamo, a number of children were detained alongside those accused of being active enemy combatants.

Six hundred and sixty males from 42 countries were held on suspicion of having links to al-Qaeda or Afghanistan's ousted Taliban regime. They were not charged or allowed access to lawyers. Extra-judicial detention, otherwise known as detention without charge, has been one of the hallmarks of totalitarian states. However, the US government is not a totalitarian state.

The United Nations condemned the US for breach of international law. It did nothing, however, to prevent the transfer of prisoners to Guantanamo Bay where the sovereignty of Cuba allowed the US government to violate the rights of those prisoners. The US administration under President George W Bush claimed that the prisoners of Guantanamo were not entitled to the protections of the Geneva Convention. The US Supreme Court ruled against this on 29 June 2006. Many supporters in the Bush administration argued for the summary execution of all unlawful combatants.

Back home in the quiet suburbs of Adelaide, the family and friends of David Hicks were forced to accept that he might be the very first Australian executed in Cuba by a so-called democratic government—its ally, the United States.

The 'Fair Go for David' campaign rallied together with four specific aims in mind.

It would call on the Australian government to ensure David Hicks would be treated in accordance with the Geneva Convention.

It would seek to have the law of *habeas corpus* applied to David Hicks to safeguard his individual rights against arbitrary state action.

It would appeal that David Hicks be repatriated to Australia and given access to a fair civil trial, without the fear of a death sentence if convicted of a crime.

And finally, it sought that any other Australian in a similar situation to David Hicks' be entitled to these same rights.

I joined this campaign because of my fundamental belief that no matter who we are, where we are, or what it is that we are alleged to have done, we all should have our rights upheld in accordance with the Geneva Convention and other UN mandates. I knew first hand what it felt like to have been denied the basic human rights and dignity most people take for granted. I knew exactly how it felt to be violated and detained against international mandates and laws, and labelled something I knew I wasn't.

My husband had once been labelled a spy, which in Laos where he had been detained, is akin to terrorist, enemy combatant or rebel and considered an offence punishable by death. It was fortunate that the Australian Defence Force addressed that issue early on and saved my husband from a bullet to the back of the head. It could have so easily gone another way, with news headings spreading untruths of why he was in Laos. How would anyone back in suburbia ever know the truth? Do the media always report the facts as a true representation of the facts? In my experience as a former detainee and as a human rights advocate, I've often discovered that the facts have become distorted and, in some cases, incredibly far from the truth. But still some people believe everything they read and base their judgements on an opinion formulated by another, who may or may not have a complete understanding of the facts.

I've heard all manner of justifications from people in my community as to why western governments should have the right to arbitrarily detain someone.

They must have done something wrong to get arrested.
You don't go to Afghanistan to picnic.
He was Muslim.

Regardless, there should be a proper process of detainment and investigation. There should be transparency and lawful governance over the arrest of any and all persons, regardless of race, nationality and gender. All people should be equal before the law and should be entitled without any discrimination, to the equal protection of the law.

David Hicks was not the first Australian to be detained in the War on Terror. Fellow Australian, Mamdouh Habib, had been arrested on 5 October 2001 while travelling by bus to Karachi in Pakistan. The bus was stopped by local police who arrested the Egyptian-born, father of four. Two Germans were also arrested with Habib, but released shortly thereafter. Habib was deported to Egypt and detained there for five months before being transferred to US military custody.

Both Habib and David Hicks were detained at Guantanamo along with hundreds of other so-called terrorists.

Mamdouh Habib was released by the US military and returned to Australia on 28 January 2005. Not a single charge was laid. Since his release, Mamdouh Habib continues to put his life back together, despite the Australian government warning that his activities will be constantly monitored to ensure he does not become a security threat. He is not under any control order at this present time, nor should he be. Habib is a free man and was never convicted of an offence in either Australia or elsewhere. He and his family have suffered a great deal and only time will tell if they will be able to recover fully from their horrific ordeal.

Freedom comes at a price and, with it, great responsibilities. Generally, when one loses and then regains their freedom, life tends to take on new meaning. Certainly life is never the same as it was before. Life becomes more precious and we learn that our freedoms ought not to be taken for granted.

The idea of arbitrary detainment angers me. The idea that any citizen can be detained in violation of their rights, in the name of democracy or the War on Terror or any other reason, is deplorable. Human beings have rights!

I was outraged to think that an Australian citizen could be impounded by a so-called democratic state, kept like an animal in a small wire cage for more than five months, and then transferred to a small prison cell with only a bed, no chair and no window, particularly when that Australian had yet to be subjected to an open and fair judicial process.

The Australian government denied the torture allegations raised by David's lawyers, as they had done previously with Habib's lawyers. Attorney General Phillip Ruddock said that sleep deprivation and sensory deprivation were not forms of torture, and that the lack of exercise periods per week was also nothing to be concerned about. Yet when my husband and I were unlawfully detained by the communist government in Laos, the fact that we weren't allowed exercise and were confined 24 hours a day to our cells was argued by the Australian government as ill-treatment.

To the average Australian, David Hicks didn't deserve to be treated humanely. The US government disseminated propaganda that David Hicks had taken up arms to kill American troops on the battlefield. However, David Hicks had never fired a single shot and the only physical forces fighting in Afghanistan at that time were, in fact, Afghani forces.

It was a story of old that dated back to when the Mujahideen defeated the Soviet Union and forced its withdrawal from Afghanistan in 1989. The problem was that the Mujahideen did not establish a united government. Many of the larger Mujahideen groups began to fight each other. A village Islamic clergy (mawla) organised a new armed movement of Afghanis with the backing of Pakistan. This movement became known as the Taliban. The factions or the tribes in Afghanistan have been killing each other for years. They didn't need any prompting to wage war against each other. All those not on the side of the Taliban allied themselves together again, just as they had done during the Soviet invasion, and formed the United Islamic Front for the Salvation of Afghanistan (Northern Alliance). It ousted the Taliban from power with the help of the United States and its allies and a new official government was formed. It was what they should have done when they first defeated the Soviets.

Democratic governments are supposed to lead by example. To establish justice where there is injustice and to defend liberty and freedom where there is oppression. They are supposed to uphold the law and adhere to the agreements they sign in principle, designed to protect the rights of mankind. How can they condemn totalitarian regimes for applying extra-judicial process and then turn around and do the same?

David was fortunate that his father Terry never gave up fighting for his rights. His unwillingness to allow the world to condemn David created strong support within the legal community and amongst Opposition Members of Parliament.

'Retrospective, prospective, the bottom line is this. I am no defender of Mr Hicks. I am a defender of his legal rights and his human rights and under these circumstances he will not be getting a fair trial,' said Kevin Rudd, the then leader of the Labor Party of Australia.

David was once hidden behind a wall of diplomacy and secrecy and very few people at that time cared. Even fewer cared that his family were suffering.

Who could ever forget the image of Terry Hicks inside a Guantanamo Bay-sized cage on the sidewalk in New York? He showed remarkable courage in the way he took up the campaign for his son. He never once claimed 'my son is innocent'. Terry only ever stood up for David's right to be given proper legal representation and a fair trial. What father wouldn't do that for his son? Terry even travelled to Afghanistan, trying to retrace David's footsteps in order to satisfy himself that his son was not a terrorist.

While in Afghanistan, Terry spoke to the arresting officer at Pul-e-Khumri, a garrison 237 kilometres north of Kabul. This was the checkpoint where David was stopped in December 2001. The officer told Terry that his son should not have been handed over to the Americans. He added further that he believed David Hicks had done nothing wrong and that there was nothing to indicate David was not there as a tourist or a journalist.

According to Terry's account of the encounter in a later television documentary, Terry asked the key question: 'Had David ever fired on Australian or US troops?' The response recorded on film was that he was told that there were none in the area. Furthermore, it was alleged that there were no Americans, no foreign troops in the area at all, only the Northern Alliance Forces and they were all Afghans.

Another turning point in the Hicks case was the appointment of Michael Dante Mori, a major in the US Marine Corps. He was appointed in November 2003, by the US Department of Defense, to represent David Hicks. Mori featured frequently on Australian television and continually expressed concern over David's extended interrogations and detainment.

> *Laws can embody standards. Governments can enforce laws—but the final task is not a task for government. It is a task for each and every one of us. Every time we turn our heads the other way when we see the law flouted—when we tolerate what we know to be wrong—when we close our eyes and ears to the corrupt because we are too busy, or too frightened—when we fail to speak up and speak out—we strike a blow against freedom and decency and justice.*
> —Robert F. Kennedy, 21 June 1961

Why did the Australian government allow the rights of one of its citizens to be so inexcusably violated? Is it simply politics? Are bilateral relations and trade agreements more important then the right to a fair trial? Are there double standards for people in our community? Or is it simply that life is complex and not everything goes the way we expect. Not every problem is easy to resolve.

On 3 February 2007, the US Military Commission announced that it had prepared new charges against David Hicks. They would include the charge of attempted murder and providing material support for terrorism. Each offence carried a maximum penalty of life imprisonment, but the prosecutors said they would argue for a jail term of 20 years, with an absolute minimum of 15 to be served.

On 1 March 2007, the charge of attempted murder was dismissed by Judge Susan Crawford, who concluded that there was no probable cause to justify the charge. This left the remaining charge of providing material support to terrorism. It created quite an outrage in Australia, particularly when the charge wasn't even an offence at the time David was detained.

The US Military Commission decided to apply the law retrospectively. Ex post facto laws are seen as a violation of the rule of law as it applies in a free and democratic society.

Even the then Australian Prime Minister, John Howard, commenting on the David Hicks case in 2004, stated: 'It's fundamentally wrong to make a criminal law retrospective.'

But in 2007 they were doing just that.

There was no proof that David Hicks was a terrorist and yet he was being portrayed as one. The media did such a good job of spreading the US President's propaganda message that few people believed David would escape execution.

At the end of the day, it will be politicians who decide the fate of David Hicks and others detained at Guantanamo Bay, regardless of the truth and regardless of any presumption of innocence or the rights of humans to defend themselves without prejudice.

On 26 March 2007, David Hicks entered a guilty plea to the charge against him of providing material support for terrorism. His father said it was the only way his son would ever return home. A plea agreement was drawn up by 6 am AEST on 27 March 2007.

'David Hicks is a desperate man in desperate circumstances,' the Australian Democrats' Attorney-General's spokesperson, Senator Natasha Stott Despoja said. 'The fact that this seems to be the only way David Hicks can escape the hell hole that is Guantanamo Bay, is shameful. However, it is unsurprising given how long Hicks has been detained and the flaws in the military commission process he faced.'

On 31 March 2007, a US military tribunal decided that David Hicks would receive a seven-year suspended sentence and serve nine months in an Australian prison. It was stipulated in the plea bargain that he would be subject to a media gag and would not take legal action against the United States.

David would also be required to withdraw previous allegations of abuse and torture that he alleged he suffered throughout his detainment. By the time the US military tribunal disclosed its judgement to the world, the majority of Australian citizens came to realise that David Hicks had been given a reprieve, not through justice, but as a result of a pending election and political power plays.

Was he a terrorist? It really didn't matter anymore. Terrorist or not, he was denied a fair trial.

Australian Foreign Minister, Alexander Downer, said that David Hicks received sufficient legal representation. I can accept that may be true, but what most people found unacceptable was that his legal representation and trial appeared more challenging than the biblical stand off between David and Goliath. Ironically, the Hicks case was soon dubbed 'The President v David Hicks'.

Different courts and different jurisdictions do have different practices, but should any of us accept, or expect our government to accept, that another jurisdiction can convict its citizens without the right to an open and transparent trial? For David Hicks, and for others who are detained on political grounds, pleading guilty is often the only option available. No one seemed surprised by David's guilty plea. It seemed a foregone conclusion that he just wanted to go home.

On 20 May 2007, David Hicks was flown back to Australia in a private jet under intense security. Under the terms of the US agreement, he would be required to stay in a South Australian prison until 31 December 2007.

It was a huge relief for his family to see the plane touch down in Adelaide and David walk across the tarmac in those same orange-coloured overalls we'd seen many 'Gitmo' detainees wearing on the news. Finally, an Australian citizen was no longer being subjected to arbitrary detention in violation of international law. Maybe in the end justice was more the victim in this situation than David.

A worldwide campaign is now in motion to close Guantanamo Bay forever. The people who are still there lingering in limbo need to be given a fair and legal trial, particularly since it has been proven that not all of them are terrorists. Children in Guantanamo have been given no indication of whether they will be released, whether they will be returned to their native countries, or when, if ever, they will see their parents and families again.

Terry and Bev would be the first to admit that they are incredibly lucky to have David home.

As for David Hicks, he says he had never set out to cause such a fuss or hurt anyone. He's looking forward to getting his life back and is a little overawed by everything that took place.

One day he was travelling along a road in Afghanistan and the next thing he was in the eye of an international storm.

David Hicks will inevitably face intense scrutiny from the Australian Federal Police, most likely for the remainder of his life. He will be subjected to a control order as part of the new federal anti-terrorism laws, a media gag, and a curfew that will see him reporting to the Adelaide police in person three times a week.

What I hope people will try to understand from the Hicks case is that regardless of what they think they know about David Hicks, his case highlighted the frightening reality that nowadays governments are using the War on Terror to erode civil liberties. There is now more of a presumption of guilt when it comes to people accused of terrorist offences, long before they have their day in court.

In our society everyone is supposed to be innocent until proven guilty. Sadly, this is an ideal that is disintegrating rapidly. Before too long, we might all be in danger of losing many of the freedoms that those who went before us sacrificed and died for.

Since the Australian government placed a media gag order on David Hicks, everyone will have to wait until at least March 2008 to hear if he has anything further to say about the way he was treated in Guantanamo. Personally, I expect he'll have quite a lot to say.

On the 29 December 2007, David Hicks was released from an Australian prison. He had prepared a statement read by his lawyer, David McLeod. The content of that statement is below:

Thank you for coming out on a Saturday and during the holiday period. I know you all hoped I might appear and answer some questions. I had hoped to be able to speak to the media but I am just not strong enough at the moment—it's as simple as that.

I am sorry for that.

As part of my conditions of release from Guantanamo Bay, I agreed not to speak to the media on a range of issues before March 30, 2008. It's my intention to honour this agreement as I don't want to do anything that might result in my return there. So for now, I will limit what I have to say—I will say more at a later time. I would ask the media and the public understand and respect this. I do however want to take this opportunity to say some overdue thank yous.

First and foremost, I would like to recognise the huge debt of gratitude that I owe the Australian public for getting me home. I will not forget, or let you down. Next, I would like to thank my family and friends who have been so supportive of me. Words cannot adequately express the level of my feelings for them. I love them very much. Also my team of lawyers: Major Dan Mori, Josh Dratel, Michael Griffin, Steve Kenny and David McLeod, as well as their legal teams in Adelaide, Sydney, Washington and London. Much of their work was carried out pro-bono and they know I owe my freedom to their efforts.

I also thank the legal profession within Australia, including the Law Council of Australia and the state law societies, and those abroad, who strove to uphold the ideal of a free trial for an Australian citizen. Many thanks go to the Fair Go For David campaigners and organisations such as Amnesty International, GetUp, the International Committee of the Red Cross, Dick Smith, church groups including the Catholic Church, and various anti-torture and human rights groups.

The Red Cross played an important role by trying to improve conditions and the treatment of detainees at Guantanamo Bay. I thank them from the bottom of my heart for their efforts.

There are certain politicians I would also like to particularly mention and thank: Senator Natasha Stott Despoja, Danna Vale, Sandra Kanck, Senator Bob Brown, Senator Kerry Nettle, Mark Parnell, Senator Linda Kirk, Nicola Roxon, Bob Debus, Rob Hull, Frances Bedford, Kris Hanna and many others who preferred to work behind the scenes.

A huge thank you also to the members of the media who wrote about and increased public awareness of my detention and treatment over the years. Without you, the court of public opinion would not have been as informed or influential.

There are many other groups, both large and small, and individuals involved in the campaign for my return to Australia, and to them I offer them my heartfelt thanks. This list is in no particular order and to anyone that I haven't mentioned, I am very sorry. I hope to thank all of you personally at a later date. Right now I am looking forward to some quiet time with my wonderful Dad, my family and friends.

I ask that you respect my privacy as I will need time to readjust to society and to obtain medical care for the consequences of five-and-a-half years at Guantanamo Bay. I have been told that my readjustment will be a slow process and should involve a gentle transition away from the media spotlight. Thank you for respecting my privacy and allowing me some breathing space to get on with my life.

16
INVISIBLE BARS
Belmarsh 12, UK

Punishment without trial has been imposed on several foreign nationals. Labelled 'terror suspects', they have been released from prison to virtual house arrest. Some face the threat of deportation to regimes notorious for torture. Their liberty has been restricted under 'control orders.'

In light of September 11, when people from all over the world were detained as 'suspected terrorists', including women and children, new legislation was devised specifically to prevent 'persons of interest' from becoming a threat to society. Thousands of Arab and Muslim immigrants to the United States were fingerprinted and registered under the Alien Registration Act of 1940 that made it a criminal offense for anyone to knowingly or wilfully advocate, abet, advise or teach the duty, necessity, desirability or propriety of overthrowing the government of the United States or of any state by force or violence. It prevented anyone from organising any association which teaches, advises or encourages such an overthrow, or for anyone to become a member of, or to affiliate with, any such association. Some 8000 Arab and Muslim men were interviewed and 5000 foreign nationals were detained on the basis of deterring and preventing acts of international terrorism against the United States.

The British government believed that it had an emergency so great that it threatened national security. Australia too followed suit to introduce new legislation that gave special powers to police to enable them to search people and property without cause or specific warrant. This gave them the justification to enact a system of arbitrary detention.

Arbitrary is a term given to choices and actions which are considered to not be done by means of any underlying principle or logic, but by whim or some illogical formula. It is a practice condemned by western nations yet, when it comes to the war on terror, suddenly it becomes acceptable?

During World War I the Australian government interned almost 7000 people, more than half of whom it classed as 'enemy aliens.' They were housed in remote prison camps set up in each state of Australia. It was the government's response to those it thought posed a threat to Australia's security. Initially, internment was reserved only for citizens of those countries that were at war with Australia, but this expanded to include citizens of enemy nations, naturalised British subjects and Australian-born descendants of migrants.

The camps were established to prevent residents from assisting Australia's enemies, to appease public opinion and to house overseas internees sent to Australia for the duration of the war. In later years, Japanese were interned en masse, along with Germans and Italians. In fact, over 20 per cent of all Italians resident in Australia were interned. One and a half thousand British nationals were interned. By 1942, over 12,000 people were interned in Australia from over 30 countries, including Finland, Hungary, Portugal and Russia.

Sixty years on, and the justification of arbitrary detention is discriminated against and in many cases now defended by governments.

Many still argue that breaching a small number of people's human rights may save the lives of many others. In the words of Leonard Nimoy as the Star Trek character, Captain Spock: 'The needs of the many outweigh the needs of the few, or the one.' It may have been a one liner in a fictional movie, but how true the sentiment.

In acknowledgement and respect to the many thousands of good men and women working in law enforcement and intelligence throughout the world, theirs is a selfless undertaking to uphold justice and to protect the needs of the many. However, and I'm sure even many of those officers would agree, we live in complex times. Sometimes the issues become so many different shades of grey that it's hard to determine where lies the truth.

Civil rights lawyer, Gareth Peirce, has represented some of Britain's most high-profile cases, including detainees at Guantanamo Bay. She made a valid point in an interview with Jessica Carsen, *Time* magazine (24 August 2006). In it, she said: 'What is not just unacceptable, but plain wrong, is to say that a person suspected of terrorism deserves the rule book being torn up —basically a retreat to medieval rack and thumb screw, and that's what Guantanamo is all about.'

Guantanamo Bay detention camp, a prison established at Guantanamo

Bay US Naval Base in Cuba became notorious for detaining persons in violation of their rights, particularly those the US suspected of being terrorist operatives; 775 detainees have been detained in Guantanamo; 420 have been released.

While many might argue that it's necessary to detain such alleged violent and criminal offenders, surely nothing could be more important than making sure that anyone detained, for whatever reason, retains their right to have proper legal representation and full access to any and all evidence against them? Surely humans must have some interest when governments attempt to convict people by association or hearsay in the absence of proven criminal activity.

'There's a lot of criticism of Guantanamo. But I believe we are holding the right detainees, the right people. We are holding them in the right place, and I believe we are doing it for the right reason, and in the right way' according to Rear-Admiral Harry Harris interview with '*60 Minutes*'.

Another senior military officer begged to disagree. 'Sitting in solitary confinement for over two years is abuse. I think not allowing a person to go outside and have access to sunlight for over eight months is abuse—that is mistreatment, clearly', said Major Michael Mori.

Persons of interest should be answerable to authorities, but what is an acceptable timeframe in which to detain them, and where? It was, of course, impractical to send every person of interest to Guantanamo and unacceptable to many civil rights lawyers to detain people on home soil indefinitely, so an alternative had to be considered.

The 2005 Prevention of Terrorism Act, gave the British government the power to replace indefinite detention with control orders. So detentions without trial continued, but in the form of house arrests.

A group of Muslim men, dubbed the Belmarsh 12, were singled out and locked up indefinitely without charge. They had not been subjected to any trial or notified of any release date. They were simply left in limbo, clearly in violation of their human rights. Following the introduction of control orders, the men were released from the high security Belmarsh Prison, in the London Borough of Greenwich, and placed under control orders in their homes.

Initially, such orders were introduced solely to deal with foreign terror suspects, but there are now several UK born control order detainees. The highly secretive Special Immigration Appeals Commission issued control orders on at least 40 non-UK nationals, subject to partial house arrest.

In many of these cases, the men cannot even walk from one part of the house to the next or even into the yard area. If they do, they will be in breach of their control order. Many would argue that such legislation is justified because there are people from whom we need to be protected. In my opinion, there are violent sex offenders and paedophiles who rate highly in that category.

My interest in control orders is not to represent a view that 'persons of interest' or 'terror suspects' are in any way beyond the law or should be. I am merely suggesting that where the powers-that-be have reason to suspect a person has some association with terrorist activity, that the person be given full disclosure of the evidence against them. Such persons should be allowed proper and immediate legal support and given the right to appeal their convictions all the way up to the Supreme Court if need be. If there is evidence that they are wrongfully detained, then they should be released from the control order. They should not be denied access to their families at any time, or to proper medical care.

What is the impact of control orders on detainees and their families and what is the effectiveness of control orders? In my research, I came across some rather interesting facts. According to several prominent civil rights lawyers, anti-terrorism laws allow innocent people to be held and questioned; and they restrict those persons from unrestricted access to legal representation. These same civil rights lawyers believe that control orders circumvent justice because they can be used for political purposes against individuals who are released from detention, or who have not even been convicted of any criminal offences.

Several cases, in the UK in particular, revealed that the so-called 'persons of interest' were never charged with an offence and were never found guilty of any crime. The most obvious question: How did the Home Office ever come to the conclusion that such persons were terrorists or supporters of terrorism? Surely they must have had a valid reason to arrest these people? Surely their evidence was more than just circumstantial?

Much of the intelligence gathered to place some, not all, of these persons of interest under control orders could not be relied upon or deemed accurate. So their lawyers argued. There were many inconsistencies. Evidence was submitted based on hearsay. Much of it was given in secret and was protected under national security. The detainee's lawyers were not permitted to access the evidence because it was deemed a threat to national security if they did and could jeopardise secret sources. This is certainly a valid concern, but in the absence of full disclosure of the facts or the case against a person of interest, it was, and is, impossible to know the truth.

A proper legal challenge, under such circumstances, is invariably unattainable. However civil rights lawyers continue to challenge the process of issuing control orders through various high court appeals.

How then do persons under control orders impact on our sustainable communities? Do control orders provide any guarantee to the community that the control order detainee is prevented from breaking the law? Unfortunately they do not. Where there is a will, there is a way. A control order detainee may go into the community on their own and if it is their intention to harm others, then they will. The same as a thief will steal if they are so inclined or a murderer will murder if compelled.

Control order detainees are generally required to stay within an invisible boundary as a pre-condition of the control order, but this doesn't mean that they are physically watched every minute of their daily comings and goings. They may be given permission to travel three stations by rail but not four. They may be given permission to visit their mosque or other place of worship.

They may shop in a busy city shopping centre, if that is included in their designated allowable area, and they may speak to whomever they choose in public. The restrictions placed on them are supposedly designed to protect the public from serious terrorist threats, but one has to wonder how effective they are.

When you think about it, if the control order detainee was a real threat to society, then it would be easy for them to plot to kill a lot of people. Does that mean that they are not a threat to society? Those currently living under control orders compare it to a neverending mental torture that is worse than any prison.

In my search to understand what effect control orders have on families of detainees, I contacted Saiyeda Ravalia, chairperson of a registered British charity known as HHUGS—Helping Households under Great Stress. HHUGS was set up in September 2004 in response to the increasing number of 'anti-terror' arrests across the United Kingdom. It provides practical support and advice to households devastated by the arrest of a family member under UK anti-terror legislation. Saiyeda explained to me the difficulties many families face. Daily tasks have become difficult, they are struggling to make ends meet and transport to visit their loved ones is infrequent. On top of this, their friends have disowned them, their mosques have abandoned them and their communities have shunned them. They are lonely, vulnerable, and desperately in need of help.

Saiyeda directed me to watch a documentary, 'Dispatches—At Home with the Terror Suspects.' I was rather troubled by the reality that these families endure. They are forced to live an incredibly invasive existence. Their home life is completely disrupted. The children of the house are not permitted the basic liberties that our children take for granted. They cannot have friends drop over impromptu. They must first have them properly vetted and approved by authorities. In most cases, their friends are either too afraid to visit and don't, or the children themselves are too embarrassed to invite friends over. They are usually banned from using the internet to do their homework or assignments because it may breach the control order imposed on their father. These households are subjected to raids by police where all their belongings, their clothes, their personal effects are thoroughly searched sometimes two and three times a week, and at any time, day or night.

One woman was left alone without the support of friends and neighbours when her husband was admitted to hospital. Although her husband wasn't there, her house was still under control orders and no one was allowed to enter. I can almost hear the cynics and hard hearted people saying, 'so what?' This woman's husband was placed under a control order in the absence of a trial, a hearing, a court process.

Women who are married to control order detainees lead difficult lives but they do so in silence. They don't complain to anyone when they have no way of fixing the broken door to their house following a police raid. They just find a way to manage, or they don't. Many wives are terrified whenever they hear a police car passing by. Many are wary of visitors. There is no real normality in their lives. They are constantly watched and, just like their husbands, constantly monitored.

How can anyone not consider these women who endure this loneliness, knowing that once their lives amounted to so much more than being shunned in the street? Even their closest friends have broken contact as they are scared of being associated with the wife of a so-called 'terror suspect'. Their only crime was to love a man, suspected of being someone of interest, yet not actually proven to be.

In a single moment, a decision might be made that turns her life completely upside down. Her husband may decide to return to his country of birth, taking his young family with him rather than endure the appalling conditions of being imprisoned without charge in his own home.

Although his wife is terribly upset by this decision, she will not be able to change his mind. She and her three small children, under the age of five, will take one last look at the sofas and chairs that were ripped apart during a police raid the night before. The stuffing strewn all over the floor exposes the springs that once held her furniture in place. She will be forced to accept that her life will never be the same and the country that promised so much freedom, has become a jail to her children.

Her friend, also married to a control order detainee, hours away, has lost her Post Office card for child benefits. As a result, she has run out of money for food and her children have spent many days hungry. Her husband is in prison because he hasn't yet been placed under a control order. She finds it difficult to visit him because the prison is so far away. She doesn't understand it when his lawyer tells her that there is no evidence to keep her husband detained. Why, she asks, but no one gives her an answer.

When she does manage to catch a train, an hour's journey to her husband's prison, dragging their children into a world they have never known before, she almost cannot bear to return to her empty existence. She wishes to stay with her husband because without him she cannot possibly manage. Her children cry day and night because they want their father home. She is isolated. She doesn't go out because she fears going out alone. She does not let her children out of her sight, not even to play in the park across the road. She is afraid that they too will be snatched, just as her husband was.

As a result, her children do not go to nursery school, nor do they interact with other children. They need a father figure. She needs a husband. Their family needs to be reunited. It needs to be whole.

A control order detainee is required to call the control order monitoring centre every day whenever they leave and return to their place of residence. They are fitted with an electronic tag, usually around the ankle, that cannot be removed. It tracks the control order detainee's every movement, even where he walks inside his own house to kiss his children goodnight. He is confined to the home for up to 22 hours a day. If he leaves the house without prior approval, his tag will signal an alert to the police and he will be arrested. He cannot suddenly go outside if his child needs him or to help his wife with the shopping. He cannot sit by the bedside of his mother if she is dying in hospital unless he has prior permission to do so. If an accident occurs outside his house and he can see that with his assistance he might save someone from dying, he cannot respond. He can only stand by his window and watch. He must report in at the designated times or he will be arrested. He may be required to telephone the control order monitoring centre each evening at 3 am. If he does not call at the designated time then the police will be dispatched to his house.

Again, I am not saying that persons of interest should simply be let loose in our community. What I am questioning is whether, when they are let loose, the means of monitoring them are effective and conducive to promoting a sustainable community? Some would argue that these conditions promote anti-social behaviour in control order detainees and there is sufficient research conducted that lends support to that theory.

In relation to the practical aspects of monitoring, quite often it has been reported that the control order monitoring equipment fails. When this occurs, the police are dispatched, as it is recorded as a breach of the control order. One detainee's control monitoring equipment failed 40 times and the police came to his house each time. This in itself can be a traumatic experience for a family, in particular, young children.

What long term effects does this sort of exposure have on a child? According to those who have some form of professional association with such families, there is obvious emotional trauma on the child. So much so that foreign control order detainees contemplate escaping the nightmare of living under such restrictions by agreeing to return to the country of their birth. In several of the cases documented, however, this would see them returning to countries that practise torture.

It is impossible for the British government to secure assurances from these countries that the deported will not be tortured. Two detainees who returned, went missing. Many foreign control order detainees, however, have families who are not citizens of the country to which they would be deported. One control order detainee has lived in the UK for over 17 years; his children were born in the UK. Such families would have very little knowledge of the culture and language that they would need to help them assimilate into a society which would be foreign to them. I imagine there would be serious practical and emotional difficulties for a teenager to face under such circumstances, particularly one who has lived all their life under a Commonwealth system. To be suddenly taken out of a system that you know and understand to be thrust into the unknown, would be incredibly daunting.

An eight-year-old boy named Mohammed cried for his father, Jamil El Banna, who was taken to Guantanamo Bay detention centre in 2002. Every day this broken child prayed along with his brothers and sisters to call on Allah for his father's return. 'I love you dad ... I miss you so much!'

Five long years later, Jamil was finally released from Guantanamo to the UK (19 December 2007), largely due to his lawyer, Gareth Peirce, who campaigned tirelessly for his release. Jamil now has to wear an electronic tag as part of a control order. His family are glad to have him back, but now they are all effectively prisoners in their own home.

One control order detainee is contemplating returning to his country of birth (Algeria) but his wife has been trying to convince him not to go because of the potential dangers of torture or death. He has been detained without charge at HMP Long Lartin in the UK since 2005.

Where does it end? What if the government ever planned to broaden the control orders to the extreme? Currently, the British government is seeking to do just that for persons suspected of fraud and drug dealing.

It is, as many would argue, the first semblance of the erosion of our civil liberties.

> *The government's system for monitoring terror suspects was thrown into jeopardy today when the High Court ruled that control orders were 'conspicuously unfair'. In a judgement that threatens the entire anti-terror scheme, Mr. Justice Sullivan declared that a British suspect's order was 'incompatible' with the Human Rights Act, as it denied his human right to a fair hearing.'* —**Sam Knight**, 'UK terror suspect wins challenge against control order', *Times Online*, 12 April 2006.

Every night a young child thinks of his father locked up behind invisible bars for a crime of which he was never convicted. That child cries in a very low voice so that his mother does not hear him. He dreams of life before his father was placed under the control order,

A mother sits alone in a nearby park. Her husband must stay behind in the house because he doesn't want to breach the control order. She encourages their children to run about the park, to laugh and have fun, so they cannot see her tears. She cries day and night when no one is looking.

'I wish people could see the human side of my dilemma. The effect this has on my children. I am not alive. I merely exist.'

She doesn't want to reveal who she is because she fears the repercussions. Her husband could not cope with suddenly re-entering the world after being detained six years in a maximum security prison. He is completely damaged, psychologically and physiologically.

'We are all suffering under the control order, all of us, and the stresses on my children are obvious. There is no way to know when this will ever end and what will happen next. We wait and constantly worry that they will come again for him in the night.'

Her husband is medicated. He takes sleeping tablets because he cannot sleep without having nightmares.

He sets the alarm on the bedside table to wake him at 2 am so that he can call the control order monitoring centre. His wife worries that he won't wake. She sets a second alarm by her bedside table just in case, then sleeps on and off, waiting for it to buzz. She cannot talk to her mother on the telephone or tell her how she truly feels. Somebody is listening to every word she says.

'It's driving me to madness. It's torture on my children. We are paying a price for something we did not do', she cries in desperation.

Her life is unfamiliar to her. She is no longer happy. She suffers depression and wonders how she can endure. 'My health is getting worse. I have headaches and cannot sleep at night because of the telephone call that has to be made and because I worry too much. I have lost hope and my life means nothing. Sometimes I wish that I would never wake up or that this life would begin again.'

Imagine being shunned by your local community and branded an outcast or being constantly abused by your neighbours. Imagine being too scared to leave your front door because you fear that you may be attacked. What if your children are harassed and bullied at school? Many of these families cannot visit their loved ones because they have been put in prisons far away from where they live. Many control order detainees have contemplated suicide because they feel helpless. Many children cry to sleep every night not sure what the next day will bring. Welcome to the lives of those affected by the anti-terror legislation, who have not been convicted of an offence.

Equally, and in fairness to all the law enforcement officers throughout the world who are charged with responding to and enforcing control orders, theirs is a difficult and demanding job. They are, at times, condemned for what they do, but they too feel a strong sense of responsibility for keeping our communities safe and I don't believe this is something for which they should ever be condemned.

In conclusion, I wish to acknowledge two very special women who have given me tremendous support in accessing this information. I thank them both sincerely and admire them for their outstanding commitment in fighting for the rights of others.

Thank you Saiyeda Ravalia, and all the volunteers at HHUGS for allowing me to glimpse into your lives and into the lives of those in your care. Thank you Maryam Hassan, Executive Director of Cageprisoners, who is always willing to remind others that people need to be treated within the civilised norms of justice, to ensure that they are given their due rights, namely humane treatment, an open fair civilian trial, access to medical care and, most importantly, access to their families.

HHUGS
PO Box 415, New Malden, KT39AF United Kingdom
Web: http://hhugs.org.uk

Cageprisoners
27 Old Gloucester Street, London WC1N 3XX
Web: http://www.cageprisoners.com

17
IT'S ONLY PRESCRIPTION MEDICINE

American grandmother, South America

On the brink of suicide and feeling that life was completely out of her control, one young mother of three begged her doctor for a prescription drug to stop the anxiety and depression that threatened to overwhelm her. She went from Valium to Xanax and Temazepam. Eventually, she found herself becoming more and more dependent on drugs. She was becoming an addict.

Two out of every 100 Australians take some form of prescription tranquilliser, otherwise known as benzodiazepines. If they take them long enough, they run the risk of becoming addicted. Their drugs don't come from street corners or even the internet; they get their prescriptions from their local GP. Prescription addicts are caught in a cycle of anxiety and the need to increase their dose. It may not be heroin they're pumping into their bodies, but it can be just as addictive and as equally destructive to people's lives as any other illicit drug.

Addictions don't necessarily take away your freedom to choose, but they can take away your freedom to make the right choices.

The United Nations reports that in some parts of the world, the abuse of prescription drugs has surpassed the abuse of illicit drugs such as heroin and cocaine. In fact, trafficking in prescription medicine is a multi-million dollar business. One prescription drug dealer netted himself a profit of $700,000 in a single month. Young people can easily be convinced by these conmen that trafficking prescription drugs carries no penalty—after all, they are legal, right? Wrong! Without a prescription—they are just as illegal as street opiates like heroin and street amphetamines like cocaine and speed.

Trafficking prescription medicine is sometimes more appealing, because there is a perception that prescription drugs are relatively safe when compared to street drugs. This is most probably because prescription drugs are produced under strict laboratory conditions. Just because prescription drugs are not produced in backyard labs, it doesn't make their active ingredients any safer.

Curiously, there is less stigma attached to the trafficking of prescription drugs because many people feel that if a doctor can prescribe them, then they can't be too bad for you. This is certainly not the case. Taking prescription drugs without a doctor's advice and constant supervision, unrelated to a medical condition, can be a dangerous, even deadly, decision.

According to the Journal of the American Medical Association, over 100,000 people die each year in the United States from problems relating to prescription medication. A report released in 2005 by the National Center on Addiction and Substance Abuse at Columbia University suggested that between 1992 and 2003, more Americans were abusing controlled prescription drugs than cocaine, hallucinogens, inhalants and heroin put together. In the same report, 2.3 million 12 to 17 year olds (almost one in 10) abused at least one controlled prescription drug. Girls were more likely than boys to be abusers.

There are generally two types of drug dealers—the user and the non-user. The user has turned to dealing to fund a drug habit. The non-user is in it for the money and justifies trafficking prescription drugs by maintaining they are not hard-core substances that kill people. Drug dealers are always looking for new and ingenious ways to hook people into their web of deceit and the illegal drug trade. Those who are already addicted to drugs don't need much of an incentive too, with excuses like: 'I didn't know it was illegal ... it's only prescription medicine'.

Drug-Free America reported that the average age for users to start experimenting with prescription medication is between 13 and 14 years old. One in five teens has abused a prescription pain medication. Girls are more likely to be abusers than boys (4.3 per cent versus 3.6 per cent). Alcohol and cigarettes are still the most commonly used drugs by teenagers, but more and more teenagers are experimenting with prescription medications. Prescription medications are only legal for the name on the label.

Most people who try prescription medications do so once or twice and then stop. However, some will continue to use and, before too long, they're hooked. Telling yourself that you won't get hooked is just kidding yourself. These are highly addictive drugs. The cravings will come day and night, with or without someone convincing you that you need them. The drug that you took socially will soon become far more important to you than the friends you were socialising with when you first ingested the drug. It doesn't take an Einstein to figure out that your friendships will be affected, your cash will go to calming the cravings and, when you are broke, a one-off overseas holiday with a lot of drugs and cash thrown in, may seem quite appealing.

Unfortunately though, it is usually a one-way trip to hell—no money, no drugs and sometimes no life. The traffickers back home aren't travel agents who you can sue for a holiday gone wrong.

It's impossible to tell who will and won't become drug users and drug addicts, so it's best to make sure prevention programs and positive role modelling are available to everyone. We need clean parents to be good role models if we are to have any hope of diverting children away from drugs. There's no point saying: 'Do as I say, not as I do'. Parents can teach children many things, but first they must take responsibility for their actions. Young people need good role models to learn by example. If a young person is constantly exposed to a parent's pill popping or drunken behaviour, then it is likely that young person may develop a mindset that these behaviours are normal.

The fact that some children of parents who have done their very best still choose to enter the insidious world of drugs, doesn't let any parents off the hook. It's still essential to be good role models, to explain responsible drug use and the need to avoid drug abuse. It reduces the chances, even if it doesn't immunise.

Keeping the lines of communication open is important. Being able to share with each other and staying alert to the dangers of taking prescription drugs should be everyone's priority. Prescription drugs are far from harmless.

Anyone can be susceptible to drug abuse. Take this case of a middle-aged American woman who was arrested in South America for buying prescription medication and she is now awaiting her trial in a South American penitentiary.

While incarcerated, she has been subjected to all manner of ill-treatment including beatings and rape. She was told a number of times that she would be free but that was 12 months ago and all her family are still waiting her return. Every single day is a day of struggle. She is doing her best to cope with life away from her family, all the while knowing she did nothing to deserve this. She was forced to get her medication from over the border after she was made redundant at work. She was no longer covered by medical insurance and simply couldn't afford it. She didn't think there was anything wrong with buying it cheaper across the border and, because it was too expensive to travel to and fro, she decided to buy in bulk. Once she got there, upon leaving the pharmacy where she normally shops, she was stopped by police demanding to see her purse. She gave it to them without hesitation. The police then told her that she was breaking the law and would be arrested, unless she gave them a few hundred dollars. She refused. She believed she hadn't committed any crime. She tried to show the police her prescription, but they said it was invalid and needed to come from a local doctor to be legal. She was charged with possession.

After making the trip to where she was being detained, her son was advised by the American consulate to hire a lawyer for his mother. He hired one of those on the consulate's list. After hearing his story, they assured him that she would be out in a couple days, but he would have to pay $1000 in legal costs. He paid it immediately, but a few days later they asked for more. The son believed his mother would be free and, not wanting to make her situation worse, he again gave them more money.

They said he could hire a local doctor to explain why she needed the medication, but that it was going to take months to build a case and inevitably, this would also incur additional 'costs'. The woman was forced to sign a statement that was completely different to the truth as she told her son. But she had no other choice, because the lawyers he had engaged told them this was the way it was done.

On the day the woman went to court, an officer of the court demanded more money. There was no money left to give because it had all gone to the lawyers. Her son was flat broke and had nowhere else to turn. The deal was off they said. The woman is still in that prison. She was sentenced to five years.

The family's last remaining hope was the promise that she would receive a transfer to the United States and the case would be reviewed again. They would see all the facts and with a fair trial, she would be set free. As of 2008, the woman is still waiting to be transferred.

The woman is a caring woman who doesn't deserve what's happened to her. She has missed Thanksgiving, Christmas, New Year's Eve, Easter, and many family birthdays. And she has never seen her new grandchild. Her family have exhausted their resources in an attempt to bring her home. It has cost them thousands of dollars they didn't have in the first place. But money aside, it has cost them even more from an emotional standpoint. Ever since that day the family haven't been able to stop worrying about their mother's wellbeing. They have done everything they can. They fear their mother will die in there if no one helps!

Cynics will say 'Come on…it sounds dodgy. She can pay to go to another country, but she can't afford to buy locally? Why didn't she just borrow from her family if they could afford to pay her legal expenses? Surely they could have paid her medical insurance so she wouldn't have to go over the border?' Indeed, the circumstances are questionable, and most people who have been caught out seldom admit to it. Then again, there have been many reported cases of innocent people getting arrested. I don't know the woman in this case or her family. She may or may not be innocent, but either way she is now in a situation that for whatever reason has changed her life forever.

Her own family living peacefully in the suburbs have now discovered that there is a huge jump to make from life as an average family in an ordinary community, to a family thrust into federal and international politics.

I've heard hundreds of stories like this. For some, it's not always easy to share the truth, but sometimes the best lessons can be learned from someone else's tragedy. People are bound to make mistakes, because they are human. We are never immune to tragedy. It can strike at any time and we need to cultivate compassion for those who find themselves in such desperate situations.

Friedrich Gustav Emil Martin Niemöller exemplifies this theory in something he wrote while imprisoned in concentration camps in Germany from 1937 to 1945. He narrowly escaped execution and survived imprisonment. He wrote:

> First they came for the communists and I did not speak out because I was not a communist. Then they came for the socialists and I did not speak out because I was not a socialist. Then they came for the homosexuals and I did not speak out because I was not a homosexual. Then they came for the trade unionists and

I did not speak out because I was not a trade unionist. Then they came for the Jews and I did not speak out because I was not a Jew. Then they came for me and there was no one left to speak for me.

While some may be claiming they are innocent and may well not be, there are many who are innocent, railroaded and are unfairly treated and sentenced, just as there are many who are guilty, make their bad choices and still unfairly treated and sentenced. There's not a whole lot that can be done to secure an early release when a person is sentenced in an overseas jail because they are effectively part of a foreign correctional process. Their situation is unlikely to change simply by saying, 'but really, I didn't do it!'

For those who may be tempted to make some quick cash by trafficking in drugs or by any other crime, I'd urge them to think again. The same as I would urge anyone who has a drug habit to deal with it within their own country and not in a country that allows the death penalty. There may never be another chance to make another choice.

Remember, having the best lawyer in the world may not save someone from a firing squad. Some people may think that they are smarter than the next person and maybe they are, but plenty more law enforcement officers out there are a whole lot smarter. Why gamble with your life?

We are each responsible for our own actions. Sometimes there's nothing anyone can do to dissuade another person from making a bad choice. Sadly, sometimes it takes something really bad to happen before some people realise their mistakes. Only then, it's usually too late!

The Dangers of Prescription Drug Abuse
http://www.medicalonline.com.au/medical/drugs/prescription-drug-abuse.htm

Say No To Drugs!
http://www.saynotodrugs.org.uk

18
MY BROTHER BRAD

Bradley Peake, Australia

Today it is 26 August 2007. I had a bit of a cry today. I found a letter Brad wrote to me on Christmas Day 1994 from prison. He asked if I could bring him in two plain blue towels. I cried because I couldn't remember if I did or not. I remembered going down to visit him in Bendigo a couple of times, but can't remember anything about the towels. He never asked for much when he was in jail and I just hope I did this for him
—Julie-Anne Peake.

Julie-Anne's brother, Bradley Thomas Peake, was born on 2 September 1972 in Burwood, Victoria (Australia). He died from a fatal combination of prescription drugs (Xanax, Rivotril and Oxy-Contin) on 20 July 2006. He is sadly missed by Julie-Anne, his father Bill, his mother Barbara, niece Amy, sister Eliza, brother-in-law Rob, wife Jen, stepdaughter Stacey and stepson Michael, along with countless friends and other relatives.

Brad had a long and unfortunate history of poly-drug use. (This is when a person uses two or more psychoactive drugs in combination. For example, cannabis and alcohol, or cocaine and caffeine, or cocaine and heroin.) Combining these drugs makes the whole drug-taking experience far more dangerous than taking the substances alone.

Brad's drug use varied over the years from alcohol, marijuana, amphetamines, heroin and prescription medication—often being a combination at once. He served a number of years in jail for drug-related offences to feed his addiction. He had only been released from prison for three days before he took his last breath. Unfortunately, his story is not uncommon.

Brad's family have suffered. Living with someone who has a drug addiction is a hard struggle, but they learnt tolerance and they stuck together through the bad times. They learnt the true value of unconditional love and never once gave up on Brad. He always had a safe place to go if he needed it. They understood that drugs affect people's personalities. Brad was a good person. It was just the drugs that were bad.

'Hang the addict, he deserves everything he gets!' someone says carelessly. How devastating that must be for Bradley Peake's family and others like them, who know first hand what it is like to watch someone you love slowly lose themselves and kill themselves through drug use.

Brad's sister, Julie-Anne, has kindly agreed to share her brother's story because there are some very valuable lessons in telling it.

> Brad always called me "Kiddo" and he was always my hero. Despite all the normal sibling rivalry, he always stuck by me. I remember how he never wanted to walk on the same side of the road as me when we'd walk to primary school. And when he tried to drown me in the pool when I threw a golf ball at his head. And him standing at the front of the high school bus telling the driver to knock me off my bike as they drove past. I will always remember the times he dobbed on me for kissing boys behind the shelter shed (when he was doing the same thing to girls!) and when he told Mum and Dad I stole a nail polish pen from a local shop.

Julie-Anne says that in a strange way, Brad was always looking out for his younger sisters and wanted the best for them. As the eldest child, he believed that was his responsibility. His sister, Julie-Anne, remembers many times when he came to her rescue. One time on one of their many trips along the Murray river, Julie-Anne was in a canoe and started drifting out further and further from the bank. Brad, aged 12 or so, swam the width of the Murray to save her.

Brad and Julie-Anne were close.

He was always well liked by friends and put most of his energy into playing football for Hallam, Oakleigh Districts and ROC Football Clubs. He could have gone a long way with his footy, and everyone said that he had so much potential. It's funny how things turn out. We can dream dreams and hope to become everything we want to become but sadly some don't realise their dreams, no matter how hard they try.

When Julie-Anne was 14, she was suspended for being drunk at school. She told Brad: 'You're so straight, you don't drink or smoke, you don't sneak out at night, you don't have a girlfriend, you work in a library and all you ever listen to is that horrible country and western music.'

At this point in their lives, Julie-Anne was the one getting into trouble. And to this day, she regrets ever saying that to Brad. He began to emulate her behaviour. They 'partied' together more and their friendship grew. His friends became Julie-Anne's friends and hers became his. They drank and smoked and listened to Guns 'N' Roses. All Julie-Anne's friends drooled over Brad and were attracted to his spunky, bad boy image. Julie-Anne fell in love with his friend, John, and Brad fell for the girl next door.

The parties continued. There was always a competition to see who could drink the most, smoke the most, who could sing the loudest to the music, or who could steal the most jugs and pots from the Hallam Pub.

The tables turned for Brad when 'the girl next door' broke his heart according to his sister. He was devastated. He took off to Wangaratta when she moved up there to live with her aunty. He wasn't allowed to see her. That was when he was first was arrested for stealing a chainsaw from a barn he was sleeping in. In his naivety, at 17 years of age, he tried selling it at the local pub to get some cash. He ended up doing jail time for this. Maybe the judge thought he would teach him a lesson. Brad swore he would never go to jail again.

But he continued to party, continued to drink and got into even harder drugs. These were his downfall time and time again. Drugs became a way of life, a way to numb out, to stop his thoughts, to stop his emotional pain.

Julie-Anne says that the things Brad did under the influence of drugs are what continued to land him back in jail. There were more girls, more heartache and always more drugs. Jail became a way he could clean up and get his life back into some sort of order. It offered him a break from the real world, where structure and routine provided some sense of certainty to his life.

In Brad's letters to Julie-Anne, he wrote that he wanted to make something of his life, but said it was easier said than done.

> *I'll try my best, that's all I can expect of myself. I don't want to disappoint Mum and Dad anymore. I can tell from the times I've seen them that they feel kind of responsible for me being in jail. They are good parents, the best anyone can ask for. The only reason I'm in jail is because I abused drugs and the reason*

I used drugs in the first place had nothing to do with not being brought up right. Tell ya the truth, I don't know why I turned to drugs. Maybe it was to escape reality, I don't know,' wrote Brad. Brad was obviously searching for answers. He longed to have his life over.

I wish I was a little kid again sometimes, so I could have a try at life again. I know so much, I have seen more than most people in such a short amount of time and I have so many answers, but at the same time I know nothing, have seen shit and got no answers to anything.

Julie-Anne says that Brad always maintained his sense of humour, no matter what amount of physical or emotional pain he was experiencing.

Christmas and holidays are always difficult for prisoners and their families. Julie-Anne's family was no exception. With Brad in jail, all they could do was carry on without him. All he could do was imagine them opening presents and joke that the judge had frozen his assets, hence he couldn't send them anything special.

Julie-Anne says her brother never blamed his childhood, their parents or her for his mistakes. He took responsibility for his actions and sometimes he took responsibility for the things his friends did. He was a loyal friend.

In jail, Brad worked hard to earn back his self respect. He frequently took the younger kids under his wing to teach them the ropes and keep them out of trouble. In jail, he had learnt to cut off his emotions in order to survive but he had not lost his humanity, according to his sister.

When he was released from jail, he was confronted by a world where he had to learn to feel again. He had trouble coping. When he dropped his guard, in would creep the emotional pain and insecurities.

In fact, most of the time Brad felt it was easier to be in jail, which highlights the depth of his struggles. He felt he didn't fit in in a world where people looked down on him for having a drug addiction.

Although Brad's family suffered a great deal because of his drug use, they stood by him unconditionally. They knew, despite what he did, that he was essentially a good person, a strong person. Even through his years of addiction, he showed an enormous amount of courage, love, compassion, loyalty and determination.

Brad wanted to survive by looking at the bigger picture, but as time went by, that picture began to blur and it became harder for him to focus on it. He knew what he wanted and where he wanted to be in life, but so many internal and external pressures blocked his path.

Everyone struggles with life at times and they cope in different ways. Like Brad, every struggling person has a story. If you listen hard enough, and don't judge, you will hear it.

It is funny really, because if someone has a troubled upbringing, it is more acceptable to people that they use drugs—it helps people understand their behaviour and they can excuse it, to a degree. Julie-Anne says she felt sometimes that others looked sideways at her family, when they didn't know the situation and history. In the absence of a troubled background, Julie-Anne believed that Brad used drugs because he wanted to. But did he really want to or was it a way he could escape his private traumas and deal with his pain and guilt? Julie-Anne is certain Brad would have chosen a different lifestyle, if he could. But that is the hold drugs can have on a person. The only thing stigma succeeds at is isolating and ostracising families.

The government and society are learning and things are slowly changing in Australia. For example, bringing in Medicare rebates for psychologists is a good move, utilising a workforce that is quite capable of treating people with mental illnesses and taking the load off GPs and psychiatrists, making services more accessible to those in most need. Also, that arbitrary line between mental and physical illness is diminishing. Alzheimer's used to be classed as a mental disorder before its biological basis was found. Depression is recognised now by the medical community and is being identified much earlier. This has all been the result of lobbying to reduce the stigma of depression by educating the community.

So things are slowly changing. Further change is needed, however, in the way that drugs of dependence are prescribed—especially to those with a known drug or alcohol addiction. Punishing people with a mental illness is not the answer. Getting them the help they need, no matter where it comes from, is a start. Teaching them the survival skills they need to get through this sometimes harsh and trying life, is a good first step.

'Brad's addiction was his way of coping. His story has a sad, tragic ending for those of us left behind, but at least for him, his mind is at peace after a long, hard struggle. He will always be my hero and I, like the many who truly knew him, will miss him dearly,' says Julie-Anne.

The exact number of families who are grieving the loss of a loved one as a result of a drug overdose is not recorded. However, there are millions of people who die each year from drug overdose. For families living with a dependent drug user, it can be a prolonged frustrating process of trying to find help during the crisis and afterwards, when they are left to pick up the shattered pieces of their lives. Where do families go for help and what help is available for them?

Australian Drug Information Network
http://www.adin.com.au/content.asp?Document_ID=1

Drug Arm
www.drugarm.com.au

Youth Substance Abuse Service
http://www.ysas.org.au/

ADFAM
A leading UK organisation working with and for families affected by drugs and alcohol.
http://www.adfam.org.uk

In Loving Memory of Bradley Thomas Peake
2 September 1972–20 July 2006
www.bradpeake.piczo.com

19
FALLEN ANGEL
Randy Sachs, Vietnam

'Don't be stupid ... if you do drugs you could be tied to a post and shot!'

Sometimes it takes a harsh reality check to make people realise the true consequences of their actions. Death penalties for drug-related crimes may seem like a harsh form of justice, but in Vietnam a conviction for drug possession can lead to public execution. It's reported the Vietnamese government does this to deter people from getting involved in the country's increasing drug trade. It's a practice criticised by human rights groups.

I received a letter from a very distressed Dee Hogle, the mother of a young Canadian man, Randy James Sachs. Her son and his Vietnamese student friend from Canada had been arrested in Ho Chi Minh City in May 2003. Vietnamese police reported that the two had in their possession 1000 prescription stimulants, otherwise known as amphetamines.

Amphetamines are not illegal, but trafficking them is. Used appropriately under medical supervision, amphetamines are commonly used to treat Attention Deficit Hyperactivity Disorder (ADHD) in adults and children. They are also used to treat symptoms of traumatic brain injury and the daytime drowsiness symptoms of narcolepsy and chronic fatigue. Unfortunately, the illegal drug trade sells them as a recreational drug and as a performance enhancer. So now, in the UK for example, amphetamines are regarded as Class B drugs. Internationally, amphetamines are Schedule II drugs which are only available by prescription in small quantities and distributed under careful control. In the US, amphetamines are classified as Schedule II drugs and are monitored by the Drug Enforcement Agency (DEA) because they have strong hallucinogenic qualities which make them highly attractive to illegal drug dealers.

It was around midnight when Dee Hogle returned home from a very busy midnight sale at her family clothing store. The phone rang. It was her eldest son's fiancée. She was calling from their home in Ontario. She was frantic as she told Dee that her son, Randy, had been arrested on drug charges in Ho Chi Minh City, Vietnam. Dee's life, as she knew it, changed forever in that single moment.

'My spouse, Robin, tucked Randy's siblings, Colbie, (then 10 years old) and Robbie (then five years old) into bed. We immediately placed a call to the Canadian embassy in Ho Chi Minh City. We had great trouble getting through to them with the time zone difference. The language barrier and very thick Vietnamese accent was a definite challenge for us. We received no answers that evening, other than confirmation of Randy's arrest. I cried myself to sleep … the first of many nights like that,' says Dee.

Randy Sachs may or may not have thought about the consequences of his actions. He might have been foolish, believing, like so many others, that prescription drugs aren't as bad as illicit drugs. In countries like Vietnam, however, they take a much stronger view of the illegal trafficking of *any* drugs. Mere possession of drugs can result in the death penalty.

According to those who know Randy, they believe he did not set out to intentionally hurt his family, but everything that happened after the police slapped those handcuffs on his wrists, affected them. They were completely devastated. His mother Dee, his family and his closest friends were all helplessly drawn into a nightmare, his nightmare. Not only did they have to immediately come to terms with Randy's arrest in a foreign country, but they were now being asked to pay in advance for the body bag that would be used to transport his remains home.

Funeral arrangements are never pleasant and many people these days tend to do their planning well in advance, in order to lessen some of the emotional trauma associated with death. Dee and her family were expected to make such arrangements. They were forced to visualise Randy's demise, a slow and lonely walk to a single post where he would be bound, blindfolded and possibly gagged, before being shot. No mother's arms would comfort him, no whispers of 'I love you son', no final goodbyes and no second chance to make things right.

♓

Soon after her son's arrest, Dee received a call from the Canadian consulate in Ottawa. Her family's nightmare had begun. The realisation that Vietnam has harsh penalties, including the death penalty, was quickly becoming a reality. Randy had no human rights and, as his mother soon discovered, Vietnam's laws and court procedures were very different to the West.

Randy admits that he was not always on the straight and narrow in Canada. He had once been charged with some minor offences but nothing on this scale. Randy Sachs was once hailed a hero in his hometown of Hamilton. It was Christmas Eve 2002 and Randy had just finished work and was driving to his mother's Beaverton home when he came across a car crash. The victim, a 22-year-old student, was still inside, unconscious at the wheel. His car had left the road and landed in the icy waters of a shallow ravine. The car doors were locked. Randy grabbed a hammer from the trunk of his car and broke the window of the victim's car just before the Chevy burst into flames. He managed to drag the student free. A *Sunday Sun* reporter wrote the headline 'Angels Among Us'.

Within months of that story, Randy was arrested in Vietnam with 1000 ecstasy pills. The newspaper dubbed him 'The Fallen Angel'. Randy didn't suddenly sprout horns, a pointy tail and transform into an evil person. Essentially, he is still a good person; he just made wrong choices.

> *We were at my sister's home in Kitchener when Robin brought the newspaper in. This was not good. My niece, Rachelle, then 14 years old, wanted to read it. She and Randy have always been very close. Reading about her cousin in that way broke her heart and there was nothing any of us could do. I cried with her and it seems that every day since, I've cried,* says Dee.

Following his arrest in Vietnam in May 2003, Randy was housed in a district jail with 5000 prisoners. His cell was a concrete box (3 metres by 4 metres) that he shared with seven others. They slept on straw mats and ignored the rats and roaches scurrying back and forth in the darkness. Randy developed rashes and scabies amidst the stench of stale urine that dropped from the cracked ceiling above.

In September 2003, Randy welcomed a new addition to his cell, Samuel Dong Sung Kim, an English teacher from Vancouver. Sam was charged with swindling students after his English school went bankrupt. His family sent him a small amount of food each week. Sam shared everything he had with Randy and used the money his wife sent him to purchase more water, and to get a doctor to treat the rashes and scabies that ravaged Randy's body. Of course, the doctor was a fellow inmate with no medical experience and prescribed medicine to other inmates for a fee. Then Randy was moved to the pre-trial unit, ED 24, another dilapidated room filled with more rats and roaches. Sam soon joined him. The room was in a shambles with pieces of the ceiling falling on him daily. The stale stench of urine was ever present. The Canadian consulate intervened as best it could and eventually all foreign inmates were granted access to the infirmary once a week.

Randy and Sam were always examined last at the infirmary because they weren't able to pay Dr Dong, head of the infirmary in Chi Hoa Prison's high fees. Sam began having chest pains and dizziness for one or two days. His blood pressure was high, but Dr Dong insisted he was fine. Seven days later, Sam had a heart attack. Fortunately, he survived the heart attack but the treatment that followed almost killed him. The officials told the consulate that Sam was receiving the very best care and probably by their standards he was. But everything came at a price and Sam's wife constantly had to pay guards to ensure her husband received medical care. Where else would the money come from to maintain a minimal standard of care?

Christmas was approaching. It would be the first time Dee and her family would be without Randy over the holiday season. The thought of it scared her. Randy was always home for Christmas. He would climb up on the roof and make reindeer tracks in the snow and put reindeer grain up there for them to eat. Of course he had to do it just right because his younger brother, Robbie, would always want to check if Santa did park on their roof the night before Christmas.

Dee says her older son went to a great deal of trouble to make Christmas special for his younger brother and sister. He would help decorate the family Christmas tree, join them singing Christmas carols and reminisce about all the Christmases before and all the crazy things each of them did.

Before they knew it, Christmas Eve was on their doorstep. Dee went to the midnight service at the church alone. She sat in the pew and felt the icy cold winter wrap around her heart. Her son, who usually sat beside her on such occasions, was sitting half way around the world in a dark and dirty prison cell. There was no joy in Dee's heart. No Christmas spirit or

Christmas cheer that could erase the agony she was feeling. Closing her eyes, she prayed and thought of Randy. She prayed harder than she ever knew how, that this horrid nightmare would end. 'Please God. Please bring my son home!'

Dee barely slept that evening despite her husband's loving arms wrapped around her, to protect her from the nightmares. Dee's last thought before sleep was how she was going to explain to Colbie and Robbie that Santa hadn't brought their one wish this year.

The morning came all too soon and the house seemed quieter than usual. Our first Christmas without Randy certainly had a devastating impact. He was the one who always woke up Robbie and Colbie by spraying them with silly stringy stuff. In turn, Robin and I would be woken by their squeals and giggling and running through the house, laughing, 'stop, Randy, stop!'

We woke to the sound of silence. I made breakfast for my family in silence. Of course, there was plenty of chatter going on around me, but in my heart, there was silence. There was an empty space beside me at the table, an empty space where my son should have been. I felt lost. How could I pretend that I was enjoying Christmas when my heart felt like breaking into a million pieces. I sat quietly watching Colbie and Robbie take their stockings from the mantelpiece. They were so excited by the array of brightly wrapped gifts inside and those waiting for them under the brightly lit Christmas tree. My eyes stayed momentarily on the Christmas stocking still hanging where theirs had hung. I saw my own handwriting inscribe the words 'To my beloved Son, Randy. With love Mum'. We would send them to Vietnam.

I don't recall how I managed to get through the rest of the day. In all his innocence, Robbie kept asking: 'Where's Randy? When's he coming?' I felt that someone had stabbed my heart with the same red-hot poker that my father prodded the fireplace with. We went over to Grampa and Nanny's house to exchange our gifts. I had an extremely difficult time trying not to cry, when I saw my Mum and Dad. I saw in their eyes the same hurt that I was feeling and later when we went to Grammie Harris's house to exchange our gifts, we wore brave smiles and pretended that everything was fine,.

Randy was detained for 18 months before being officially charged. His family was suffering along with him, even though they were separated by half a world. They were forced to close their clothing store because Dee could not deal with the stress and anxiety of being totally helpless. She said: 'I needed to fight for my son's life. I needed to focus on that.'

Randy's grandparents became preoccupied with the fate of their eldest grandchild when they learned of the harsh conditions that Randy was now enduring. Randy's younger sister, Colbie, was totally devastated and very angry when she learned of Randy's situation. None of them could tell Robbie at this time. He was only five years old and would not have understood. Yet Robbie knew something was not right because it was obvious their lives had all changed. Randy's stepfather, Robin, was the family's pillar of strength. He kept reassuring everyone that they would do everything to get Randy back home, safely. This trauma strengthened their relationship and Dee says that she knew that with Robin's compassion, support and understanding, she could get through this.

Such situations can often break marriages and whole families. It's important that everyone stays focused on enduring together, to weather the storms.

Dee received a letter from her son via the Canadian embassy in Vietnam. It was a birthday greeting. Randy had drawn a picture of a birthday cake with several candles and a picture of a beautiful, gift-wrapped parcel with a dorky sign: 'Open' … followed by the words 'Your Song—EJ. Listen to Feb 17/04. I love you Mom XOX'. The song was by Elton John and was one of Dee's favourites.

On 18 February 2004, Randy's family received a letter from the Vietnamese officials stating that Randy would receive a 10-year sentence. They were told official confirmation would be sent in due course. Immediately, Randy's family began preparing themselves. The consulate negotiated an agreement that consideration would be given for time served. The family formed the impression that Randy would have only eight-and-a-half years to serve. This was something they could deal with, and for the first time since the terrible news of his arrest, they began to hope. They received some good news in the meantime. They were reimbursed the money for the body bag that was to be used to transport Randy's remains back to Canada.

Nine months later, on 8 November 2004, Randy Sachs was sentenced to 16 years. His family were completely devastated.

When the phone call came from Ottawa that Randy had been sentenced to 16 years hard labour, his family could not grasp the number 16. They were utterly unprepared for this amount of time. Randy's mother physically collapsed from shock. She literally screamed and hysterically sobbed for hours.

Thank God that Robin was home for lunch with me when the call came in. All he could do was hold me, cry with me and try to reassure me that Randy will be alrigh..

They decided not to keep anything from Colbie as she would be directly affected by Randy's situation. Colbie cried with Dee and Robin, asked many questions and grew up a hell of a lot that evening. Randy's grandparents were also shocked by the sentence, yet they found strength to help Dee and Robin cope and kept faith that they would all survive this horrific nightmare.

Following the trial, Randy was transferred to Bo La Prison for a month, then onto Z30D Thu Duc Prison K4 Ham Tan in Binh Thuan province. The conditions of the prison were unimaginable to a Westerner. Rats, roaches and all things creepy occupy your space. If you're lucky, they won't bite. If you're luckier still, you can catch them, as some prisoners do, to supplement their diet.

Months later, he wrote to his mother pleading for her to help him return to Canada. According to him, his life had become one of survival as he, being one of 63 prisoners, was allocated exactly 84 centimetres of floor space to sleep. His daily diet consisted of two bowls of rice and one bowl of soup. He was allowed a ration of 18 litres of water per day to drink, shower, wash clothing and clean his dishes. He lost a further 15 pounds (6.8 kilograms) and developed more dental problems through tooth decay.

Randy was housed in the 'United Nations Room'—as dubbed by the prisoners—because it houses all foreigners, not because there was anything united about it. He was detained with every type of hardened criminal, murderer, rapist, sex offender and drug courier.

Randy's life became increasingly difficult. His family didn't know exactly what was happening because his letters always went missing in transit.

They did receive one letter and the contents of this letter perplexed them even more.

Randy wrote: 'I've seen enough. I wonder how many more [prisoners] I will see die before I'm done here?'

The conditions inside prisons in South-East Asia are tough. They are designed to break the criminal will of every man and woman who finds themselves there, in order for them to suffer and truly understand the consequences of their actions. Some suggest that it is thought that because they are criminals, they must not expect any measure of mercy.

Communications with Randy were almost non-existent in the early stages of his detainment. His mail and parcels were always being lost or misdirected. His family sent letters and care packages when the Canadian Consuls visited him every four to six weeks. He had no phone privileges. Their visit reports were Dee's only indication as to how Randy was coping, mentally and physically. Dee suspected that Randy was 'sugar coating' his actual situation, so as not to upset the prison or Vietnamese government officials. Randy was not permitted visitors unless they were relatives, and his family have none in Vietnam.

Thank God that he can speak and write Vietnamese. His health has deteriorated due to malnutrition and dehydration. He was denied medical attention in the first months, but that changed when pressure was put on the prison officials and their human rights violations were exposed in a smuggled letter,' says Dee.

Dee and her family continued to appeal to the Vietnamese government for mercy. Randy's grandfather, Bob, wrote a letter to the then Canadian Prime Minister, Paul Martin:

I am 70 years old. I doubt I will see my grandson again. Not because of my dying first but because of Randy not getting the medical attention he deserves.

On 22 December 2005, the Canadian consulate confirmed that as a result of repeated requests and with the provision of costs provided by Randy's family, he could be transferred to a local Vietnamese hospital approximately 45 minutes from prison for treatment. Randy's mouth was X-rayed and examined by a local dentist who indicated that he would require five bridges/implants and four root canals. The cost would be approximately

US$1000. His family would have to pay that bill.

> *It would be another black Christmas and I don't think I shall ever enjoy trimming the tree or making Christmas turkey until I can do it with my son by my side, as he should be.*

On 11 January 2006, Randy's family received confirmation from Canadian consular staff that Randy had received the first of three sessions of dental treatments and would need to see another doctor for his kidneys. The consular staff advised the family to prepare for these additional expenses. While Randy's family continued to rely on the generosity of relatives and friends to cover the costs of the escalating medical bills, they hoped to impress upon the Canadian government officials the urgent need for Randy to be repatriated. Only Vietnam doesn't have a parole system. There is no Prisoner Exchange Treaty with Canada. The best anyone could hope for was clemency, but a pardon was rare. Their local MP, Barry Devolin, and Minister of Foreign Affairs Peter MacKay, were doing all they could for Randy. The family continued to hope that with the support of their government this horrible situation would change for the better.

On 5 October 2006, Dee Hogle was informed that her son was to be transferred to another prison in North Vietnam (Hanoi). This news was initially met with welcome relief, thinking that Randy would not be so isolated. The conditions were reportedly better but still extremely difficult. Dee worried that her son would not survive.

The Canadian consuls visited Randy in jail on 14 December 2006 and reassured her by saying that he seemed to be in good physical and mental health despite appearing to have lost more weight. The authorities arranged for him to undergo tests for HIV, Hepatitis A and B and the results were negative for all. They allowed Randy to go to a local hospital for a medical examination, dental treatment, eye examination and vaccines for Hepatitis A and B.

The Vietnamese authorities allowed Randy to purchase reading glasses. Consul staff gave Randy some basic supplies—food, pillow, toiletries, books and magazines. They also gave his family the bill for all of this.

As the years creep by, Randy's family patiently pray and continue to hope that his jailers might consider their fallen angel worthy of a second chance.

Wendy Harris, Randy's grandmother says:

> *My heart is filled with worry and he is always in my prayers. We wish that he could come home to Canada and finish his sentence here instead of somewhere we have no contact with him. He is a good man and knows what he has done wrong, but he most certainly doesn't deserve this horrendous burden. We worry for his health but know that he can pull through because he's got his family and friends to back him up. Please let him return to Canada to finish his sentence!*

One of the most difficult things to face when someone is imprisoned is how and what to tell young children about what has happened. How difficult would life be for Colbie and Robbie to find out that their brother, whom they've idolised all their lives, is facing a long prison term in a foreign land, thousands of miles away.

Dee finally told Randy's young brother, Robbie, the details of Randy's situation. He was now eight years old and old enough to understand. Robbie knew Randy was in Vietnam, but not the details. After she told him, Robbie's behaviour at home and school changed dramatically. He was angry, disruptive and disrespectful to everyone. He seemed to not care about anything, including consequences and privileges. Their family doctor said Robbie was lashing out and was depressed and angry about not being included in Randy's affairs. Dee now agrees that they should never have kept Randy's detainment from Robbie, but at the time they thought they could protect him. They told him the story. They gave him his very own journal to be able to write to his big brother. This could be a private journal or he could choose to share its contents, but this was his decision. This helped greatly and now the whole family could share their true emotions and pain ... together.

Children often sense that something is wrong, but they don't understand what's going on and so they get confused. They absorb the emotional turmoil around them and worry even more when they feel they aren't allowed to ask questions. Keeping a diary or journal to record what we are feeling is an excellent way of letting out the anger and frustration. Feelings, no matter how painful, should be felt, not locked away, or they will only fester.

Dee and Robin kept encouraging Colbie and Robbie to write to

Randy, to tell him the exciting and not so exciting things that happened in their week.

On 11 August 2007, Randy informed the Canadian consulate that he was joining several other prisoners on a hunger strike to protest the violations of his human rights. His family was naturally fearful and took the news as an admission that Randy was giving up. Five years in a Vietnamese jail was obviously taking its toll.

Talks of hunger strikes, however, won't get him any closer to home. He cannot force the hand that holds him there. All too often Westerners think they can apply Western logic to every situation, but it doesn't work like that. Randy must learn to accept the things he cannot change or he will live in torment. He needs to conserve his energy to survive. He needs not to follow others because there is no safety in numbers. Randy must be humble. He must show his captors that he has learnt his lesson. He must not keep fighting against these authorities. He will never win his freedom that way. For now, he has to endure his imprisonment minute to minute, and just survive.

It can be frustrating for families to feel as if nothing is happening while the world continues to move forward.

Randy doesn't want his family to visit him. He doesn't want them to see his pain. He doesn't want them to see him struggling to disguise his pain. Randy must be patient. His family must be patient. They must all focus on maintaining their health, their sanity, their control. His mother says:

> *Isolation from Randy has been the most painful experience of my life. He will not allow me to visit him in Vietnam. He says he doesn't want that image in my mind, the squalor of where he is detained. Not being able to hug him and tell him that we love him unconditionally rips my heart apart every single day. Not being able to look into his beautiful blue eyes, hear him laugh, smell his cologne or yell at him to stop teasing Colbie and Robbie, are the things that I miss.*
>
> *My guts churn when I think of the last five years of our lives, Colbie and Robbie's lives in particular. They have watched me become consumed with Randy's case. They have watched me fight depression without medications. They have seen my fingernails fall off due to stress. They have watched my long hair fall out by the handful. I was put on medical stress leave until I could regain my physical health. Colbie and Robbie feel sad, angry and helpless as well, not being able to control or understand this.*
>
> *I have become so very serious now. I feel very guilty enjoying life when I*

> know what kind of a life Randy will have to endure for the next 11 years. Some days it takes all my strength to dig deep in my soul and just get out of bed. On those days, I tell myself that I still have two beautiful young children here who desperately need their mother to be strong and take care of them. I would definitely be locked up in a rubber room if I did not have Colbie and Robbie. They are amazing lifelines for me, and as well for Randy. Colbie and Robbie are still dealing with anger issues. They cry and desperately miss their brother, everyday. They look at their pictures with Randy and see the physical changes and growth in themselves. They wonder how old they will be when he comes back home. They wonder if Randy will be home for their high school graduations or their weddings. They wonder how Randy will have changed. They worry that he is frightened and all alone. They still wonder if he will come home alive or dead. They find it difficult sometimes to tell their new friends about their big brother's incarceration.
>
> Embarrassment of his grave mistake weighs heavy with Colbie. Being a gorgeous teenager these days is difficult enough, without having to deal with this kind of stress.'

Dee says her two children have had so much to deal with since their brother's incarceration and life has been an emotional roller-coaster for them.

> Holidays are depressing for us all who love Randy. He is constantly included in our thoughts, prayers and funny little memories that we all cherish. We have tried to learn new ways to cope with this trauma like looking at his photos and going to some of his favourite places like Manitoulin Island, our family cottage, shopping in Toronto, ice fishing and dancing. We all make a big deal out of eating rice, as Randy has sustained himself on two cups of rice a day for five years now. Colbie and Robbie never waste food or water, as they know how thirsty and hungry Randy is everyday. We appreciate each other more often now. I too have learned that I am not alone in my despair and that there is a network of distraught families who are experiencing the same situation. I must remain determined to bring my son home safely. I forgive him for making this huge mistake. I will be here to help him heal when he comes home. I will continue to be thankful for all the good days we have and to remember how very fortunate we are to have such a close-knit and loving family. My circle of friends are heaven sent and I will always be grateful to them for their understanding. Along the way, I have also

made many new friends because of Randy's incarceration, including other mothers in the same situation. I have experienced one mum's jubilation when her son was released from Thailand after six years of a life sentence. The courts acquitted him of all charges. I will always cry happy tears for Lorna Aggett, knowing that she endured the pain of having her son detained in a foreign prison. I have faith that this long, winding road will have an end and that like Lorna and her husband Tony, I too will get my son back!

Another year is coming to a close. Another Christmas that Dee and her family don't want to face. The thought of hanging Randy's stocking on the mantelpiece depresses her, along with the photographs she dusts that reveal how much they have all changed while Randy's photo remains just as it was when he left. Dee often wonders how she will cope.

'I will go to the midnight service at the church alone and pray as hard as I can for this nightmare to finally end. It's all I can do now. There's really no point blaming myself or anyone else for the choices my son made. I can only hope that he will come home and perhaps something good will come from all this suffering!' says Dee.

30 August 2009, Randy's family received the news that he would finally be repatriated to Canada.

On 17 September 2009, Randy arrived home!

It was the miracle they'd all been praying for.

20
Zambian orphans

Gilbert Mwamba, Zambia

The death penalty creates orphans. It robs children of their fathers and mothers, of their primary carers.

Zambia in southern Africa experiences relatively high orphan rates. The practice of capital punishment further exacerbates the crisis. In Zambia, there are over 11 million orphans—children under the age of 15 who have been robbed of one or both parents, usually through drought, flood, food shortages, malaria or HIV/AIDS. The issues affecting these children are well documented through United Nations reports. The leading killer of children in Zambia is malaria. And many are born with HIV as a result of mother-to-child transmission. At least 50 per cent of children under the age of five are affected by malnutrition, anaemia and vitamin A deficiency. Zambia's healthcare system faces severe shortages of drugs, equipment and qualified personnel, especially in rural areas. Only 36 per cent of the rural population has access to improved drinking water.

The government in Zambia has endeavoured to improve the economic outlook, but many Zambians are still forced to live on less than $1 a day. As a result, many Zambians have turned to extreme survival strategies, including high-risk behaviour such as exchanging sex for food or cash. They may also steal for survival, which may, and often does, result in lengthy prison sentences. Zambia has the death penalty. Capital punishment is frequently used for crimes of survival, though they are crimes nonetheless.

When the sole provider of the family is imprisoned, the family falls into an even deeper and more desperate economic struggle.

In many parts of Zambia, people are eating what people have never eaten before. Things like the soft tree leaves or soft tree roots. The only news sources is the radio, and the only news is hunger.

One prisoner writes:

Although I am here in prison, I feel I am doubly oppressed. I am thinking about my children because hunger can claim their lives at any time as they under the care of my ageing mum who is not doing anything at all. My wife divorced me while I am here in this prison and dumped my children on my aging mum. At this time I don't know where my wife is. I am requesting anyone to assist my children. If you scan the internet about hunger you will believe me that Zambia is facing starvation. To us prisoners, our government does not consider us as their fellow human being. We eat once per day, breakfast, porridge without sugar, daily. What do our children eat? Many of us are sorry that our lives have come to this.
—Costa, a death row prisoner in Mukobeko Maximum Security Prison, Zambia.

So where does this leave their children?

About two years ago, I became aware of Reverend Gilbert Mwamba who heads the New Life Community School and Orphanage in Zambia. He himself was once a prisoner in Zambia—a thief in fact—and had spent more than five years behind bars. It was during his incarceration that he found God and turned forever from the destructive path he was on.

In 2004, he began the Zambia Ultimate Prison Ministry, which was developed to identify the social, spiritual and physical needs of the Zambian prisoners. He pledged to raise awareness about the plight of inmates in Zambia in order to maximise community support while prisoners were detained and following their release. Those, of course, who would be released and not die from disease or death row sentencing.

Reverend Gilbert committed himself fully to this need. He extended the program into other areas of Zambia and was met with an outcry from prisoners who had thought life had well and truly forgotten them.

Reverend Gilbert was transforming lives. He was giving back hope to those who were walking that same self-destructive path that he had walked. He developed programs under the school of discipleship and offered intensive discipleship courses for inmates, prison leadership seminars and one-to-one discipleship.

Before too long he came across the sad reality that many of the inmates to whom he was ministering had orphaned children scattered all over Zambia.

Reverend Gilbert decided to take them into his care. By this time he had married and had the support of his loving wife Mary. Together they began to build new dreams and, in doing so, gave hope to children currently living without it.

> *The children in our care are housed in a small three-bedroom style house that I manage to provide through the salary I receive from my congregation. I am afraid the house is in a very bad state because there are no toilets or proper bathroom facilities. We do not have the money to install them and we cannot get money from the government because this problem is endemic to Zambia. We use a pit-latrine. All of the children must sleep on the floor because we do not have enough room for beds and, of course, we do not even have beds. Each room accommodates between eight and ten children. It is not the ideal arrangement but it is far better for the children to live here, under shelter, then to be on the streets,* says Gilbert.

In fact, the children in his care don't get a proper education because there is hardly any funding available. But the level of education they do get is better than no education at all. Reverend Gilbert is able to offer tuition from grade one up to grade seven.

The standards are far lower than western standards, but provide a basic platform for the children to help break the cycle of hopelessness. There is no free education in Zambia. They do not receive any assistance from the government or world organisations because they are simply villagers trying to sustain their community. They must somehow manage by themselves and take responsibility to care for those in their community for whom there is no help available. They struggle to pay for the needs of the school and orphanage through generous donations from members of the church and from those who may hear of their efforts. Sometimes they do not know how they will continue from day to day. It costs about $1500 per child each year to provide all the essential care to give them a chance in life. Those who can afford it, try to take this responsibility on their shoulders, believing that if they help others who are struggling, even while they too struggle, then perhaps there will be a reduction in the poverty they face.

Everyone in the community is affected by poverty, and if they do not try to help each other then none of them will survive. There is no World Vision sponsorship for Reverend Gilbert's orphanage. They exist on faith and continue to pray for miracles.

Currently his orphanage is only able to care for the children aged five to 15 because they do not have the resources to engage more care mothers and staff. When the children eventually leave, they must go to some other institution, if there is a place available for them. Hopefully, they will continue on with their education up to grade 12, but that depends on many things. They depend on the availability of sponsorship. Without it they cannot possibly receive an education. If these children are fortunate enough to make it to adulthood and if they have education then they have job potential. But there are no guarantees. In Zambia it is very difficult to get a job. Even those who have better qualifications still find that there are not too many opportunities for them.

There are some who have acquired some valuable life skills through Reverend Gilbert's early intervention and they have a more positive outlook on life.

We try to strengthen their belief that if they have faith, and work hard, miracles will happen. I believe there are always miracles waiting just around the corner, but we must be patient.

Reverend Gilbert is a man with a vision. He is determined that the lives of the children of death row prisoners will not be bleak. By helping them gain access to free education, they will have a better chance of not ending up in prison like their parents. Education is the key to success in Zambia. It is not the guaranteed solution, but without education many children may be doomed even before they have a chance to live. Reverend Gilbert and those in his community are trying to help the children understand their situation and to learn how to cope with all the struggles that come their way. It is not their fault that they are poor or that they are orphans. It is not their fault that their parents are in prison or dead. He says:

I always feel humbled to receive a child into my care because I know that it is one more child that I might be able to help survive this life. There are times, however, when this work is a terrible burden and I must give some of the weakest back to God. I feel heartbroken when I must conduct the funeral of the orphan boy or girl who has not the strength to endure despite our best efforts.

'It is a sad fact of life in Zambia that many children will not survive. We can only do the best we can do and pray for miracles.'

Reverend Gilbert is just one of many thousands of caring individuals in Zambia who have accepted the challenge of seeking to overcome seemingly impossible odds. He is a role model, a living example that there is another way. Through his intervention and through the support of his congregation and caring individuals like Lori Hart and her son Ronnie, Clive Jacobsen and his team at www.prisoncare.org, there are now 26 children who know that they do not have to grow up to become prisoners. While 11 young boys and 15 young girls may not seem like a significant number compared to the millions of other children orphaned in Zambia, they nevertheless represent real lives, and lives worth saving.

There are, on average, about 62 more children that Reverend Gilbert is still searching for because he has located their fathers on death row and now has the task of tracking down and retrieving these soon-to-be orphaned children. It may seem to some like a drop in the ocean but Reverend Gilbert shares the view of many other caregivers in Zambia, that the orphans of death row prisoners must not be overlooked. They must be given the same opportunities as other children orphaned by HIV/AIDS and others deemed by the government as vulnerable children. They must be able to have hope and maybe even realise their dreams to become doctors, lawyers and teachers, so that in doing so they will give hope to the tens of thousands waiting in line for their chance of attaining those same dreams. If there is no hope, then there is no reason to endure. There is no reason to dream, and when there is no reason to dream, there is no reason to care about the future or those around you.

When people talk of the overwhelming crisis in African states like Zambia, they think the task of rebuilding lives is too difficult. They forget that the tallest tree once grew from a tiny sprout. Without a doubt it is an extremely difficult challenge to restore broken lives, and at times quite hopeless, but many people are doing the best they can, in the hope that it will make a difference in some way and to someone. Countless Zambian caregivers are now undergoing teacher training so that these children and others like them might be given some sort of education opportunity. The schools are often not much more than dirt floors and concrete walls, and sometimes not even that, but they are filled with the promise of hope. Here is one:

> *My name is Julius and I am 10 years old. My father is on death row for murder. I had no one to care for me until I was taken to the orphanage. I am thankful for every day because I can have my dream to become a doctor. I will then live to help others.*

This child, who has not yet lived out his childhood, already understands that his survival and his success will affect those around him. In many ways, he has the hopes of a whole community planted firmly on his small shoulders even before they are strong enough to carry such a burden.

Many children are forced to live on the street, if you could call it living. They become like rats that forage in waste bins for scraps to eat and sleep anywhere they can find shelter, usually in some filthy, dark corner that might offer them safety and some degree of comfort. They struggle in absolute poverty. They are susceptible to many dangers. A large number of them may even end up in prison themselves because of the challenges they face.

Imagine comforting a child who has been told repeatedly by their frustrated grandmother that they will be hanged by their neck if they keep asking the whereabouts of their father. This happens, and more, because the children are passed around the families when one relative can no longer care for them. They become an endless drain on an already weakened family structure, through no fault of their own. They do not understand why it is so wrong that they should ask where their father is or why he is on death row. Their father may have only been trying to help their family survive. That his behaviour was criminal doesn't register in their young eyes. That they miss their father is all that registers in their young hearts.

They cannot understand why it is so wrong to ask questions about why their mother has left them and now wanders the streets, selling her body for money. They do not understand why their grandmother is so angry with them or why she says they will be hanged for being so inquisitive about the whereabouts of their parents. They do not understand why she says that they must now leave her care and fend for themselves on the streets where danger lurks with every small step they take.

These children have not only been traumatised by the separation of their parents, but they face very real survival issues. They are also often emotionally scarred by the reactions of those who are left behind and given the additional burden of their upkeep.

These children often don't get the chance to laugh and play like children should. Essentially, they have become prisoners themselves, trapped by the circumstances into which they were born. They are forced to steal food in order to survive. They are forced to pay the price for being born into a country that cannot sustain even their basic needs. They must become both mother and father, in a world that every day threatens their very survival.

Despite the reasons behind some of these crimes and the all-pervasive destitution in Zambia, there is a cultural shame about committing crimes of survival. The children left behind are often told repeatedly that their mother or father is a worthless, no-good criminal, who deserves to die in prison. The children are told that as the children of criminals, they have the same qualities and they themselves will end up just like their parents—worthless prostitutes and thieves. The children's minds can be polluted with hatred for their parents, without forgiveness or compassion for their parents who have veered from the straight and narrow, but often in extenuating circumstances.

If a child is taught from an early age that they are worthless or that they have no hope but to become bad, then how can they possibly be otherwise? How does one shortcircuit this vicious cycle of poverty and crime?

My name is Babbrah and I am eight years old. My father is on death row for robbery. I have no one else to care for me. I live at Reverend Gilbert's orphanage because I have no home and no place to go. One day I want to become a teacher. My life is difficult but I hope God will make a way for me.

Children will not remain children for long while this cycle of poverty, crime, neglect and abuse continues. Parents can no longer protect their children when they are detained in the squalor of a filthy prison cell, sometimes for petty offences. Similarly, mothers who are forced by poverty into prostitution can no longer protect their children. It is also not uncommon that children are forced into a life of slavery and abuse.

After my mother died and my father was put in the jail, I went to my mother's mother. She died, so I stopped school. Then I went to my aunty. I was told that if I do not keep having sex with my uncles then they will throw me away on the street and there will be no one to keep me. So I keep quiet.

There is not a country in the world that doesn't face an uphill battle in protecting its most vulnerable members, its children. While it is difficult enough in affluent Western countries to protect, nurture and guide children, the pure desperation and struggle for survival present in developing nations exacerbates these issues.

In Zambia, the sexual abuse of children, especially orphans, is very common. Not surprisingly, families will go to great lengths to conceal this abuse. Children who attempt to report the crime are often scolded by authorities for being promiscuous. The community structure in Zambia encourages all children, especially girls, to be submissive to men. There is little or no protection for a victim of abuse, whether it be psychological, physical or sexual abuse. Child abuse is an often hidden crime. Perpetrators are rarely exposed for their crimes. Their crimes are difficult to prove. Sadly, many families, friends and associates often protect the more powerful perpetrators, rather than protect the vulnerable child. As such, the perpetrators remain free to continue abusing children, unhindered.

When the basic needs of a child are met, that child will then have a fighting chance to improve all other opportunities. They will have more choices and they will not be forced into prostitution or slavery. The challenge is to keep providing care to these vulnerable children, so they are given a chance to survive and improve their quality of life.

> *My name is Moses and I am 14 years old. My father died in prison while serving a life sentence for aggravated robbery. My mother died in 2005 from HIV/AIDS. This is a problem in my country because many millions of people now have this terrible illness. I do not know if I too will get it one day. I do not need many things because it is only important to be safe. I miss my parents very much and sometimes I cannot bear to think of them. I was left alone with no one to care what happens to me and I became hungry and thought that my existence would be finished until I was taken into the care of Reverend Gilbert. Now I have hope that I can become a lawyer to defend people like my father and people who cannot find help to keep them from death row. I am one person, but if I can succeed then I can help others to make a better life!*

Why should the children of Zambian death row prisoners not be given the same rights as any other child in the world—the right to safety and a meaningful relationship with both their parents? Why should these children not be given opportunities and facilities to enable them to develop physically, mentally, morally, spiritually and socially in a healthy and normal manner and in conditions of freedom and dignity? I contend that the situation of their parents does not and should not deny these children their basic human rights.

In August 2007, the President of Zambia, Levy Patrick Mwanawasa, downgraded the death sentences of some 100 prisoners to life, and then released 823 prisoners on a parole-like status from 53 prisons throughout Zambia.

The release of these prisoners came as a mixed blessing. While many prisoners have been reunited with their children, they also now need emergency assistance from Reverend Gilbert and others like him.

With support from their community and with the support that people like Reverend Gilbert give, these prisoners have a second chance to try to make the best possible effort to care for themselves and their children, without breaking the law.

Reverend Gilbert says: 'Consequently I have a lot of these brothers at my home. Most of them have been asking me for financial assistance for their transport to find their way back to their own villages. Others need clothes, blankets and food. I am trying to find them accommodation so that they can start their lives again. We have just started building a drop-in centre so that we can provide temporary emergency care. It is an incredible challenge but we will continue to do what we can because there is simply no other alternative in this life.'

We must never underestimate the power that each of us holds to make a difference to someone else's life—the smallest act of kindness has the potential to turn a life around! Through intervention, these children can rebuild their lives and embrace hope.

Children in Zambia may be poor for generations to come, they may find life a constant struggle to have even their most basic needs met, but if people take an interest in just one young life, it will create the starfish effect in Zambia.

An old man was walking along the beach, when he came upon a part of the sand where thousands of starfish had washed ashore. A little further down the beach he saw a young woman, who was picking up the starfish one at a time and tossing them back into the ocean. 'Oh you silly girl,' he exclaimed. 'You can't possibly save all of these starfish. There's too many.' The girl smiled and said, 'I know, but I can save this one,' and she tossed another into the ocean, 'and this one', toss, 'and this one ...'
—Randy Poole, the Starfish Effect.

Support Rev. Gilbert Mwamba and his Orphans
PO Box 35538
Lusaka—Zambia
Email: zupministries@yahoo.com

Prison Care
www.prisoncare.org

21
KEEPING THE PROMISE
Eugene Debruin, South East Asia

What could be worse than having your loved one detained in a foreign prison not knowing how to contact them, how to verify their existence or, if worst came to worst, how to learn of their final moments?

As it stands today, there are over 78 000 missing US servicemen from World War II, over 8000 missing from the Korean War, over 120 missing from the Cold War and over 1800 missing from the Vietnam War. Britain recorded losses of around 200 000. The USSR reported 33 million dying in German Prisoner of War (POW) camps in World War II.

Over the years I've had a great interest in POWs and those Missing in Action (MIA). My own great uncle died as a POW on the famous Sandakan Death March in Borneo during the war.

When my husband and I were unlawfully detained in Laos we met Lao and Thai POWs. Some of them had been detained 15 or so years. Their only crime was that they were accused of wanting democracy and freedom. No one had a clue they were still there, trapped behind the razor wire. Others were scattered in various other POW camps throughout the country.

I remember asking them about foreign POWs since quite a few US pilots had been shot down over Laos during the Vietnam conflict. I had always wondered if they were still alive. I was told that it would be highly unlikely. Too much time had passed for anyone to survive such appalling conditions, particularly an enemy of the state.

The general consensus by these Lao and Thai POWs was that all foreign POWs had perished in the death camps in northern Laos or in Vietnam, to where they had presumably been transferred.

One Thai POW had completely lost his mind. I talked with others in the camp about their experiences and quietly watched him scurrying from tree to tree, pretending to shoot at the enemy.

Another told me his incredible story. He'd lived in the village of Phonthong in Laos and was going to become a doctor. He ended up in Thailand as a refugee and then a freedom fighter. He had returned to Laos to help evacuate others to the Thai border. He was shot and captured by the Lao authorities in 1984. During interrogation, they broke his jaw and beat him against a tree for seven days. The police bashed his feet so he could barely walk back to the dark room from where they'd dragged him. The small, desolate cell was only one metre square, with no lighting, no bedding and no toilet was his home for the next 12 months. He survived. He told me that he dreamed of freedom and that's all that kept him alive. He wanted his family to remember him as a good man, even though he had no way of getting word to them that he was still alive in that hell.

Meeting the POWs in Phonthong made me realise that my own survival was more important than ever. One day I would share their struggle with the world.

To think that some prisoners might not ever see their freedom or families again is unimaginable. Most families who have loved ones detained in foreign prisons at least know where their loved one is. Even if getting to them is difficult, they can go to bed at night knowing that in the morning they can, if they want, write a letter. They can tell their loved one how they spent their week or who won the World Series in baseball.

They can share news about births, marriages and all the things that might help them and their loved one endure the long days ahead, until they are eventually reunited.

The families of POWs and MIAs are not so fortunate. They have nowhere to send birthday cards or letters. They have no contact with their loved ones at all. In fact, they don't even know where they are. They spend years searching for clues to their loved one's final days. Often over 20, 30, 40 years or more.

One elderly widow, who was married 10 years to a soldier who went missing, said this of her husband:

He went away on the tram and he just waved. I never saw him again.

Many such families agonise every day trying to figure out why their loved one never came home. One widow spoke for many:

I don't think we ever lost hope. I didn't. But I remember feeling cross at the pessimism expressed over their fate. I remember it upset me a lot. You see, I still remember! It's only now, talking about it. It was almost like betraying him even thinking he could be gone.

MIA/POW families hear that their loved one is missing in action or is a prisoner of war and they are initially shocked, but then, typically, they may spend years wondering when and if their loved one will be rescued or, at the very least, the remains of their body found.

Soon after I returned home to Australia in 2001, I was contacted by an American, Jerome 'Jerry' DeBruin. He wanted to know if I had heard anything of his brother, Eugene, who was captured by Lao military forces in the early 1960s. Of course, to most people it would seem ludicrous to expect me to have run into anyone who might have known his brother, but in Laos, where time is itself a prisoner, it is possible.

The Lao government had admitted holding American POWs following the Vietnam War and insisted that the US negotiate directly with them to ensure their release. The US has never recognised the Lao government since it illegally seized control of Laos in 1975. As a consequence, not one of the nearly 600 Americans lost in Laos (many of whom were known to have survived) was ever released.

Eugene DeBruin's family believe that American POWs are still alive in South East Asia and for the past 40 years they have searched for a trace of their beloved Eugene or one of his crewmen. They simply want to know what happened, so that they can finally put his memory to rest. Of course, the chances of Eugene being alive at 74 years of age are slim, but it doesn't make the situation any less difficult for his family. Perhaps the truth will never be known, perhaps it is too late, but for a family of a POW, the questions inevitably remain.

Eugene 'Gene' DeBruin was the second eldest in a Wisconsin farm family of 10 children. He was a quiet, unassuming person who was neither boisterous nor a troublemaker. He was honest, emotionally stable and felt strongly about helping others.

Gene was working as a 'kicker' (Air Freight Specialist) for Air America in 1963 when his plane was shot down.

According to various sources, including American government agency sources, correspondence with POW/MIA families, published sources and interviews through the POW Network and through discussions with the DeBruin family, Eugene disappeared over Laos on 5 September 1963, when his Air America C46 aircraft was hit by ground fire and crashed about two kilometres from Tchepone in Savannakhet Province. The actual loss coordinates were recorded as 164245N 106102E (XD250480).

Eugene DeBruin, YC To and three Thai nationals (Pisidhi Indradat, Prasit Promsuwan and Prasit Thanee) parachuted to safety, but were immediately captured by the Pathet Lao. The pilot, Joseph C Cheney, and co-pilot, Charles Herrick, were killed in the crash.

Later, the Pathet Lao photographed DeBruin and the four other prisoners and published a leaflet naming the five as their prisoners.

Numerous times during their captivity the entire crew was moved to different locations within Savannakhet and Khammouane Provinces. Once, in May 1964, the five escaped for seven days, only to be recaptured and returned to prison. Eighteen months later, two US pilots joined the five to make seven. They brought news of the outside world, including the assassination of President John F Kennedy and the build-up of American troops in Vietnam. Meanwhile, the secret war in Laos continued.

In early July 1966, Eugene and his six cellmates made another escape. However, only two of the seven, Dieter Dengler and one of the Thai nationals, Pisidhi Indradat, who was part of Eugene's crew, reached safety.

One report stated that DeBruin was killed in the escape attempt, but the Thai national reported that DeBruin and YC To were last seen attempting to reach high ground in a classified location.

Eugene's family was able to uncover a report that Eugene may have been alive as late as January 1968. His brother, Jerry, travelled to Laos in 1971 in search of information. He met Pisidhi Indradat who had escaped from Ban Houei Het prison camp with Gene. He said that they had been recaptured near Seno, 30 kilometres from Savannakhet, in an area that had been taken over by the communists at that time. He told Jerry how he and Eugene had been taken to a prison complex located in caves near Mahaxay. This camp had once contained a large number of Royal Lao POWs, but no Americans or other Thais.

In early January 1967, information about this prison complex, Ban Na Dene, was received by CIA personnel responsible for operations in Laos. They had devised a rescue plan which was successfully implemented on 7 January 1967. They rescued 53 prisoners—52 Lao and one Thai—Pisidhi Indradat.

According to unconfirmed intelligence reports obtained by road-watch teams, Gene DeBruin was moved to a POW camp at Muong Nong which contained seven other American POWs under the joint control of the Pathet Lao and North Vietnamese. While in this camp, Gene was strictly guarded by the North Vietnamese Army (NVA), given intense indoctrination lectures, yet allowed to talk to the other Americans.

According to these reports, in January 1968, the eight Americans were moved out of this complex by the North Vietnamese Army. The person responsible was Ong Lui. Their destination unknown.

Since the end of the war, live sighting reports continue to surface indicating Gene DeBruin remained alive well into the early 1990s and possibly beyond.

No one knows for certain.

When I was detained in Laos, the prison interrogators assumed everyone in the Western world was connected to the CIA. If a prisoner couldn't explain why they were in Laos, they were CIA. If a prisoner was deaf and mute (as one I met was), then he was obviously CIA. If a prisoner was crazy and couldn't string two logical sentences together (like Joe Hay, a Frenchman I met in Phonthong Prison in 2000), then he was clearly a CIA operative.

This paranoia was sparked by the Air America (AA) and Air Freight Specialist (AFS) pilots, Eugene Debruin included, who were amongst the first Westerners detained in Laos. AA was the CIA's covert airline and supported the frontline of unconventional war. AA and AFS pilots, like Eugene, flew 'black missions' all over Laos.

Eugene had been in Laos only one month and his mission was to deliver rice and freshly slaughtered buffalo meat to an outpost near the Vietnam border. No 'hard rice' weapons. (Hard rice weapons are things like ammunition, howitzer shells, rockets and bombs and 55 gallon drums of aviation gas). During 1970, Air America delivered 46 million pounds (20,000 tonnes) of food in Laos.

I don't know if Jerry will ever find out the truth about what happened to his brother Eugene. I believe that Eugene would have endured many great hardships and most likely he would have succumbed to the horrific conditions of the prison camps. Jerry, however, remains optimistic, yet realistic.

'On 5 September 2007, we began our 45th year in the search for Gene. We're both realistic and optimistic. The search goes on. The goal of finding Gene, either dead or alive, remains in crystal clear focus and is attainable,' says Jerry.

He continues to track various prisoners and people who stayed behind after the war. He is covering all possibilities to find out if Eugene is alive.

The US government established the Joint POW/MIA Accounting Command (JPAC) to account for all United States POWs and MIAs from all past wars. The 2008 schedule encompasses more than 52 recovery missions and 18 investigation-related missions. Recovery teams are led by a team leader and a forensic anthropologist. They travel throughout the world to recover those missing from the Vietnam War, the Korean War, World War II, the Cold War and the Gulf War.

Their continued efforts have given closure to many families and hope to those like Jerry Debruin. The search continues.

> *I will never forget the day we got that dreaded phone call in September telling us that Gene was missing. It was a real nice sunny day and none of us could believe what we'd just been told of'* says Jerry. *'In the minutes that followed, our family draped a map across the table to find out where Laos was.'*

My own mother did pretty much the same thing when Kerry and I went missing in Laos. She pointed her index finger onto a map of the city of Vientiane and allowed her eyes to slowly scour the endless, unpronounceable names of nearby villages, wondering where we were and if we were ever coming home.

Jerome DeBruin and his family are left to pore over similar maps, wondering if they'll ever find a trace of their Eugene.

> *All the prisoners took the same risks. All made decisions that ultimately led to their own fate, known or unknown. To the families and friends, all are heroes,*

whether fate allowed them to live or not,' says Jerry. 'Every day, my brother, Eugene DeBruin, and the others, are loved and missed by their families.

www.rescuedawnthetruth.com

Joint POW/MIA Accounting Command (JPAC)
www.jpac.pacom.mil

22
OUR RIGHT TO HUMAN RIGHTS

They affect our everyday lives

The value of human rights and human rights values mean different things to different people.

Some may see the right to life and freedom of thought and expression to be more important than the right to practise one's religion without fear of persecution, since in some countries one has the right to think but not to act. Or the right to choose who one marries, or the right to work a 38-hour week. To me, human rights values mean to confront injustice in support of human freedom. Having seen so much injustice in the world, I believe that it is vital to commit oneself to ensuring that all people have human rights.

> *We all struggle to transcend the cruelties and the follies of mankind. That struggle will not be won by standing aloof and pointing a finger; it will be won by action, by men who commit their every resource of mind and body to the education and improvement and help of their fellow man.*
> —Robert F. Kennedy, 1966 South Africa.

I believe that we have an obligation to contribute to upholding human rights, in both a global sense and within our local community. Of course, it is important to fight injustice and free the oppressed in the world, but we also need to question ourselves from time to time about what human rights mean to us, specifically. How do they affect our ordinary lives?

If all else in life fails, if we lose our way, our job, our sense of justice, our freedom, then what do we have that cannot be taken from us? What is the essence of who we are? It is our dignity. We should vigorously defend this dignity. It is our sole human right that cannot be violated, unless we let it.

According to the *Macquarie Dictionary*, the word dignity means the quality of being worthy of esteem or honour; worthiness; i.e. the quality of being highly valued.

I believe that dignity is the highest human value. But what is my value to society? How much importance do I place on my dignity? Is my dignity worth defending? These were questions I asked myself when I was unlawfully detained in a communist prison.

When I lost my freedom at the hands of the communists, I was humiliated. I feared losing control over my life. When I was tortured, I feared not existing. I did not fear death or dying. When I was thrown into a tiny cell where the temperature exceeded 100°F (45°C), I feared that I would be trapped in that place forever. I feared never knowing again the feeling of a cool breeze on my skin.

Even with my freedom stolen and my life taken out of my control, the one thing I felt could not be taken away from me was my dignity.

A person can only be humiliated if they allow that humiliation to take effect. A person can only feel shame if they allow that shame to envelop them. When a person has dignity and a person values that dignity then nothing, not even death, can take that remaining human right from them.

Cultivating human rights values, such as the preservation of human dignity, in our communities, is something we all must seek to do.

'Injustice anywhere is a threat to justice everywhere' said Dr Martin Luther King.

We all should seek to uphold the dignity of others. who are wrongly detained. We should not fear standing to defend them. Respecting the rights of others sadly, is something that appears to be disappearing in our societies. If this simple rule were adhered to, then a good deal of human rights abuses would be curtailed—but how lofty and unrealistic is that ideal?

An English philosopher by the name of John Locke, born in 1632, said that people should use thinking to search for the truth, rather than simply accepting the ideas of those in power, or the ideas of superstition and other unscientific beliefs. He also believed that it was the government's obligation to protect the rights of the people.

Unfortunately, issues such as taxes, inflation and the cost of living, all seem to feature more highly and more regularly on the political agenda than the issue of the protection of basic human dignity.

When we look back over the years to some of the world's worst violations of human rights, we ought to have learned many valuable lessons. Have we? Take the mass persecution of those 16 million Jews at the hands of Nazi Germany. They were tortured, enslaved and killed. In the aftermath of those atrocities, it became apparent to the world community that the price of human dignity was not clearly enough defined.

On 10 December 1948 at the Palais de Chaillot in Paris, the Universal Declaration of Human Rights was adopted by the United Nations General Assembly. It is composed of 30 articles representing the view of the United Nations on the human rights guaranteed to all people throughout the world. These guidelines, in their entirety, are designed to remind us all what it is to be human and how we ought to treat each other. They show us how we can achieve human dignity and how we can preserve it. Included in these guidelines is the International Covenant on Civil and Political Rights, the ideal of free human beings enjoying civil and political freedom and freedom from fear and want. The Second Optional Protocol to the ICCPR was created to preserve human dignity by abolishing the death penalty.

The International Covenant on Economic, Social and Cultural Rights was created to be the foundation of dignity to preserve freedom, justice and peace in the world, to ensure economic, social and cultural rights for all individuals.

Many other mandates have been written and disseminated by governments around the world, each one designed to support our human rights, our human dignities. Sadly however, these are not enforceable and are too often ignored, abused and violated. No matter where we are or who we are, we need to work to promote tolerance towards others and to truly care about the struggles that the person beside us may be enduring. We need to foster a community that affirms human rights, sees respect for people as the highest value we collectively share and honours their right to dignity. We must do what we can to build a culture of mutual respect for human rights.

We cannot assume that we are immune from human rights violations. Often, for our own sense of security, we need to believe that bad things cannot happen to us. We tend to view people who have had their rights violated somewhat suspiciously. We want to believe that if we live our lives well, we will not suffer the same fate. We want to believe that 'victims' have somehow contributed to their own situation, because if they haven't, that would make us vulnerable, and it is difficult to live with such insecurity.

We cannot afford to live in our community thinking that bad things happen only to bad people. Have you ever heard someone say: 'That could never happen to me!' 'She must have done something to deserve it!' or 'I never thought that could happen in my family.'

The challenge for us all lies in what we can learn from others and how we act on that. The challenge is to believe that our personal dignity and the personal dignity of others is truly the highest human value.

If a person is raised from childhood with their dignity intact, then surely that person will form the right image of themselves and the world. However, if that person is humiliated from childhood and throughout life they often lose their sense of dignity and their self-esteem will be low. They may or may not learn to value other people. They can either attract further abuse or externalise the pain they have suffered by visiting it upon others. It is a very difficult challenge to transcend primary victim hood (or secondary perpetrator roles) to heal and go on to live one's life with renewed psychological integration.

It is possible to manage prior trauma, but often the scars remain indefinitely. It is very easy for a decline in human dignity (as the highest human value) to pass from generation to generation, often compounding.

In contributing to the preservation of human dignity, we should never be afraid to ask for goodness to encompass our lives, or for good things to happen when we are in turmoil. We should never be afraid to ask for the seemingly impossible—to not be violated when our situation allows no immediate escape. We should not be afraid to speak out even though in doing so we may face uncertainty and persecution. We should not be afraid to stand up for those who need our help, even if it might endanger our freedom. We must never lose our compassion or inclination to help others in need. We must foster dignity in our lives.

Having stood at the door to death and waited for it to open and close on me, I can honestly say that the only fear we should have is the fear of giving away our dignity. We can lose our freedom, we can lose our life, but our dignity will remain long after we are gone. It will serve to remind others of what we believed in, what we stood for, and how we changed the world for the better.

United Nations Mandates and Treaties
www.un.org/rights

The Universal Declaration of Human Rights
www.un.org/en/documents/udhr/index.shtml

Australian Human Rights Commission
www.hreoc.gov.au/human_rights/index.html

What are Human Rights—Office of the High Commissioner of Human Rights
www.ohchr.org/en/issues/Pages/WhatareHumanRights.aspx

23
EXONERATED

Rickey Johnson, USA

During his 26 years of wrongful incarceration, Rickey Johnson has missed watching his four children grow. One was born just after he went to jail. According to the Innocence Project, eyewitness misidentification is the single greatest cause of wrongful conviction in the United States.

Aside from political prisoners I've known, who were generally only ever guilty of wanting democracy or freedom from oppressive totalitarian regimes, there have been a number of cases that I have either worked on or observed, where evidence has strongly suggested the absence of a fair trial or that the defendant was, in fact, wrongfully convicted and, in some cases, innocent.

Granted the percentages for wrongful conviction are not exceptionally high, as opposed to actual convictions that have been properly processed, however research shows that quite a number of innocent people have gone to jail and some have served and are serving extraordinarily long prison terms. It further shows that no judicial system is completely infallible.

It is imperative that we don't just push these issues to the back of our mind, thinking that we could never be affected by something so unimaginable. Wrongful convictions happen to ordinary people, everywhere throughout the world. They happen to people who are in the wrong place at the wrong time. They happen to legitimate foreign investors who follow all the rules of the country they may be operating in, but still fall foul of the law, at no fault of their own. Wrongful convictions also happen to people who may have been party to a crime, but were perhaps charged under the wrong penal code or sentenced in excess of the crime or, even worse, put to death.

If we are to support the notion that imprisonment is an avenue for rehabilitation and not simply a place to punish people, then we have to ensure justice is delivered fairly and appropriately. Sadly, it is a fact of life that courts don't always get it right. When it is our life or our loved one facing wrongful conviction, then it tends to mean something.

In the United States, a Louisiana man by the name of Calvin Willis was arrested in 1981 for the rape of three girls aged 10, nine and seven years old. In 1982 he was sentenced to life imprisonment. Most people observing the case would probably have thought that life imprisonment was too good for Calvin Willis. Many, I'm sure, would have wanted him to go straight to the gas chamber.

Issues can become complicated when emotions and innocent victims are involved, hence the need for a proper judicial process to ensure fairness, transparency and accuracy.

In 2003, having served 21 years for a crime he did not commit, Calvin Willis was actually exonerated through DNA testing and released from Angola Prison. Calvin Willis had spent half his life behind bars because the eyewitness had misidentified him as the perpetrator. The evidence was unreliable and, sadly, the real perpetrator was never found. Calvin Willis missed seeing his children grow up. He missed out on being a father and lost two decades of his own youth. He now has to rebuild his life in a world that must be completely unrecognisable to him.

When he went to jail, it wasn't compulsory for people to wear seatbelts. When he was released, it was. The 1980s were a time of tremendous population growth, in fact among the largest growth throughout the world in all of human history. Calvin Willis missed seeing the first Apple Macintosh computer introduced. Big hair and fashion changed drastically, as did music and culture. All these changes were indicators of how much Calvin Willis had lost.

When Calvin Willis left Angola Prison, he could have absorbed himself into the daunting task of rebuilding his life, but he knew, better than most, that there were others in Angola who had been wrongfully convicted too, despite the opinions of the impassioned lynching mobs. One such man was Rickey Johnson, whom Calvin recommended write to the Innocence Project to seek assistance.

The Innocence Project was founded in 1992 by Barry C Scheck and

Peter J Neufeld at the Benjamin N Cardozo School of Law at Yeshiva University, to assist prisoners who could be proven innocent through DNA testing.

Rickey Johnson had nothing to lose. He had lost so much already.

'I am not the man that did this rape ... all I want is to go home,' said Rickey Johnson to the media.

In 2005, Johnson's daughter, Lakeisha Butts, wrote a heartfelt appeal to the Innocence Project on behalf of her father.

> *My father, Rickey Johnson, was wrongfully charged and sentenced to life ... 21 years have now passed and my dad has been stripped from his children and family on a charge of which he is not guilty, while the real perpetrator of this heinous act was granted the priviledge of walking free and having the opportunity to be surrounded by his family ... We, the children of Rickey Johnson, need your assistance in exonerating our father.*
> Lakeisha Butts.

Over 212 people have been exonerated by DNA testing in the United States. A number of these were serving time on death row.

The Innocence Project carefully examined the Johnson case and in 2006 they agreed to take it on.

Rickey Johnson had already spent two decades behind bars for the rape of a woman in 1982 in the state of Louisiana. When the matter went to trial, the distraught woman had told police that a man, whom she later identified as Rickey Johnson, broke into her home at 1 am and raped her over several hours. The police had shown the woman an eight-year-old photograph of Rickey Johnson and photos of two other men from Many, Louisiana. In her testimony to the police, she claimed that she saw her attacker's face during the four hours he had been in her room, but she was not able to remember any distinct marks, such as Johnson's gold front tooth. Yet despite this, the woman identified Rickey Johnson as her attacker.

During the trial, the prosecution stated that the victim had contracted syphilis during the rape. A medical examination of Rickey Johnson showed that he did not have syphilis.

Johnson was then a young man of 26 who had everything to live for. He was convicted of rape, solely on the victim's identification, in January 1983 and sentenced to life without parole. He was transferred to Louisiana's State

Penitentiary, also known as 'Angola' or 'The Farm'.

Angola is one of the largest prisons in the United States with approximately 5000 inmates and over 1000 staff. It is located on an 18,000-acre (73 square kilometre) plantation in West Feliciana Parish, near the Mississippi border. Flooding of the Mississippi River is a constant danger. Inmates of Angola are generally interned for a very long time. The average prison term is 88 years. Most inmates have no prospect of parole. Most die of old age or illness and are usually buried at the prison cemetery.

The Louisiana Crime Rates for 1960 to 2006 show that there were 2957 cases of aggravated assault, 279 cases of forcible rape and 270 murder cases in 1960. By 1981, those figures rose to 16,325 cases of aggravated assault, 1782 cases of forcible rape and 673 murder cases. Then by 2006, the state of Louisiana reported 22,098 cases of aggravated assault, 1562 cases of forcible rape and 530 murder cases.

The majority of those detainees would have been justifiably detained. Those who commit crimes should be punished, removed from society and given every opportunity to rehabilitate. But just how many prisoners in the world are detained in the absence of evidence, fairness and proper judicial process? Even if the figure was one in every 100, then is that an acceptable ratio? Do we then accept that one train might crash in every 100? Or one school bus might go off the roadside into a raging torrent so long as 99 don't?

Does losing one innocent life justify the odds so we can proudly say that we found twice as many guilty people rightly convicted? Is one innocent even worth fighting for when the cost is often insurmountable and the time and effort all consuming?

Believing that a terrible injustice had robbed Rickey Johnson of his life, the Innocence Project team urged Sabine Parish District Attorney, Don Burkett, to allow DNA testing to prove Johnson's innocence. It wasn't until late December 2006, that his DNA profile was actually compared to the vaginal swab that was previously taken from the victim. The results revealed a match, but not to Rickey Johnson.

The DNA matched another Angola prisoner by the name of John McNeal. He too was serving a life sentence for a rape he committed in April 1983. Ironically, Johnson knew that McNeal was an inmate in Angola, since the two men were both serving life prison terms, but he had no idea that his life had been destroyed through some horrific deed committed by McNeal for which he had never been held accountable.

Perhaps it was fate that Rickey Johnson had met Calvin Willis, who encouraged him to write to the Innocence Project.

Without their support, police and prosecutors would not have been compelled to focus more on Rickey Johnson's case.

Sadly, a woman was still raped and who's to say that this horrific incident might have been avoided had the real perpetrator been brought to justice sooner. Imagine the victim's guilt in sending an innocent man to prison for half his life. Imagine her anguish at having to relive that horrible experience and go through another judicial process to bring the real perpetrator to justice. Imagine her guilt knowing that another woman endured the same hellish nightmare that she endured at the hands of John McNeal. Most rape victims feel a great deal of anger towards the person who assaulted them, and justifiably. But for all those years, that Louisiana woman would have been directing her anger towards the wrong man. It would be understandable if she felt cheated and then frustrated at having to go through the long and difficult healing process yet again.

'Anyone who doubts that our criminal justice system is stronger when we take steps to prevent wrongful convictions should take a close look at Rickey Johnson's case.' **Vanessa Potkin**, Innocence Project Staff Attorney.

Rickey Johnson had endured 26 years of hell knowing he had been detained for the brutal rape of a woman he had never met. What an incredible moment it must have been to sit and listen to a Louisiana judge exonerate him of any wrongdoing.

Rickey Johnson's joy would have been obvious to those observing, but if truth be told, it would also have been impossible for him to truly comprehend just how much he would have lost to Angola Prison.

What impact would that have on him in the future? Vanessa Potkin: *'Watching Rickey taste freedom for the first time in more than a quarter of a century is mind-boggling, naturally he was overjoyed, but the fact of the matter will always be that an innocent man spent two decades in prison for a crime he didn't commit.'*

According to the statistics recorded at the Death Penalty Information Centre, as of 12 December 2007, there have been 126 exonerations in 26 different states in America alone. Sixty-three of these were black prisoners, 50 were white, 12 were Latino and one from another race, not listed. The highest number of those exonerated (22) was recorded in the state of Florida, followed by Illinois (18) and Louisiana, Texas, Arizona and Oklahoma (eight in each state).

Since 1976, there have been over a thousand prisoners executed, and some of these may have been innocent.

Rickey Johnson was incredibly fortunate that he didn't become one of those statistics. He was given an opportunity to clear his name and have his freedom restored, largely because Sabine Parish District Attorney Don Burkett gave him that chance.

'I'll just take one day at a time. That's the way I learned it in prison; one day at a time. Wherever the Lord leads me, that's where I'll be,' Rickey Johnson said on his release.

Rickey Johnson became the tenth person exonerated through DNA testing in Louisiana and the 211th nationwide, according to the Innocence Project.

Johnson never knew if he would ever be free. He could have opted to commit suicide, but he didn't. He chose to survive, as did his family who were agonising on the outside of Angola Prison. They learned to cope as best they could by sticking together and never giving up hope that someday, the wrong might be made right. They were held together by their belief that Rickey Johnson was innocent, despite what the world said, or what the court decided. Despite the lynch mob, with their angry red faces, waving their placards, demanding justice for the innocent.

Unfortunately, Rickey's mother died in 1992. His sister Shirley died four days before Rickey learned the results of the DNA testing that exonerated him. Had Johnson's family the money to hire an attorney to properly defend him at the beginning of his nightmarish ordeal, then perhaps they might all have been spared a lifetime of anguish.

It is perhaps one of the saddest realities families face when their loved one is wrongly convicted, that they cannot afford proper legal representation to ensure the defendant's rights are protected and upheld. The struggle against a wrongful conviction often takes years, through numerous appeals and even then there is no guarantee of ever righting the wrong.

DNA testing can lead to revealing the true perpetrator of a crime, as happened in the Rickey Johnson case. It is not an exact science, however, as there is always a possibility that DNA evidence may be contaminated, misplaced or lost. And whilst it is not a perfect method of proving innocence, it certainly goes a long way to justifying why a particular case should be further examined or re-examined.

Of course, many countries do not allow DNA testing and others simply reject it outright.

Wrongful convictions will continue to occur because human beings are not infallible and neither are the courts. And while the majority of law enforcement officers are honest, there are many who are corrupt. Facts can be distorted. Evidence can be tampered with. Judges can be opinionated and biased to the detriment of the accused. Juries can be susceptible to misdirection. Courts don't always get it right.

Above all, regardless of innocence or guilt, we should concern ourselves that persons subjected to the law, for whatever reason, are brought to trial and convicted through 'due process of law', lest we wrongly condemn the innocent.

For those who have endured injustice there can be no turning back the clock and rewriting the life they've missed out on due to a wrongful conviction. Living beyond bars, knowing that they have been robbed of reputation, dignity and so much more than precious memories, is often harder to deal with than enduring the wrongful internment itself.

These lives are sometimes impossible to restore, but they deserve to be restored and sustained. The road to recovery can be an extremely difficult one. It takes both courage and determination to recover from any traumatic experience.

Many exonerees do experience a feeling of elation. Walking through that prison door, knowing it will be for the last time, is indescribable. It can also be incredibly daunting.

Loved ones thought to be waiting on the other side may have passed on, moved away to another state, or simply lost faith. Some families may have spent their entire life savings on legal expenses. They may have gone bankrupt, mortgaged the house or sold everything of value that either they or their loved ones owned, in order to win back their freedom. The costs some families face in sustaining their loved one, particularly when there's no clean drinking water are incredible. A simple bottle of water can easily amount to tens of thousands of dollars over a ten-year period of incarceration. All this significantly impacts on families.

An innocent person wrongly convicted of a crime is robbed of so much more than memories and personal mementoes. They suffer a great deal of mental anguish. They suffer humiliation, as do their families. Sometimes it is simply too much for them. Sometimes the families are forced to leave their community because of the shame they feel.

Exonerees and their families may experience initial jubilation in gaining legal justice but then plummet into despair just as quickly, when the realisation hits them of all they've lost; the friendships that cracked under the pressure, the stigma, the special occasions that can never be revisited. Their lives are completely shattered and, understandably, they feel victimised.

The exonerees may exist in their community, but it's most likely that they will always be known as 'that man who did this ...' or 'that woman who did that ...'

How do they begin to piece together their broken lives?

For some it becomes impossible. Counselling services may repair some of the damage, but, ultimately, exonerees face a long and difficult psychological struggle. They may experience terrible bouts of fear and anxiety as they wait for their mind and body to digest what happened to them. Every person processes their feelings and experiences differently.

When I was released from a communist prison after being wrongly convicted, I felt tremendous elation being free, but I also felt guilty about leaving friends I'd made behind. This soon transferred to depression.

Exonerees can plunge into a depressive state, become bitter, over-sensitive to everything around them, loud noises, large crowds, life travelling too fast. All these things can make a person want to crawl into themselves. Sometimes reality is unreal.

I hadn't driven a car for over a year because of that year I lost in a Lao prison. When I returned home, the first time I drove, I automatically went to the wrong side of the road. I was accustomed to the American system in Laos, which is quite different from driving in Australia. I had to learn to think in Lao Language because I had been detained in a foreign country and, in order to survive, I had to submerge into that language and culture.

Most exonerees—who have been detained for long periods in a foreign country—forget what it is to be British, American or whatever their nationality. They lose their sense of identity, surprisingly, quite quickly. It is true to say that no one who goes into prison ever comes out the same.

Anger is the most extreme feeling that exonerees face and anger takes a long time to get over, control, manage and resolve. The feeling of being cheated can be overwhelming. It's completely natural to feel intense burning rage about the violaton of rights which should never have been violated. We should never be hamstrung fighting injustice, but we are.

Many families, like exonerees, feel isolated emotionally because their experiences are often incomprehensible to ordinary people in their ordinary communities. Wrongful convictions impact on everyone, therefore everyone should be more involved in helping those who have endured such horrific, life-shattering experiences. The first step is empathy, the second, is willingness to act, the third, to become more aware and educated about these issues and, not least, to support those who undertake the fight against such insurmountable odds.

Bad things *do* happen to good people.

> *The Universal Declaration of Human Rights [Article 11]*
> *(1) Everyone charged with a penal offence has the right to be presumed innocent until proved guilty according to law in a public trial at which he has had all the guarantees necessary for his defence.*
> *(2) No one shall be held guilty of any penal offence on account of any act or omission which did not constitute a penal offence, under national or international law, at the time when it was committed. Nor shall a heavier penalty be imposed than the one that was applicable at the time the penal offence was committed.*

Innocence Project
To free the staggering numbers of innocent people who remain incarcerated and to bring substantive reform to the system responsible for their unjust imprisonment.
100 Fifth Avenue, 3rd Floor
New York, NY 10011
http://www.innocenceproject.org

Life After Exoneration Project
Address the injustice of wrongful conviction and incarceration by assisting

exonerees and their family members in re-building their lives on the outside.
http://www.exonerated.org

Death Penalty Information Center
An exhaustive store of information and scholarship regarding the death penalty.
http://deathpenaltyinfo.org

Justice Action
http://www.justiceaction.org.au/index.php?option=com_content&task=view&id=80&Itemid=360

Other links
http://forejustice.org/wc/wrongful_conviction_websites.htm

24
WAITING FOR A REPRIEVE
Linda Carty, USA

A black British grandmother who once sang for the Prince of Wales faces death by lethal injection in Texas unless her final appeal can persuade the US Supreme Court that she deserves a second trial.

The Mountain View Unit, for women on death row is an easy 45 minute drive from the more famous Texas town of Waco, where cult leader David Koresh and seventy-four branch Davidians, died in a fiery blaze following the 1993 shoot out with the FBI. The first woman to be executed in Texas since the US Civil war was Karla Faye Tucker. The most recent female executed was Frances Newton. She was executed on 14 September 2005 for killing her husband, Adrian, 23, her son, Alton, 7, and daughter, Farrah, 21 months. Capital punishment has existed in Texas since 1819. As of February 22, 2011, there have been 1,217 individuals (all but six of whom have been male) executed. Linda Carty stands to become the first black British woman to be executed in more than a century.

Born on the 5th of October 1958, in the eastern Caribbean island of St Kitts, Linda Carty lived as a British Overseas Territories Citizen, teaching children with special needs. She had a two year old daughter named Jovelle. Her daughter's father had emigrated to New York previously, leaving Linda as a single mother.

In 1982, Linda and Jovelle emigrated to the US to live the American dream. She pursued higher education studies at the University of Houston. It was here she was raped in the car park and which resulted in a pregnancy. Linda gave up the baby girl (born 23 June 1989) for adoption. Two months prior to giving birth, Linda's beloved father died. She was deeply distraught. Linda felt a deep sense of shame at her rape, and concealed the pregnancy from her family. Later, she found herself in an abusive relationship and was a victim of domestic violence.

It was when she was at university that Linda was approached by a police officer who she claims introduced her to an agent who was recruiting and running Confidential Informants (CIs) for the Drug Enforcement Administration (DEA). Linda was intrigued by the offer for her to become a confidential informant. With her linguistic background and knowledge of pharmaceuticals she must have seemed an ideal candidate. The work would be exciting, but certainly not without an element of danger. The financial incentives were an added bonus. CIs usually go deep undercover and tell no one of their role in the DEA. Linda's family would not know of her secret life, not even her daughter or her mother.

On 16 May 2001 Linda Carty's world came crashing down around her. She was charged with the murder of Joana Rodriguez, aged 25. If convicted, she would be sentenced to die by lethal injection.

Texas sentences more people to death than any other state in America. Up until 1965, prisoners were executed by the electric chair but the US Supreme Court deemed it 'cruel and unusual punishment'. Nowadays, it is all done by lethal injection and costs the state only US$86.08 per execution. As at December 2007, a total of nine females have been executed in the state of Texas as opposed to 362 males.

Linda's daughter, Jovelle, was studying political science at the University of Houston, following in her mother's footsteps to become a pharmacist. When Jovelle heard the news that her mother had been arrested, she was shocked. She was visiting her father in Florida when she got the call from her grandmother. She knew instantly that something was wrong, but had no reason to believe what she was about to hear. Her grandmother's tears were a dead giveaway that something was terribly wrong. Then she hit Jovelle with the news that her mother had been arrested for murder.

The drive to the Mountain View Correctional Facility in Gatesville, where Linda Carty is detained, takes four hours by car. Northwest of Houston on the edge of the Texas hill country, it prides itself as the sort of hometown everyone dreams of, full of friendly people and fond memories, set in beautiful surroundings, abundant recreational opportunities, low taxes and low crime. Jovelle would make that journey as often as possible.

> *I would have to travel four hours out of town to get there. I have to mail her a letter, which I'm not for sure she's gonna get. So I have to wait until the next time I see her to see if she received my mail.*

It would have to be one of the worst situations to be in, especially with the strong bond that existed between mother and daughter. Not being able to talk face to face but having to speak through a glass partition that separates you from your loved one, would have been horrendous. Not being able to take comfort in the loving embrace of a mother's arms would have been terribly distressing.

Knowing that your loved one is sitting in a prison is one thing. Understanding why they are is something else. Jovelle knew only the basics she'd been told over the phone. She knew her mother wasn't capable of murder, but did that matter to anyone? Did it mean anything to the jury that would decide her mother's fate when her trial eventually got under way?

Linda Carty may have lived in the United States for the past two decades but she was not an American citizen. In accordance with Article 36 of the Vienna Convention on Consular Relations, US authorities were obliged to inform Linda Carty's embassy of her arrest and detention. Somehow this was overlooked.

As a result Linda was forced to rely on a court-appointed public defender, Jerry Guerinot. Alleged incompetence from Mr Guerinot has already landed 20 of his clients on death row, more than any other defence attorney in the US.

According to the Death Penalty Information Centre, a number of foreign nationals have been executed since 1976 and in over 20 cases all indications are that none of these executed individuals were informed by US authorities upon arrest of their right to have their consulate notified of their detention.

In several instances, prisoners did not learn of their right to request consular assistance for more than a decade, by which time the treaty violation was considered by the appellate courts to be a procedurally defaulted claim.

The court appointed lawyer to represent Linda had represented defendants in 39 capital murder cases. Evidently, his record of success wasn't all that high, which made Linda want to change lawyers. The judge however refused an adjournment that would have given her family time to find a new lawyer and the necessary funds to engage that new lawyer.

The prosecutor produced three witnesses to testify against Linda Carty. Each testified that they broke into the apartment of Joana Rodriguez, assaulted the man living there and abducted Joana Rodriguez and her four-day-old son, Ray. Fortunately, baby Ray was later found unharmed. His mother, however, was found dead. Police recovered her body from the boot of a car. She had been gagged and tied up. She died from suffocation.

The three men named Linda as the mastermind behind the kidnap. They said she planned to take the newborn child as her own. State Prosecutors dropped the murder charges against them in return for their testimony.

Linda Carty was charged with murder, a capital offence in Texas. She is currently on death row.

Is it possible that there was something more sinister going on? Some people working close to the case believe that there *could* have been some connection between the murder and others who wanted revenge on Linda, possibly people she may have informed on to the DEA. Certainly anything is possible, but would the court grant more time to investigate these possibilities?

With the conviction in place, Linda Carty had few options but to appeal to the then Prime Minister, Tony Blair.

In March 2004, her daughter hand delivered a letter to number 10 Downing Street, the official residence and office of the Prime Minister of the United Kingdom. She pleaded for government intervention to save her mother's life. Linda's plight attracted a fair amount of media attention. The BBC news broadcast details of her dreadful situation, all of which supported the fact that she didn't get a fair trial because she lacked appropriate representation. British lawyer, Clive Stafford Smith, who has represented more than 200 people on death row, including British detainees at Guantanamo Bay, became aware of Linda's case and took a keen interest in it. Stafford Smith was no ordinary lawyer. He had worked tirelessly against the death penalty in the United States for nearly 20 years. He had personally witnessed the execution of six men, two of whom had been gassed, another two electrocuted and two killed by lethal injection.

Clive Stafford Smith was not only an outstanding lawyer specialising in human rights, but he also founded a UK Charity known as Reprieve, which fights against the death penalty around the world. Reprieve generated support that attracted the interest of prominent US lawyers and together they convened a panel of experts, including US death penalty lawyers and British lawyers, to work with Linda's local attorneys to prove her innocence. Reprieve also sent an investigator to Texas to continue the fight to save Linda's life. Clive Stafford Smith believes that Linda Carty was convicted of murder because her defence during her original trial was inadequate. In a statement he said: 'Up until this point, no investigation had been done on her case of any meaningful nature ... There are various appeals, but if you screw up the first one you don't get another chance in real terms because it all becomes procedural. In Texas, they just speed you on through to the death chamber'.

The prosecution had allowed evidence that should never have been admissible and crucial testimony that might have persuaded the jury that she did not deserve execution, was never called. The prosecution also said that Linda knew the deceased because they lived next door to each other. In actual fact, Linda lived two doors down and says she had no idea who Joana Rodriguez was. She says they'd never met.

There was no forensic evidence linking Linda Carty to the crime. Two eyewitnesses described four men invading the house. There was no mention of a woman.

The jury was not fully informed of Linda's undercover work for the DEA. It would have given her credibility had they known.

The DEA agent gave evidence, but only after the prosecution requested him to take the stand. He told the court that Linda had worked as a confidential informant for the DEA, but at the time of the murder she was no longer on the DEA's books.

When Linda's new legal team began digging into her case and poured over court transcripts, they were horrified to learn that crucial testimony of the DEA agent was never submitted. They interviewed him and made the grim discovery that he could have helped Linda's case. As for not being on the DEA books at the time of the murder, he confirmed that she wasn't, but that was not an anomaly. Evidently, it was a fairly standard practice for informants to come on and off the books. It wasn't proof that Linda Carty had killed anyone.

The DEA agent told Linda's new legal team that he did not think her capable of murdering anyone. Regardless of whether or not anyone thought she was guilty, under the law she had every right to be presumed innocent.

As of 13 December 2007, at least 29 foreigners are on death row in Texas, among them Linda Carty.

The prosecutor from the Houston District Attorney's office argued in the original trial that Linda knew exactly what she was doing, when he alleged she engaged the three men to kidnap her neighbour. He alleged that she had promised them drugs as payment, knowing they were involved in the drug scene. He painted a picture of Linda Carty that would send shudders down a blind man's spine. According to several media reports, he stated to the jury that Linda was afraid of losing her common-law husband and because of this she had plotted to kidnap Joana Rodriguez and then cut her unborn child from her womb. He described the surgical scissors that she had purchased to perform her cold-blooded act, but what he failed to disclose to the jury was that Joana Rodriguez was not even pregnant at that time. She had already had her baby. If Linda Carty knew the deceased as the prosecutor said she did, then why not just take baby Ray in her car and leave the state? In addition, the scissors that belonged to Linda Carty were not surgical scissors at all, they were blunt, round-bladed bandage cutters, the type that most people have in their medicine cabinet and clearly marked, 'not intended for invasive medical procedures'. If Linda Carty was intending to surgically remove the unborn baby of Joana Rodriguez, then surely she would want to remove the baby quickly to reduce the effects of foetal stress?

Had the jury all the facts, in all probability, they would have been hard pressed to return a guilty finding. Under Texan law, a common-law husband cannot be obliged to testify against his partner. Linda's common-law husband was called by the prosecution to take the stand. Little pieces of personal information were revealed to make Linda look even more suspicious. Her husband told the court that she had told him she was pregnant three times in the three years they lived together. He said that she had miscarried each time. He testified that by the third time their relationship was in trouble. The prosecutor brought it to the jury's attention that the alleged third miscarriage occurred shortly before the murder of Joana Rodriguez. Although the testimony of her common-law husband in no way proved that Linda had murdered Rodriguez, it certainly didn't help her case.

To investigate these and other anomalies in her case and trial will cost a considerable amount of money and resources. Her lawyers will have a great deal of work to do before they can appeal to the Supreme Court.

Linda Carty believes that everyone should be entitled to a fair defence. She doesn't believe in the death penalty.

> *There are too many innocent people on death row and nobody gives them a chance and nobody cares,' she says. 'I'm not really afraid of dying. I'm just pissed off that somebody decided I was guilty when I am not. Evidence was concealed and manufactured to put me here.*

Linda and her family can only remain optimistic that justice will prevail, but they are facing an uphill battle. Her daughter prays every day for a miracle. She has not given up fighting for her mother's life.

> *When I visit her she has to stay in a metal cage with a glass front. All I want to do is hug her and kiss her; but they won't even let me touch her.*

Linda has lost years of her life for a crime she is adamant she did not commit; and judging by the evidence, justice in this case may well have been blind. If Linda fails in her bid to prove her innocence and all appeals are exhausted, then the judge will issue an execution order and a date will be finalised for her actual execution. She will be moved from the general condemned housing area to a special area in the prison, death watch. This is the same area that houses the actual execution chamber.

In the final 24 hours before the execution, Linda will be given an opportunity to say goodbye to loved ones, attorneys and spiritual advisors. She will be provided her last meal before she is taken to her very last shower and told to prepare herself for execution. The witnesses will be taken to the witness room adjacent to the execution chamber. They will be told to remain silent. Linda will be escorted to the execution chamber where she will be strapped to a gurney and given a dose of sodium thiopental to put her into a deep sleep. This will be followed by a paralysing agent to stop her breathing and then, finally, the toxic agent to induce cardiac arrest. Linda Carty will then be examined and pronounced dead.

Linda appealed for a retrial in 2010, to the US Supreme Court, on the basis of her claim that she was given an inadequate defence lawyer during the original trial and that the UK government was blocked from providing support. The UK Foreign Office is on the record in support of Linda's claim that she had "ineffective counsel". Paul Lynch, the British Consul-General in Houston, called the conviction "a terrible failure of the system", from the moment the authorities failed to establish her citizenship, or notify British officials.

'In a further failure at the trial and before the trial, her defence lawyer should have gone to great lengths to find out what her nationality was. It didn't happen' Lynch said.

Martin Longden, a spokesman for the British Embassy in Washington, said the right to consular notification when British citizens were arrested in the US was 'a point of principle for us' and 'part of an individual's right to a fair trial'. He emphasised that US citizens arrested in Britain were guaranteed the same rights.

Linda sits on death row waiting for the final tick of the clock, signally that time for her has run out.

> *If I have to die, I pray that my family and my mum and my daughter will not look and feel ashamed of their daughter or their mother because I was guilty, but realises the state of Texas has failed me.... in that from day one, I was given an attorney that did nothing... didn't even bother to come to visit me... to find out the facts... he didn't even try to prove my innocence.*

Her daughter Jovelle continues to plea for her mother's life 'Please help my mum come home. To think of her not on this earth for something she did not do...makes it even harder'.

Reprieve
Representing people on death row.
http://www.reprieve.org.uk/casework_lindacarty.htm

British Consulate-General, Houston
http://www.britainusa.com/Houston

Fair Trials International.
To work for fair trials based on international standards of justice and defend the rights of those facing charges in a country other than their own.
http://www.fairtrials.net/

25
DO THE COURTS ALWAYS GET IT RIGHT?

Harry Bout, USA

> *Although legal systems vary from country to country, they are generally tied together by treaties that establish common principles applicable almost everywhere in the world. Our most basic legal right in a civil society is the right to a fair trial—the right to be tried by a competent, independent and impartial tribunal.*

Ordinarily we expect the presumption of innocence and the right to access to a judicial process compliant with national procedures, provided they are consistent with international standards. However, it doesn't always work that way. Sometimes justice is often very expensive and not always attainable.

Harry Bout is a Dutch man serving a life sentence in a Michigan prison without any possibility of parole. Under Michigan law, that means he can never be released from prison, without an order of commutation signed personally by the Governor of Michigan. No one convicted of first degree murder in Michigan has received a commutation in decades. Without court intervention in his favour, he will certainly die in prison.

Born in the Dutch town of Zeist on 19 August 1958, his parents moved the family to the United States and settled in Grand Rapids, Michigan. When Harry was eight years old, his father, Ulriech Bout, died from a massive cerebral haemorrhage. His death was completely unexpected and completely shattered young Harry. He remained close to his siblings following his father's death and throughout adolescence. Only Harry's two sisters remain living today; his two brothers are deceased.

Harry's mother remarried. Harry's younger sister, Linda, says that Harry found life extremely difficult growing up without his father's nurturing and loving support. Harry rejected his stepfather, but, regardless of any misgivings he may have had about this relationship, it didn't hinder Harry from growing into a well-adjusted, successful young man. He was well liked by many. He had more acquaintances than true close friends, but he was still loyal to the core. He succeeded in business, owned several, multiple unit rental properties and managed them on his own. He enjoyed all aspects of owning and renting these properties, and developed personal relationships with all of his tenants. He loved life.

Despite residing in America, Harry never actually became an American citizen because he loved his Dutch heritage. But even so, he loved living in the US, the land of so many opportunities.

On 7 March 1985, Harry Bout (26) and his girlfriend Dawn (17) went on a double date with their friend, Al Iwuagwu, and another woman, Vera Johnson. Later, after dropping off Johnson, the remaining three went to Harry's mother's house.

While Al and Dawn were upstairs, the unmistakable sound of gunfire rang out. Al Iwuagwu lay on the floor, dead.

On 4 April 1985, an arrest warrant was executed by the Grand Rapids Police Department arresting Harry Bout for first-degree murder. His girlfriend, Dawn, was also arrested that same day. The probable cause was based on a witness named Elvin Shaver who had participated in burying the body and implicated Harry in the crime.

On 5 April 1985, Grand Rapids police found a body encased in 400 pounds (180 kg) of concrete in the basement of Harry's mother's house. Authorities chiselled out the body, tentatively identified as Alphonsus Onunwa Iwuagwu, a Nigerian missing for almost a month.

Harry's sister Linda was obviously shocked by the arrest of her brother.

> We were in utter disbelief at the revelation of Al Iwuagwu's death. Even more unbelievable was the accusation that Harry committed the murder. We all knew that Harry and Al were very close friends and shared a unique personal bond. Harry did not have a multitude of friends, but the ones that he did have were long term. I immediately knew in my heart and mind that the accusation of murder

against my brother could not be true. Harry would never take the life of another human being. Though my brother had not lived a perfect life, because no one is perfect, he had strong religious beliefs about death and the hereafter. He may have committed many sins but he would not ever commit the ultimate sin of murder. I am certain of that.

The matter proceeded to trial.

Harry's girlfriend, Dawn, immediately claimed an insanity defence, saying she did not know why she had killed Al. The judge denied her request to be tested for insanity. She then engaged her third lawyer, changed her statement and alleged that Harry was to blame. In doing so, she avoided a custodial sentence. She testified that Harry had suggested that the three of them engage in sexual 'threesome' activity, which she agreed to and led the way upstairs. She claimed that Al and Harry followed her and in the upstairs bedroom *she* heard shots, and *she* saw that Harry had a gun.

Not a single witness, and there were numerous witnesses, supported her statement as true.

Local attorney, John R Beason, who willingly accepted the case and was retained as Harry Bout's defence lawyer, called Harry to the stand. Harry testified that he heard the shots while downstairs, he grabbed his mother's shotgun in a defensive action and ran up the stairs, partly in a state of shock and slightly inebriated, though not at all drunk. He called out to his girlfriend, Dawn, along the way to see if she was alright.

When he reached the bedroom, he said that his heart was pounding and in disbelief he saw his girlfriend beside Al's lifeless body. She was smoking a cigarette. The .32 calibre pistol was still in her hand.

Harry told the court what Dawn told him on that fatal night. She said that after Harry went back downstairs to get another beer, Al suddenly become violent and tried to rape her. So she shot him. Harry went on to explain the emotions that were coursing through him at the time and how confused he was when his girlfriend began begging him to help her cover up what she had done. 'She begged me to help her dispose of Al's body,' said Harry.

As a young man of 26, Harry didn't fully understand his reactions at the time, but over the two years that followed, he learned from a doctor that what he had experienced on that night was a rather common reaction to a traumatic event. Acute stress disorder results following a traumatic event in which the person experiences or witnesses an event that involves, threatens or results in actual serious injury or death. The response is generally intense fear and helplessness.

Harry panicked. He wasn't sure what to do, but he knew he had to do something. He called on his friend, Elvin Shaver, who was at the scene, thus making him an accessory after the fact. He suggested that they dispose of the body and pretend that nothing happened. Shaver, Dawn and Harry buried Al's dead body in the basement floor of the house. Harry and Dawn then moved the deceased's car to an airport parking lot.

Harry has since admitted to family and friends that what he did was very wrong and the most stupid thing he could have ever done. At that moment, when faced with the shock of finding his friend dead, coupled with his teenage girlfriend claiming assault and the risk to himself of being deported to Holland, Harry gave no thought at all to the consequences. It was a moment of complete and utter madness.

When Dawn turned against Harry in court, he was devastated. At that moment, the reality of his situation became clear, but Harry Bout has always maintained that he did not kill Al Iwuagwu.

Evelyn Schneider, an elderly woman who rented a room from Harry's mother, was in her bedroom at the time of the murder. Evelyn's bedroom directly adjoined the bedroom where the shots took place. She testified to the court that she had witnessed Harry Bout mounting the stairs, carrying a shotgun, *after* the gun shots rang out from the adjacent room. She also said he called out, 'Dawn, are you all right?' It was a known fact that Evelyn Schneider never stayed out at night or slept anywhere other than in her own bed. Harry Bout knew this.

If Harry Bout planned the murder, as claimed by his girlfriend, then why would he do so in his mother's house where he knew witnesses would be present?

Grand Rapids police officers, Sandra Arens and John Robinson, submitted a diagram of the house showing a wall extending in the way of Mrs Schneider's view. The police stated that Mrs Schneider's bedroom door opened inward when in fact, it opened outward. They suggested that it was impossible for her to see Harry Bout coming up the stairs from her room and that the door would also have blocked her view from her bed. These statements were completely false but the testimony of Mrs. Schneider was excluded.

Harry's attorney, John Beason, made an application on Harry's behalf for the jury to be allowed to visit the scene of the crime. Michigan law holds that, at the discretion of the trial judge, a jury can go to the scene of a crime.

Kent County Circuit Judge Stuart Hoffius refused the application.

Beason then called three people to take the stand, including Harry's sister, to testify that it was possible to see someone coming up the stairs and crossing to the room where Al Iwuagwu was shot, from Mrs. Schneider's bedroom. Seven different witnesses signed similar affidavits to that effect.

Since the jury was unable to view the actual stairway itself, due to the Judge's refusal to grant permission to visit the crime scene, they were inclined to believe the testimony of the two police officers. These same officers agreed that there was no evidence that the shotgun Harry carried that night was ever fired. In fact, it wasn't. The police testified that Mr Iwuagwu was killed with a handgun. That handgun was crucial evidence. It was never found.

The evidence was not nearly sufficient to justify a guilty verdict, yet Harry Bout was convicted on 14 August 1985 in the Kent County Circuit Court, in the State of Michigan. The verdict was first-degree murder and possession of a firearm. He would serve a natural life sentence plus two years' imprisonment.

Life without the possibility of parole.

Following the decision of the court, both Harry and his family were completely shattered, but determined to fight what they believed was a wrongful conviction.

US Attorney James Sterling Lawrence continued to represent Harry and submitted an appeal to the court for a new trial based on new evidence. Sterling Lawrence had uncovered a number of obvious inconsistencies and this convinced him that an injustice had been done. Harry Bout was denied access to a fair trial in the US. With the aid of technology, Sterling Lawrence began building a whole new case. He put together video and photographic evidence showing the approximate view Mrs Schneider would have had from her bedroom on the evening of the murder.

This demonstrated the viewpoint she would have had of Harry Bout climbing the stairs. He also engaged David G Townshend who went with him to the crime scene and compiled a forensic report which revealed that regardless of the location of the witness on her bed, she would have had a clear view of the bedroom doorway. If the view of the steps was impeded because of her position on the bed, Harry Bout would have been observable after he climbed the steps and walked from the stairway, past the open bedroom doorway.

The jury at Harry's initial trial was not allowed to view the crime scene which would have clarified differences in prosecution and defence statements. The prosecution's witness, Harry's girlfriend, was originally implicated in the murder or the subsequent cover up and received lenient treatment in return for her testimony. Under Michigan law, if a person knowingly and intentionally gives aid to a killer after the killing, but was not involved in the killing, that person is guilty of the lesser felony of Accessory After the Fact. Harry should have been charged accordingly.

Also highly relevant, but overlooked at the initial trial was the fact that Harry was a Dutch national and was denied access to consular officials. Harry's embassy was not notified until 27 October 1985, a whole two months after his conviction. This violates the Vienna Convention on Consular Relations (VCCR). The Act requires that foreign nationals who are arrested or detained be given notice 'without delay' of their right to have their embassy or consulate notified of that arrest. The notice can be as simple as a fax, giving the person's name, the place of arrest, and, if possible, something about the reason for the arrest or detention. The police must fax that notice to the embassy or consulate, which can then check up on the person.

Harry Bout was not, however, the first or the last foreigner to have his consular rights violated by United States authorities. A Panamanian citizen was executed despite an order from the International Court of Justice requesting a delay until the matter of the treaty violation had been examined. A Canadian was executed in Texas under similar treaty violations, followed by two Germans executed in Arizona in 1999. That particular case resulted in a World Court finding against the United States, claiming it breached its international obligations in regard to the Vienna Convention on Consular Relations.

Harry Bout sat in prison for many long years hoping that by some miracle, James Sterling Lawrence would uncover the truth of that night.

Having hired a private investigator, Sterling Lawrence tracked down Cecil McKinney, a friend of Harry's girlfriend, Dawn. He voluntarily provided his sworn affidavit that he knew Harry's girlfriend, Dawn, and that some time in either 1983 or early 1984, he had given her a dark blue .32 calibre hand gun. Cecil claimed that Dawn regularly carried the gun in her purse. He further claimed that Dawn confessed to murdering the deceased.

The autopsy report on the deceased revealed that he had been shot three times in the head at point-blank range with a .32 calibre pistol. It indicated that the victim would have dropped dead instantly on the spot where he had been shot after the entry of the first bullet.

Eighty-four-year-old Dutch national, Marianne Schut, began to hope that after 20 years of fighting for her son, the long awaited evidence had finally arrived. The court would agree to a new trial and her son would be exonerated from first-degree murder. Sadly, Marianne passed away in March 2005. Harry's confinement to prison prevented him from attending his mother's funeral. Then in October that same year, Harry's beloved aunt Elly also passed away.

On 10 February 2006, a panel of the Michigan Court of Appeals issued an order denying leave to appeal in the case of People v Harry Bout. James Sterling Lawrence expressed his sympathy to the family and explained that the effect of this ruling is that the conviction for first-degree murder is upheld and there will not be a full review of his case by the Michigan Court of Appeals.

No one denied the fact that Harry Bout deserved to be punished for his part in the incident, but the charge of first-degree murder did not fit with the evidence. Harry and his sister were hopeful that James Sterling Lawrence wanted to see justice served in the US Supreme Court, but getting the case there would be expensive.

Convinced that Harry Bout had been subjected to an unfair trial, two Dutch nationals, Sandra and Annabelle, began to organise themselves and the growing network of supporters in the Free Harry Bout Support group. They began fundraising to assist Harry's legal expenses. The two women also visited Harry in the prison and met with his sister, Linda, in Grand Rapids, Michigan.

Sandra and Annabelle also went to the house where the murder had occurred. They both saw for themselves that it was indeed possible to see someone mounting the stairs, just as Mrs Schneider described.

Despite their fundraising efforts, unfortunately, there simply wasn't enough time and money to proceed to the US Supreme Court. However, Harry, his sister and all those fighting for him from Holland, have vowed to keep fighting for justice.

Sabine Zanker, head lawyer for Fair Trials International, wrote to the Minister of Justice, Hirsch-Ballin, Dutch Attorney General, to bring to his attention the concerns of Fair Trials International in relation to the Harry Bout case.

Sabine wrote that it would be a grave miscarriage of justice for Harry Bout to serve a life sentence for what Fair Trials International believes to be an unsafe conviction. Further to this, she stated that Harry Bout no longer had the financial means to employ his current attorney or hire another attorney. He could not prepare or file his case himself so that the court could decide if it did in fact have merit. Harry Bout was not legally qualified to represent himself. In any case, the district court never considers pro per filed cases ('with the defendant acting on his own behalf'), to have merit. 'This leaves people like Harry Bout with no financial means in a no win situation,' Zanker concluded.

It is a common grievance among many families throughout the world that without financial resources, justice is sometimes unattainable.

Sabine Zanker urged Minister Hirsch-Ballin to consider the possibility of a prisoner transfer with parole conditions.

'I believe that the only option for Mr. Bout, apart from looking forward to a certain death in prison in many years time, is to have him transferred to Holland, where he would be released from prison at some stage. The Dutch government has the means by which to contact and urge the current governor of Michigan, Jennifer Granholm, to commute Mr Bout's sentence to one of life imprisonment with the possibility of parole, to allow him a prison transfer back to the Netherlands. The government also has the means to contact President Bush and request a pardon on Mr Bout's behalf. In both instances, I urge the Dutch government to use its diplomatic position and communicate directly and personally with both Governor Granholm and President Bush.'

The Dutch government's intervention is critical if Harry Bout is to obtain his long-awaited and deserved freedom, otherwise, given the standard life expectancy of a man his age, Harry will most likely serve another 20 to 30 years, and then die in prison. This surely is a cruel and inhumane manner to treat any human being, particularly when the evidence strongly suggests that a grave injustice has occurred.

Another prisoner in a similar situation to Harry Bout is hoping for a commutation or pardon from the governor of Michigan. Fredrick Freeman has served 20 years of a life sentence for first-degree murder. As in Harry Bout's case, there was no physical evidence to tie him to the murder. Freeman's case, along with hundreds of others, is being considered by Michigan's newly formed Executive Clemency Advisory Council, which makes recommendations to the state parole board, which makes its recommendation to the governor's office. The council's members represent crime victims, the public and law enforcement. Since the council's formation, it has considered 140 cases.

So far, 85 cases have been found to have merit and have been forwarded to the parole board. Subject to the parole board's review, the cases that they believe have merit will then be forwarded to the governor. Out of the 85 cases it received from the Advisory Council, 33 cases were recommended for hearing. Three public hearings have been held so far. The findings are not yet conclusive. The good news is that Harry Bout's family may still have a tiny glimmer of hope that with the formation of the new Executive Clemency Advisory Council, life may not necessarily be life in prison for Harry Bout.

The rather sobering news, however, is that he may still have a rather long wait to secure any review under the system. Currently, there are more than 300 prisoners detained in Michigan jails under the sentence of life without parole. The majority of these cases occurred when the prisoners were under 18 years of age. Quite a number of them have already spent over a decade behind bars. Some of them have committed horrible crimes for which they should most certainly be punished.

Many, such as the American Civil Liberties Union, believe, however, that there should be a mechanism in place, in the event they can prove their ability to become productive members of society. The justice system has a responsibility to protect the innocent and a duty to punish the guilty. In Michigan, it has failed to do either satisfactorily in Harry Bout's case. His sister, Linda, continues to fight, but has a low opinion of the criminal legal processes that tried and convicted her brother. She believes, and rightly so, that there were obvious inconsistencies that led to the conviction of her brother.

The legal process works, but only if the system has integrity. If the real perpetrator did in fact walk free and it could be proved, then it would, without a doubt, have broad-ranging effects. It could mean a whole new trial. The family of the deceased would be forced to relive that tragic event. The emotional cost to the deceased's family, the wrongly convicted and their family, would not be quantifiable.

In 2007, Elvin Shaver finally confessed that his previous statements and testimony in the case of The People of the State of Michigan v Harry Bout were not the truth and that he made such false statements under duress. His recent affidavit was made because he could no longer remain silent. He further stated that the officers of the Grand Rapids Police Department and the Kent County Prosecuting Attorney's office in Grand Rapids, Michigan, had coerced him into testifying against Harry Bout in order to be charged with the lesser crime of accessory to murder (see www.freeharrybout.org).

> *1. On or about April 5th, 1985, I was taken into custody by detectives of the Grand Rapids Police Department, along with my then wife Carol Shaver, for questioning in connection with the disappearance of Onunwa A. Iwuagwu (hereinafter Al). At the time I was about 1 year out of federal prison for counterfeit money, and on parole. During questioning the detectives told me they were certain Harry Bout had something to do with Al's disappearance and heard Al had been killed. They threatened they would violate my parole and send me back to prison if I didn't cooperate.*
>
> *2. During the course of questioning I told the detectives Al was dead, and I led them to where Al's body had been buried. By doing this I incriminated myself as being an accessory after the fact of Al's murder (a felony) violating my own parole on top of being a 4th felony habitual criminal offender (said charge carrying a sentence of life imprisonment).*

In 2008, Harry is uncertain about what to do. He does know, however, that seeking justice ultimately comes with a hefty price tag. It takes an incredible amount of money to keep fighting cases of wrongful conviction, money he doesn't have. The courts seldom want to reopen these cases, especially when two decades have passed and a win against the court might just result in a sizeable claim of compensation.

Harry Bout has been incarcerated for more than 22 years. He was previously detained in Alger Maximum Correctional Facility in Munising, Michigan, for almost nine years. He is now detained in the Carson City Correctional Facility. He is rarely permitted to leave his one-man cell and usually stays 23 or 24 hours inside. He has filed several lawsuits against the Department of Corrections, in a bid to restore certain rights that have been denied him. As a losing party, Harry was ordered to pay US$6,000 in court costs. Since he has no income, he has no means to pay.

Harry's properties were foreclosed upon due to his continued incarceration. His wife and children were left destitute. His family's lives were changed forever.

It is true that a terrible crime was committed on 7 March 1985. It is true that the perpetrators of that crime should be punished. It is also true that a man was found guilty in the absence of a fair trial. The right to a fair trial is an essential right in all countries respecting the rule of law. It is explicitly proclaimed in Article Ten of the Universal Declaration of Human Rights, the Sixth Amendment to the US Constitution, and Article Six of the European Convention of Human Rights, as well as numerous other constitutions and declarations throughout the world.

Harry's sister Linda writes:

> *My brother has been unjustly imprisoned since 1985. He is now in his 23rd year of this wrongful conviction. The evidence in his case clearly proves that he could not have committed the crime, as convicted. He is innocent. An absolute travesty has occurred here in more than one aspect. I believe the Grand Rapids Law Enforcement and judiciary conducted themselves inappropriately and should be investigated. They failed to properly safeguard my brother's rights or investigate the facts and nor did they allow vital evidence to be presented at trial. Harry still continues to suffer excessively for his assistance in the cover up. He can't undo the tragedy of that terrible night or the part he played, but he has lived with the guilt and regret for over two decades. Knowing my brother as I do, he will never fully forgive himself for his foolishness of that night. The actual perpetrator of this senseless murder continues to walk free and, most importantly, true justice has not ever been afforded to the victim and his family. My prayer here is that each issue will be addressed and that each wrong ultimately will be righted and my brother will be exonerated and released. I have 23 years of faith that this will surely come to pass. It does not matter how long this takes, just so long as it eventually happens. This would be the true definition of justice.*

http://justiceforharrybout.blogspot.com/p/harry-bout-story.html

Harry Bout
Ionia Max. Correctional Facility (Medium Level)
1576 W. Bluewater Highway,
Ionia, MI 48846

The email address of the **Friends of Harry Bout** who run the website is:
Justiceforharrybout@gmail.com

26
A Mother's Love Lights The Way!

Patricia Gerber, South Africa

'Our lives begin to end the day we become silent about things that matter' –
Martin Luther King Jr.

'My son was just twenty when his whole world and ours was shaken to the core. I have vowed to tell the world what I have seen and heard. I'm waiting still for his return'—Patricia Gerber.

Patricia was born into a typical, closely knit, working-class family in Port Elizabeth, South Africa's second oldest city and the commercial capital of the Eastern Cape. Her father, a loving man, worked at the railways as a steam locomotive driver. His wife, a devoted stay-at-home mum. Patricia's childhood was happy and based on the Christian beliefs of 'do unto others what you would have them do unto you'.

When Patricia married Johann Gerber Senior she too wanted to give her children that same loving home she had enjoyed as a child. After a short stint as a career woman, Patricia became a stay-at-home mum just like her mother to the couple's four children. They lived in the quaint and sleepy country town of George, that lies halfway between Cape Town and Port Elizabeth along a 10-kilometre plateau between the majestic Outeniqua Mountain to the north and the Indian Ocean to the south.

The Gerbers built a stable family environment for their four children. Johann Snr worked in the IT industry. Their children succeeded in their careers in nursing, engineering and management. Patricia Gerber was happy and life was good.

That was, until on Wednesday 31 August 2005 at 3.15pm, when she received a phone call from the Department of International Relations and

Cooperation (DIRCO, formally Foreign Affairs). Her 20-year-old son Johann, had been arrested at the Maritim Hotel in Mauritius with 920 grams of heroin. Police claimed that he had 92 pellets of heroin in his stomach. They said they had received a tip-off when Johann arrived in Cape Town, and were alerted when he was collected at the bus station and taken to the hotel. Over the next three or four days, they claimed he swallowed the drugs in bullets. Each bag contained 10g of heroin.

Patricia could not believe what she was hearing—her son was working for a drug syndicate? It was preposterous! It was also very late in the afternoon, which left no time for her to do much of anything. Johann Snr returned home from work to a very distraught Patricia. Tears stained her cheeks as she looked up to her husband's grim expression, the telephone still gripped by her shaking hand.

'I was devastated. I felt helpless, as if my world was crumbling around me. I didn't know where to begin. I was shell shocked, shaky and speechless. I didn't know whether to cry, or whom to phone or how to contact anyone, especially not how to get hold of my son. My immediate reaction was that my boy is so alone and I don't have any idea how he is or where he is, or whether he has food or whether he was safe? I needed to find these things out and quickly. I needed to know who paid for his airfare and the bus trip to Cape Town [a 5-hour drive from George]. Should I get on a plane? Should I go to Mauritius? Where would we get the money to pay for all this?'

Mysteriously, the night before, Patricia had dreamed that she was all alone in a raft out in the ocean, in the dark with the giant waves swamping her. She became afraid as she cried out to the Lord for help. In her dream the response was to climb into the boat that appeared next to the raft.

'I woke up with a terrifying sense of foreboding. Something was going to happen but I did not know what,' she said.

The very next day her dream became a reality!

On Friday 2 September 2005, when speaking over the telephone to a staff member at the South African Embassy in Mauritius, Patricia was told 'Your son has been framed, there is nothing you can do, so don't even think of getting on a plane because this country has its own laws'.

The line went dead.

'What will we do?' she cried to a pasty-looking Johann Snr.

Beau Bassin Mens Prison had no public telephones. Johann and Patricia were completely cut off from their son. They couldn't ask him what was going on or how he'd come to be caught with heroin in his possession or even if he had heroin in his possession. Were the police telling the truth? Was any of it real?

The couple immediately fired up their home computer and began searching for details of their son's arrest but nothing registered. In their search they did, however, discover that there were over 30 other South Africans detained in the holiday island. Most of them were still awaiting trial; some had been waiting for as long as five years. Most of them were women.

'If our authorities knew its citizens were taking drugs out of the country why did they not stop them before they boarded the plane?' Patricia asked the Department of International Relations and Cooperation. 'And why must we not investigate what's going on? If our son is involved, as you say, then we have to find out how he got involved, surely? We have that right don't we?' she begged.

Patricia was told that doing their own investigations could be dangerous, particularly since the matter involved a drug syndicate.

'A drug syndicate? Johann Jnr involved in a drug syndicate?' she choked on the words as soon as they were spoken.

'Please calm down, Mrs Gerber,' said the officer from Foreign Affairs.

'Calm down? I've just been reading in the newspapers that the Mauritian Police ADSU (Anti Drug Smuggling Unit) waits for South Africans at their airport after they receive tip-offs from our Government's Organised Crime Drug Unit, and you want me to calm down, knowing my son has somehow been caught up in all of this?' she responded.

'Best you leave everything to us Mrs. Gerber,' the officer said with finality. Patricia found herself in a no-win situation. She was getting very few answers from the authorities and what she did learn made her feel sick. Her son had received no legal counsel, or advice or even a visit from the South African High Commission to Mauritius. Further to this, he was being held in solitary confinement, in a dark cell without a window or electricity.

For the next two months, Johann and Patricia scrimped and scraped together enough money for a single return airfare to Mauritius. Even with the help of their other three children they couldn't afford two airfares. Johann Snr and Patricia made the agonising decision that she would go for both of them. This mother of four had never travelled alone to a foreign country before. She didn't know a single soul in Mauritius, other than her son.

They searched online and found a relatively cheap apartment for rent which they calculated would be less expensive than a hotel. But with Mauritius being an island tourist destination, she would have to pay for the accommodation in either US dollars or euros. The South African Rand was very weak against these currencies, which further increased the costs. Patricia also discovered that she would not have enough money to afford the travel to and from the prison by taxi. She would have to catch four buses.

'I'll just have to manage,' she said reassuringly to Johann Snr.

Leaving behind her husband, family and all things familiar was going to be extremely difficult but it had to be done. Someone had to get some answers. Someone had to tell their son that help was on the way.

Arriving in Mauritius, the first thing Patricia noticed was the enormous difference in humidity. 'It felt as if I couldn't breathe,' she recalls.

Travelling through the streets of Mauritius to her accommodation in the township of Flic en Flac, her eyes barely drank in the beauty that surrounded her. According to the Lonely Planet guidebook, Flic en Flac is said to be a corruption of the old Dutch name Fried Landt Flaak (meaning 'Free and Flat Land'). Patricia's apartment was nestled in one of the high-end hotel areas, but was far from picture-postcard. The accommodation was best described as rudimentary and the suburb was stricken with surrounding poverty and high crime rates.

Beau-Bassin Central Prison accommodates the largest number of detainees in Mauritius. According to some reports, over half its prison population have not been officially sentenced. It is a maximum security prison which came into operation on 1 May 1887. It's the prison where every man sentenced to imprisonment is sent and then depending either upon the nature of his crime, his previous offences or his police record, he may be transferred to another penal institution. Johann Jnr was somewhere in Beau-Bassin.

The very next day Patricia wasted no time in going to see her son.

'I hailed every bus I could find on the road and asked whether they could take me to the prison,' she says.

After multiple failures she finally found the correct bus. It would take her halfway there, after which she had to repeat the process to find the final bus that would take her the rest of the way.

It took me two hours to travel the distance to the prison. I felt lost, I didn't know my surroundings, I was emotional, yet excited to be going to see him. I could not speak French or Creole and communication in English was difficult at the best of times. I was told they don't understand English, which was strange as Mauritius had been a British colony for over a hundred years! I felt extremely lonely and isolated in Mauritius.

Arriving at the prison, Patricia had to surrender all her documents and possessions. She had to remove clothing in a rudimentary booth for an officer to inspect for contraband. 'I felt violated,' she said.

The language barrier and pronunciation made it difficult to communicate her son's name and surname for them to find on their systems. After several attempts they finally found his name. The prison authorities sent the distraught mother to a waiting room and left her for almost two hours before they called her to see her son. She was led to an office upstairs.

'Nothing could have prepared me for what I was about to experience. No mother should ever be put in such a position, to be in a foreign country, to be in a foreign prison, all alone and about to face your child.'

The wardens brought her son in and immediately Patricia felt faint. He was handcuffed. He had lost a great deal of weight and he looked utterly dishevelled, even traumatised.

'I sobbed as he lifted the handcuffs over my head to hold me. We were allowed no more that 10 to 15 minutes together. Ten minutes was a snap of nothing compared to the hours, days and weeks that had brutally dragged my heart across the Indian Ocean in order to get here. There was so little time to tell my son that everything would be alright, despite the fact that I had no idea if it would be. There were seconds left to tell him that I loved him, that his father loved him and that we would not rest in bringing home. I held my son's face with hands that trembled and promised him that I would fight for him. Then he was ripped from my embrace and dragged back to his cell, they said. I was told to return again some other time.'

'I cried all the way back to my rented apartment. I just could not erase the picture I had of my son in my mind after seeing him. I could not eat knowing my son was not having sufficient food. I could not sleep knowing he struggled to sleep because of the unbearable humidity. I turned off the fan above my bed that night, refusing to take any comfort knowing my son had no such comfort. I felt completely vulnerable knowing that I had made a commitment that I could never go back on. I would never even consider going back on my word. I became quite emotional there in my room all alone with no one to talk to or pat my hand and tell me that everything was going to be okay. I didn't want to burden my family with my grief. I didn't want them to suffer any more than what they had. Somehow I would persevere. I would convince myself that I had the strength to get through this, even though I was feeling so frail. I would do whatever it takes to help my son.'

Thereafter the visits were via telephone and a glass partition. Patricia was told many times by the prison wardens that she was not allowed to have any physical contact with her son.

'I longed to wrap my arms around his wasting frame and give him comfort as only a mother can. But the wardens sternly shook their heads. I refused to leave until they allowed me access but it was useless as they again sternly shook their heads and forcibly removed me from the waiting area.'

In one of their brief encounters, Johann told his mother that he did not plan on becoming a drug mule. He was adamant that he had been coerced by a deadly syndicate in South Africa. He claimed he couldn't find the people he was meant to deliver the drugs to, so he dumped the bags in the hotel gardens. When he got back to his room, the police were waiting for him, and he immediately showed them where the drugs were. They were not in his stomach as reported.

It was possible that Johann had been used as a decoy by the syndicate. But according to his mother, he was never a drug addict. According to Johann Jnr, he says that he gave the Mauritian police permission to be tested for drugs, but they refused his request.

During her stay in Mauritius, Patricia decided to pay a visit to the Mauritius Anti Drug Smuggling Unit (ADSU) to ask them if Interpol was investigating. To her dismay, she was told that Interpol had not been notified and did not investigate such matters. Deputy Superintendent Padiachy informed Patricia that the information had been given to his friend, and opposite, an officer at the Organised Crime Drug Unit (OCDU) in Pretoria, South Africa, Superintendent Jan Rehder. Deputy Superintendent Padiachy also told Patricia that all the South Africans are connected to the same syndicate and the police will never catch them because this has been going on for seven years.

Patricia listened with a heavy heart. They were writing her son off and he had not even had the chance to defend himself.

'Surely you have to find out who's behind all this?' she demanded of the man sitting before her, shuffling a small stack of papers.

'There are many such cases,' he responded. 'I'll let you know if we hear anything further.' Patricia was dismissed but was not any less determined.

On Friday 25 November 2005, she contacted Superintendent Jan Rehder. She introduced herself and told him of her son's situation to which he replied, 'Oh... there are many such cases.'

She told him that she had been given his mobile number by Deputy Superintendent Padiachy in Mauritius. The silence down the phone line was almost deafening. 'Hello are you there? Sir?' she insisted.

After several moments Superintendent Jan Rehder advised that he was not in the office at that particular time and that she should call him at a more convenient time. They agreed that she would call back the following Monday. But when Monday rolled round, at 10 o' clock, Patricia put the call through and Superintendant Rehder simply said, 'it has nothing to do with me'.

Patricia was left reeling. She was getting nowhere with the authorities. Her son was denied access to a barrister, although the Mauritian authorities said he waived his right to one because he wanted to speed up the legal process. Patricia later learned from Johann Jnr that it was during the 21 days of isolation that he was made to believe that he would remain in those conditions unless he signed the confession that was written by the ADSU officer. He claims he did request to see an official from the Embassy multiple times but this was denied. He claims that he could no longer cope with being in isolation and in darkness, and only to be fed bread and water. In his frustration and fear, he signed their confession.

How could Patricia possibly prove her son's innocence with a confession typed, signed by her son and filed by police? How could she save her son from being found guilty, a charge that carried a penalty of 45 years in jail? It should be said that previously this kind of offence carried the penalty of death by hanging. A noteworthy point but one that offered no reassure Patricia. Forty-five years! How could anyone survive 45 years in such a place?

Patricia immediately began thinking about the conditions the prison as described by her son during their last visit, 'They let you out at 6am and at 8am then they turn the water off. If you don't have any bottled water you're stuffed. No one will give you a drop to drink of theirs. Imagine 170 people in a yard with access to four working toilets. Not the flush kind ... there aren't any flush systems. Then there's the infestation of cockroaches and bugs ... you wake up in the middle of the night and they're everywhere... cockroaches, mice, rats ... it's disgusting!'

The days drifted into weeks and soon the time had come for Patricia to leave Mauritius. Johann Jnr knew the time had to come, his mother couldn't afford to stay indefinitely.

'He became quiet and visibly stressed. But I had to start fighting for him. I couldn't just keep visiting the prison and telling him everything would be okay,' Patricia explained.

Their final visit was unbearably painful for them both. No mother wishes to see her child dragged from her arms.

'I could never describe the agony of that particular moment. It was as if my heart was being ripped from my chest'.

For the flight home, Patricia had requested a window seat.

'As the plane lifted off, I left my heart behind with Johann Jnr. Mauritius to me was not the holiday destination of my dreams, for me it had become the island of tears. It was the place that held captive my most precious thing in all the world, my son. I cried the entire way back home to South Africa.

In early December 2005, Patricia established contact with Interpol. Senior Superintendent Tummi Golding confirmed that his department had contacted the Mauritian authorities twice to request the files of the South Africans detained there and had received no response. Interpol agreed to meet Patricia and the other families in Cape Town and said they would take their statements. But when Patricia faxed a letter of confirmation as to when they would be available to meet in Cape Town, she received a call telling her that they were not interested in investigating any of the cases. They had done a complete reversal. Officers Taylor, Rodgers, Mendes and Tummi Golding confirmed this.

When asked who would investigate the matters, Patricia was directed, once again, to the Organised Crime Drug Squad in Pretoria.

Patricia, while in Mauritius, met with the Commissioner of Prisons, Mr Bill Duff, and the Deputy Commissioner of Police, Mr Jean Bruneau, who both told her to approach the then-South African President Thabo Mbeki and the South African Government to sign a Prisoner Transfer Agreement. Mauritius has signed a similar treaty with Tanzania, Kenya, India and Uganda. Mauritius is willing to sign such an agreement with the Government of South Africa but thus far, the South African Government has refused to comply.

'What were they really saying? That it was up to me to make my government see sense?'

The island of Mauritius, with its golden beaches and luxury hotels, is a dream destination but beneath the picture-postcard facade lies a dark and devastating reality. Over 25,000 heroin addicts are among the local population. And as is so typical of the drug trade, young men and women are lured by the promise of easy money:

Brigene Young, 20, sentenced to 7 years for trafficking 900g of heroin
Chanelle Ottley, 27, sentenced to 10 years for trafficking 578g of heroin
Nosipho Mdeyiya, 28, sentenced to 10 years for trafficking 504g of heroin
Noluvuyo Ntama, 32, sentenced to 32 years for trafficking 285g of heroin
Eunice Ndovela, 54, sentenced to 12 years for trafficking 577g of heroin
Arlene Parhboo, 36, sentenced to 7 years for trafficking 409g of heroin
Anneline Mouton, 33, sentenced to 10 years for trafficking 674g of heroin
Marjorie Jansen van Vuuren, 45, sentenced to 8 years for 500g of heroin
Patience Makinana, 37, sentenced to 11 years for 232g of heroin
Sylvia Ntaka, 26, sentenced to 5 years for 35g of heroin
Martha Roux, 30, sentenced to nine years for 1.175g of heroin
Amanda van Wyk, 26, sentenced to 25 years for 1.5kg of heroin
Phumla Ingebu, 29, sentenced to 14 years for 886g of heroin
Chrisella Schuster, 52, sentenced to 11 years for 530g of heroin
Annie Erasmus, 32, sentenced to 12 years for trafficking 2.5kg of cocaine
Joseph Mbokotwane, 40, sentenced to 8 years for 1kg of heroin
David Harte, 49, sentenced to 9 years for 430g of heroin
Edward Aimes, 21, sentenced to 13 years for 15g of heroin
Johan van Wyk, 27, sentenced to 7 years for 483g of heroin
Geoffrey du Preez, 55, sentenced to 10 years for 320g of heroin
Stephen Wasson, 40, sentenced to 27 years for 210g of heroin
Leon Laubeschagne, 47, sentenced to 31 years for 480g of heroin.

These detainees were merely a sea of forgotten faces in a world where no one cared because of the very nature of their offence. They were drug cases. They were classed as the dregs of society. They were to be discarded purely on the basis that they had been arrested. However, each one of them had a family member agonising over their welfare. Take Brigene Young. She was a young girl whose mother had recently died and she had broken up with her fiancé and was at the lowest point in her life. She had been befriended by a man who frequented the bar at which she worked.

'He said, "What about a trip to Mauritius?"' And she agreed. She was arrested at the airport wearing the shoes he'd given her. The police told her that they were 'expecting' her.

South Africa has become a popular transit point in the international drug trade. Many of the mules are out of work, financially desperate and unlikely to have travelled before. Many are never intended to complete a successful drug transaction. Instead, they serve as decoys to distract the attention away from the real drug-smuggling professionals.

It's been almost a year since Patricia has seen her son and during this time she's been given the run around by everyone.

'Well almost everyone...I hired a private investigator, Mike Bolhuis, from Specialised Security Services, hoping he could help me get to the bottom of all this.'

Mike learned that Johann had been threatened to drug mule and that if he didn't, either he or his family would be killed. It was an all too common scenario. Drug mules are expendable. Hundreds of them have been found dead in dry creek beds, along roadsides, in bushlands and wastelands. Many have been gutted like whales. Their carcasses left to rot. Their stomachs ripped open and emptied as their dealers retrieve their valuable cargo. It's impossible to determine the actual number of young lives lost through drug trafficking. But one thing that is known is that a mother of a drug mule, whose son or daughter is dead or detained, agonises exactly the same way any mother would if their child were in trouble or trauma.

Being a mother, Patricia's greatest fear is that her son will not return home alive. Since his arrest, three South African inmates have died. Others have died under suspicious circumstances. The South African Government refuses to investigate the circumstances or provide any assistance returning the bodies or the possessions of the deceased, to their families. Patricia silently prays every night that her son will come home but she also fears the impact this ordeal has had on him.

What impact will this separation have on his family? What impact will it have on him? What emotional and physiological problems will he have, as a result of being detained in isolation, in complete darkness for 21 days?

'I worry every day,' Patricia cries.

The drug trade continues to escalate. The number of South Africans detained overseas is ever increasing. In 1995, there was one South African prisoner in South America. Today there are over 3000. In North America there are six, in Europe 68, the Middle East there are 15, Brazil 176, in Asia there are 109 and in Australia and New Zealand there are about 45. The drug syndicates bribe South African policemen to get drug mules on and off planes unchecked. They also use drug mules as decoys. The drug syndicates themselves have been known to call ahead and tip off police. Numerous cases have revealed that police often know who exactly to arrest, what they are wearing, their name etc ... and while the arrest is being made, while the attention of the whole airport is focused on that one particular person, someone else with three to five kilograms of drugs, or possibly more, is entering the country undetected. It's a profitable business for some but completely devastating for families and mothers, like Patricia.

The Head of Narcotics at Organised Crime, Senior Superintendant Deven Naicker, believes Johann's story about being forced to drug mule is a convenient fabrication. 'When I interviewed him and asked him specifically did anybody force you to go he said no. Did anybody point a gun at you and he said no. Gerber's developed a habit of consuming drugs. He was a drug addict,' said Deven.

When asked how he knew that, he said 'Our intelligence told us. After we came back and investigated him we found out that he was a drug user. He had built up a big debt with this specific syndicate and he had to pay that. The sole purpose of his trafficking drugs to Mauritius was actually to pay off his drug debt,' Deven replied.

Patrica is adamant that these statements are false.

'My son is not an addict and he's not heavily in debt. That's utterly ridiculous!' Patricia countered.

Days, weeks, months, years.

Johann Gerber Jnr appeared in the Supreme Court of Mauritius in June 2007. He was sentenced to nine years imprisonment and given a fine of 50,000 rupees for importing heroin into Mauritius. His mother refuses to abandon him. In fact, she has taken up the fight of all South Africans detained in foreign prisons to secure an elusive Prisoner Transfer Agreement so that all these mothers' sons and daughters might return to their homeland. The South African Government refuses to enter into an agreement with the Mauritian government.

'I am devastated and disappointed by the attitude of the officials of the South African Mission in Mauritius. I have lost faith in the justice system as it has failed its citizens in their darkest hour. My son's incarceration has made me a stronger person, who is more determined than ever to find a solution, not only for him but all those similarly incarcerated. Times have been rough, often leaving me wondering and praying for resolve and strength to continue the fight. Together with the help of other families in the same situation, we have created a support group 'Locked Up in a Foreign Country'. I have changed from a person who was oblivious to people in prison to one who now has compassion for those whom society so often forgets and neglects.

'Two years after my son was arrested my husband was retrenched and was unable to secure a permanent job due to his age. My husband has not seen his son in the last six years. Both Johann's brother and sisters have not seen him in years, as they have not the financial means to travel to Mauritius on a regular basis. Often they have tried to arrange visits on a rotational basis in support of each other and Johann. But the financial cost of the court case put a tremendous financial strain on our family. We are in the process of selling our property. We are almost bankrupt,' says Patricia.

In March 2010, this very determined mother brought a High Court application against the South African Government for their failure to consider her request that the South African Government enter into a prisoner transfer agreement with the government of Mauritius. Patricia requested that they provide sufficient reasons for their decision not to do so. Nine months later, the judge dismissed the application on December 2010. Patricia immediately appealed. Without even appearing in court, the 11 judges of the Constitutional Court dismissed her appeal. There is currently no legal recourse as all the available avenues have been exhausted. Johann and 30 other South African inmates are still stuck on the island of Mauritius.

South Africa's insistence on not assisting their citizens ultimately has left more than 3000 South Africans held in foreign prisons without hope or means. Paroled citizens abroad are also not assisted to survive locally or return home, and on occasion have been left on the streets to the full knowledge of the embassies and missions, as the families back home do not have the means to pay for their return.

Peter Gray, an Australian, flew to Mauritius on business in 2005. He chatted to a woman sitting next to him on the plane and gave her his card. When the woman was arrested at the airport for trafficking heroin, she claimed she was carrying it for him. (Three years later she retracted her statement).

'They put me into isolation for 86 days and during that time I was threatened continuously with 45 years in prison. I was harassed quite a lot. I wasn't allowed to see a lawyer initially. Eventually I did get to see a lawyer of my choice and I gave a statement. They sent me to prison where I stayed for the next 16 months. I got out in December 2010 and according to my lawyer I probably will have to wait another two years before anything will happen' says Peter Gray. (Source: Carte Blanche News). Peter has now returned to Australia thanks in part to the Australian Government's assistance.

During his incarceration, he claimed police beat him up, fractured five ribs and broke his collarbone. The Australian Government had cancelled his passport so when he did get released he had no way of going home. He lived on two minute noodles and whatever support his family provided. Many would say that Peter Gray was lucky, although his South African business, which employed more than 30 people and specialised in building theme parks, was ruined. How lucky was he, having served five and a half years for a crime he had no part in?

It is for people like Peter Gray and families like his, that Patricia Gerber has dedicated her life to helping. She is extremely frustrated that the Mauritian government has presented the South African Government again with a draft prisoner transfer agreement but her government refuses to sign it. She says she is frustrated at the lack of human compassion and attitude of the South African Government. All she wants is to have her son home, even if it means he has to remain in prison.

'I pay money into the account every month for Johann Jnr to survive. He has to purchase toilet paper, soap, food, medicine, all his basic needs, and most times I have to plead with the department and the Embassy because they have failed, for some reason, not to transfer the vital funds into his prison account. Every day and every night I worry for my son and the other families who are experiencing the same anguish we are forced to experience. Not a day goes by that I do not wonder if he is safe, (South Africans have been attacked by the Mauritian inmates) or if he is lying helpless, battered and bleeding. I long for my son to be nearer to home. It's all I think about,' says Patricia.

While South Africa may have one of the most advanced constitutions in the world, Patricia strongly believes they fail appallingly in serving the fundamental human rights of their citizens detained abroad. They refuse to sign Prisoner Transfer Agreements with foreign countries and neither Interpol nor the Organised Crime Unit in South Africa has investigated any cases of a South African citizen held in Mauritius. Patricia says that families like hers are often sent from one department to another because no one person will take responsibility to address their grievances.

'We are embarking on a campaign to bring awareness to schools and universities to warn others of our situation. A petition has been drafted on behalf of all the families and soon will be forwarded for signatures. We will continue to put pressure on the South African government through the media,' she hits back. 'With my faith and the knowledge that we have come so far, we must persevere because somewhere, someone in the South African Government will have some compassion in their heart. We encourage any support we can muster. Every voice raised in opposition to these draconian measures counts.'

There are approximately 3000 sentenced South African citizens currently serving prison sentences in foreign countries. The financial costs alone are crippling many families who haven't committed a crime or been accused of committing a crime. The psychological effects on families are often devastating too. Many suffer from some form of emotional problem or depression. Some are completely bankrupt. The emotional costs are extremely high and the social stigma of having a loved one in a foreign prison often automatically generates a great deal of negative reaction.

Patricia Gerber continues to hope that good news is just around the corner. Her son is due to be released in 2016. She's hoping her son survives that long.

Locked Up In a Foreign Prison
www.lockedup.co.za

28
Justice for Jock
Jock Palfreeman, Bulgaria

Australian Jock Palfreeman left home in 2006 to travel overseas. His journey led him to a small country town, about an hour's drive from Sofia, the Bulgarian capital. During the Christmas/New Year period of 2007/2008, Jock found himself in a series of events that were to have the most tragic consequences.

Dr Simon Palfreeman, an Australian pathologist, lives a relatively quiet life with his wife Helen, in Sydney's beautiful harbour suburb of Mosman. Their now 25-year-old son, Jock, who has the Hollywood looks of a young Matt Damon, sits in a Bulgarian jail for the murder of law student Andrei Monov. The Palfreemans believe their son is the victim of a miscarriage of justice.

Former St Ignatius College school boy, Jock Palfreeman graduated from high school, enrolled in university, attended but didn't graduate. He held down a number of jobs then went on a working holiday throughout Europe before finally deciding to sign up for the British Army in September 2007. His training was to begin in November that same year. Jock arrived in Bulgaria on 22 December 2007. He planned to stay only a few days to enjoy a white Christmas with friends in Samokov, a town in Sofia Province in the southwest of Bulgaria.

In the early hours of 28 December 2007, Jock and his friends Graham, Lindsay Welsh—Graham's girlfriend—and a young Bulgarian man (Tony) were having a few drinks in a bar. Later in the evening, Graham felt unwell. He left the group to return to the hostel. Jock, Lindsay and Tony continued enjoying their last night in town. Tony said he knew a place nearby with good music. They passed Stamboliiski Boulevard on their way to the Angels Nightclub. As they were walking down the road, the three noticed a group of young men running up from Maria Luisa Boulevard towards Vitosha Boulevard. They were making a lot of noise, shouting and yelling and to passersby seemed clearly intoxicated. Tony said they were Levski Sofia football club supporters (herein referred to as Levski group). There were about 15 or 20 of them and they appeared to be chasing down two other men—gypsies, (Roma) a group often racially discriminated against in Bulgaria.

The Roma in Bulgaria are the country's second largest minority and third largest ethnic group (after Bulgarians and Turks).

One of the gypsies managed to run away towards Sveta Nedelya church. The other was thrown to the ground and kicked and punched near Serdika metro station by the Levski group.

In a split second decision, Jock ran to help the Roma man lying on the ground. His companions stayed behind and tried to get their mobile phone working.

The attack continued. Jock tried to push them away from the Roma man but they were too fuelled up on alcohol and adrenalin. A lethal combination. They turned their unwanted attention to the young foreign intruder. They probably thought he needed to be taught a lesson. Fearing the aggressive reaction of the Levski group, Jock took a knife from his pocket that he carried in self-defence, and waved it in the air to scare them. Bulgaria was a violent place and Jock had witnessed quite brutal attacks on others before. As he told the court later, during his trial, he had no intention of using the knife. He just waved it around to scare the group away. It worked momentarily. The group backed off. This gave him a small window of opportunity to attend to the Roma man on the ground. But no sooner had he turned his back on the Levski group than they became confident and launched a second attack. This time they were more violent than before and proceeded to hurl loose concrete blocks at Jock. The situation was getting out of control.

Jock was surrounded and almost knocked to the ground several times. A kiosk area was nearby but no one was coming to help. Jock slowly staggered to his feet, swinging the knife in an arc, calling out for help. His one thought: to stay alive.

'I was between them and the man on the ground. I took out the knife, raised it in the air high above my head and with my left hand I gestured them to pull back and shouted in Bulgarian 'go back, go back'. They started to retreat. Some of them tried to come close to me, but one of the friends from the group would grab his friends and would pull them aside,' said Jock. Jock was struck repeatedly with hurled concrete blocks. He somehow managed to block the blows to his head with his arm. Surely it would break?

Two eyewitnesses, guards, were watching from a carpark in front of the Sheraton Hotel, about 50m from Serdika metro station. They later told police that they saw a man being beaten. They said they then saw another man run over and intervene. They said the attack on the man on the ground continued for about 30 to 40 seconds. Jock's intervention most likely saved this man's life. Why didn't they intervene?

'All of them were throwing [concrete blocks] at me. Most of them I blocked with my left arm, raised in front of my face. I held the knife in the air and every time someone would come to attack me, I would wave the knife from left to right but not to hurt them, only to scare them. I was constantly going in circles, because every time I had my back against someone, they would attack me. Then someone hit me [on the head], I fell on the ground. They began kicking me, punching me,' Jock recalls. 'The last thing I remember is thinking "Shit, I'm gone... I'm finished".

Graham's girlfriend, Lindsay Welsh, said in an interview that she had tried to grab Jock's arm. Someone in the Levski group turned and kicked her full force in the stomach. Half-winded and more than a little terrified, Lindsay fled the scene. She didn't want to die. She didn't want Jock to die but fear forced her to retreat. In such extreme circumstances, who could blame her?

Levksi group member, Antoan Zahariev, had been stabbed, though not fatally. He lay on the ground with blood covering his shirt. His friend, 20-year-old law student Andrei Monov, the son of a prominent Bulgarian family, lay beside him. His condition was much worse. Jock Palfreeman lay on the ground nearby, beaten and bloody. When the police arrived on the scene, the only person arrested was the foreigner, Jock Palfreeman. The Roma man who had been assaulted was nowhere to be found.

As the case hit the headlines, the family and supporters of Andrei Monov began chanting for justice—a life sentence for Jock Palfreeman, the man who had murdered their son. The man who had brutally and cold bloodily killed their friend.

Could Jock Palfreeman and his family hope to secure a fair trial when Andrei Monov's funeral was flashed across the major Bulgaria news channels and attended by so many prominent figures, including Bulgaria's elite judges, lawyers and police? It was highly doubtful.

'All my life I've believed in the system. Now, for the first time, I'm faced with a system I don't have confidence in,' says Dr Palfreeman.

Dr Simon Palfreeman had good cause for concern. Not only was his son facing a notoriously corrupt judiciary but it was a well-known fact in Bulgaria that the courts can be bought. Corruption in Bulgaria is notorious all over the world.

Jock's trial began on 21 May 2008. It ran over 19 sessions. Many were shortened or aborted when witnesses (including expert witnesses) did not appear or, on several occasions, when one of the judging panel was on holiday. Despite the delays and deficiencies in the investigation, critical evidence was collected that supported Jock's version of events. This critical evidence never found its way before the judges, despite the strident efforts of Jock's defence team. The essential difference between the prosecution and defence cases was the beating of the Roma man by the Levski group before the two men, Monov and Zahariev were wounded. The prosecution denied the beating ever occurred and relied almost entirely on the testimony of the Levski group, who had instigated the assault, and claimed Jock had attacked them without provocation and at random. The prosecution said that Jock attacked the Levski group to kill as many of them as he could. He was portrayed as a sociopath who would kill again if released. In the 19 months of the trial, the prosecution failed to present one piece of evidence that would prove their claims. They failed to prove that Jock was himself motivated by hooliganism.

Jock Palfreeman admitted in his final appeal to the court that he did in fact stab Andrei Monov but that it was in self-defence. The defence submitted evidence that Andrei Monov had almost 0.29 per cent blood alcohol content, his friend Antoan Zahariev's was 0.19 per cent and Jock's was 0.1 per cent. The blood alcohol content analysis was carried out by a Bulgarian state forensic lab. These figures were never challenged in court despite them showing that Monov and Zahariev were highly intoxicated. Monov's intoxication was almost six times over Bulgaria's drink-driving limit of 0.05 per cent blood alcohol content. He was very drunk. Then the prosecution called on the chief pathologist who characterised the knife wound as 'forceful'. When cross examined, the defence showed that every textbook of forensic pathology supports the claim that a pathologist cannot be dogmatic about the force, direction or characteristic of knife wounds. Yet the prosecution's witness was adamant. Antoan Zahariev's initial pre-trial statement revealed that, according to him, there had been a physical altercation before Jock had arrived on the scene. But this statement was not permitted to be heard during the trial. The statements of the two witnesses, who were in the car park at the time, were also overlooked by the judge, as was an account given by a nearby kiosk attendant who said he saw a group of men throwing concrete slabs at another man.

Bulgaria's leading human rights group believes the trial has been grossly unfair because it overlooked a great deal of critical evidence, including CCTV footage that police claimed 'a freak blackout wrecked its hard drive'.

Andrei Monov's closest friends told the media that Jock Palfreeman was a cold-blooded killer and would kill again. The media picked up on this, and the claims escalated. They said that if released, Jock Palfreeman would kill not only others in Bulgaria but people in Australia. Bulgarians became fearful and called for Jock Palfreeman to be detained for life. Allegations arose too that Andrei Monov's father, Hristo Monov, one of the country's most prominent and expert psychologists, and former head of a Child Protection Agency for the Bulgarian government, used his considerable influence to sway the court.

Following his son's death, Monov issued a heartfelt statement pledging to protect Bulgaria's children as he could not protect his own.

Bulgarian political and social scientist, Dr Evgenii Dainov, took a keen interest in the case. He told media 'I don't have to imagine cases when witnesses are harassed and pressured to change their statements because it happens all the time. I'd expect the victim's father to put pressure on the entire structure of the law enforcement and judicial structure. I'd expect the judicial system to collapse under that pressure ... Under normal circumstances you can get justice in this country. If at any stage anyone puts any pressure on any link in the chain, it seems that you can't get justice. So (in such cases) the rule of law does not apply because the law is different for different people and so this is a completely unsatisfactory situation'.

Dr Palfreeman believed his son's actions were heroic. 'While as a parent I would have preferred he stayed safe and out of harm's way, as a human being I am proud a young man tried to help despite such dangerous circumstances.'

Dr Palfreeman also expressed compassion for Andrei Monov's family 'I feel for the Monovs. The fact that they've lost their son. That has to be acknowledged ... but the reality is that I've got a son too, and I don't want to lose him.'

Hooliganism is rife in Bulgaria. Case after case filed by police highlights the extreme violence that Bulgarian citizens are forced to live with. Sofia's Chief of Police has, on many occasions, been forced to deploy over a thousand police for any one football match, including over 40 members of the riot squad. 'We also use horses, dogs and specialised equipment to prevent public order offences,' he said in anticipation to one up and coming game between two of the most popular clubs in the Balkan country—Levski and CSKA.

Nasko Sirakov, managing director of Bulgaria's Levski football club is on the record stating that Bulgaria needs a law on football hooliganism. Sirakov claims the violent conduct of the club's fans, who disrupt games by throwing smoke bombs, signal flares and ripped out seats at the pitch, is out of control. He called such people 'pure provocateurs and have no place in the stands.' Clearly, their behaviour in the stands is carried over into the streets.

Jock Palfreeman perhaps had no idea just how violent the Levski football fans were that fateful night he rushed to the aid of the Roma man. Bulgaria is still desperately poor and gypsies are often the target of racial abuse. This is a notable fact according to the human rights watchdog, the Helsinki Committee. According to one opinion poll conducted among non-Roma Bulgarians, less than one per cent of them can imagine marrying a person of Roma origin, and less than ten per cent of them would welcome gypsy neighbours next door.

The court panel that was assembled for the trial comprised two judges and three 'lay' panel members. One of the judges was the senior 'reporting' judge and ran the whole process.

The young wounded man, Antoan Zahariev, recovered and attended the court, along with the parents of the deceased, Andrei Monov. The Monovs were admitted as civil claimants which gave them the same rights to participate in the trial as the prosecution and the defence team. In effect, the civil claimants and the prosecution worked as a team throughout the court hearings. According to Bulgarian law, a direct descendant or ascendant of the defendant can be appointed to the defence team. Jock's father, Dr Simon

Palfreeman, was appointed to the defence team. Father was pitted against father. Neither one wanted to concede defeat.

The first court session was held in May 2008 and it took 19 months to hear all the evidence that was allowed to be heard. Had the court permitted all the evidence to be heard, then perhaps the case might have gone on for much longer. Incompetence or foul play? Who could dare to say out loud? The management of witnesses was appalling. Often only one turned up for the hearing despite others having been subpoenaed. In addition to this, one of the lay panel members did not attend for over five months. Conveniently, he was overseas on holiday. This was typical of how the trial was mismanaged and defence efforts were frustrated by a particular lack of appropriateness and protocol. But this was Bulgaria and not Australia.

On the final court day the prosecutor, civil claimants and their representatives, the defendant and defence team gave their final statements before the panel of judges. Jock's lawyer argued that his client had to face an extremely hostile audience both in court and in the media. In fact, it could be successfully argued that Jock Palfreeman had a trial by media. This complicated an already difficult undertaking—to get justice for a young foreign man who had, in self defence, killed the son of one of Bulgaria's most prominent citizens. No one was under any illusion that the odds were stacked well and truly against Jock Palfreeman.

> *The social consciousness from the very beginning, and after that, was subject to the purposeful influence of the one-sided and totally disadvantageous to my client media coverage and interpretation of the case, in which Jock's behaviour was always defined as an arrogant murder not provoked by anything, assessed as the dark culmination of a purely hooligan behaviour. The defendant himself was called "a butcher", "the cold-blooded and cynical murderer", "cunning and aggressive back-stabber", "an Australian gone wild with a knife in the centre of the capital". Unfortunately the prosecution willingly fed the press with materials and data from the investigation from the very start of the court investigation. A glaring example for this was her interview with 24 hours of 24.03.2008. Moreover—in that same interview, prosecutor Nikova allowed herself, violating the presumption of law innocent until proven guilty as a major constitutional right of every defendant, to give peremptory qualifications of the defendant's behaviour, to divulge information selectively with regard to some evidence and to interpret the evidence in a biased manner, to set the punishments. If this interview*

> *can be of any help, it is that it makes it clear how one-sided and prejudiced this investigation was, and the only way it could be so is with the relevant orders by the prosecutor.*

Jock's lawyer pleaded with the jury and judges to judge the case fairly. He urged them to assess the evidence sensibly and not let the extensive media coverage prejudice their decision. But the prejudice was there, spread across the case like a thick blanket of Sofia snow. That prejudice occurred immediately after the tragedy of that night when only one version of the incident was chosen and followed through until the end of the trial. The version of truth relied entirely on the information provided by the drunken Levski group.

> *And because one-sidedness and prejudice always go hand in hand, from the very start of the investigation, consciously or not, the investigating body, acting under the prosecution's supervision, has allowed for significant and irreparable omissions/mistakes/gaps in the investigation, which in the following stages have multiplied exactly because of keeping to only one version, chosen at the very start.*

So many vital pieces of evidence were never allowed to be presented to the court. As Jock's lawyer presented page after page of complaint as to the way in which his client's case had been handled, it became obvious that a miscarriage of justice was in the wind. The writing was on the wall for Jock. Yet still, his lawyer fought a good fight.

> *In the testimony delivered in court hearing of 21 May 2008, Antoan Zahariev gives a very detailed description of the injuries, while for other details of the incident he's quite unsure, or claims he can't remember them. This very selective amnesia is able to cause doubt in what he says. It is also not true what Zahariev said, that he was stabbed in the back. This was refuted by the forensic medical report pertaining to his injury. Again Zahariev lied to the court that before being interrogated in the court investigation, he had mentioned to no one that between his friends and the unidentified Roma people, there was a fight and exchange of punches. In my view, these are not witnesses that can be trusted and what's more, whose testimonies could not be used as grounds for the verdict.*

No one ever searched the Levski group for weapons. The crime scene was never cordoned off. The Roma man was never found. The knife was never actually proven to be Jock Palfreeman's and nor was there any evidence that his fingerprints were even found on the knife. Witness testimonies were discarded. Statements made by the Levski group changed frequently. At one time it was so, and then another time it was a completely different story. So many inconsistencies, so many failures to properly process evidence, so much corruption of an event that transformed so many lives, most of all Jock Palfreeman's.

In conclusion, Jock's lawyer pointed out that, regardless of the outcome, the main reason for the trial was through tragic circumstances. A young man died. Another was praying for a fair trial.

The Judge delivered the verdict on 2 December 2009.

Jock was charged with 'murder with hooliganism' and sentenced to 20 years. He was ordered by the Sofia City Court to pay 400,000 leva ($A326,238) to the family of the victim Andrei Monov and 50,000 leva ($A34,195) to Monov's friend Antoan Zahariev, who was injured during the incident.

The Judge then took five and a half months to write the report that explained the verdict and ought to have taken a month to write. The delay in reporting significantly delayed the appeal process, which occurred on 21 October 2010, before three Appeal Court judges. A number of requests were put forward by the defence but only one was accepted. This was a request to re-question five witnesses to explain the discrepancies in their previous testimonies. Two of the witnesses were from the Levski group that attacked the Roma man and Jock. The other three were policemen. All five witnesses had stated in their original police statements that there was a fight between the Levski group and Roma man. Yet during the first trial they denied ever having said this.

The Appeal concluded after five sessions on the 19 January 2011. As this book goes to press, the Appeal judge is yet to provide a written report on her findings. Hopefully it won't take as long to write as the initial verdict. Hopefully it will enable the truth to come out.

It's April 2011. Dr. Simon Palfreeman and his family continue the fight for their son's freedom as Jock sits 23 hours a day confined to a cell in Sofia

Central Prison. He spends a great deal of his time helping other prisoners and though he's allowed an hour for exercise each day, he says he much prefers to spend the time writing letters to friends. It's important to him that he not lose touch with reality. It's a challenge, considering he has no access to the internet or to the telephone. He can't simply jump on skype and chat to his dad. Nor can he follow the Rugby League matches in Sydney or what the weather may be like today in Bondi. He is totally isolated from all things familiar. His only communication with the world outside comes in the form of letters and visits, twice a month, from friends. The financial burden on his parents is incredible. The emotional burden doesn't compare.

When one analyses the concept of what a miscarriage of justice really is, some might suggest it is when a court or judiciary has attempted to deliver justice but that somehow everything went off the rails. Those close to this particular case believe there were greater powers in play. Some believe it was more a case of wilful covering up of the facts, and a wilful wrong decision. This is not a case of taking sides. Some can choose to believe Jock Palfreeman's version of events. Others can choose to believe the Monovs or the drunken Levski group. Taking all the emotion out of the equation, the facts speak for themselves. Had all the evidence been heard, Jock Palfreeman would not be in the situation he finds himself in today. His options are few. In fact, he has more of a chance of winning the lottery than he has of overturning the decision made against him in Bulgaria, but that's not to say he and his lawyers and family should not continue to fight for justice. He could appeal to the European Court of Human Rights in Strasbourg. Unlike the International Court of Justice, whose function is to settle legal disputes submitted to it by states, the Strasbourg Court can hear cases brought directly by individuals. However, there is no guarantee that an application to the court will be admissible or successful and it could take years for the outcome to be known. Jock could be transferred back to Australia to serve the remainder of his sentence, but that would require the signing of a prisoner transfer agreement between Bulgaria and Australia, and that could take years. Jock could pray for a miracle but that too could take years. Either way, his future is grim.

At the moment, Jock Palfreeman will remain in Sofia Central Prison for at least a further 17 years, unless the Prosecutor shows leniency. It's highly doubtful he will.

If anything might inspire Jock Palfreeman to hope, to hold out, to survive until that day he gains his freedom, then surely the words of William Ernest Henley must do just that:

> Out of the night that covers me,
> Black as the Pit from pole to pole,
> I thank whatever gods may be,
> For my unconquerable soul.
>
> In the fell clutch of circumstance,
> I have not winced nor cried aloud.
> Under the bludgeonings of chance,
> My head is bloody, but unbowed.
>
> Beyond this place of wrath and tears
> Looms but the horror of the shade,
> And yet the menace of the years
> Finds, and shall find, me unafraid.
>
> It matters not how strait the gate,
> How charged with punishments the scroll.
> I am the master of my fate:
> I am the captain of my soul.

Please support the Palfreeman family as they continue to fight for Justice for Jock.

Justice for Jock
http://www.freejock.com

Jock Palfreeman
Sofia Central Prison
21 General Stoletov Boulevard
Sofia 1309, BULGARIA

29

WORDS

Can Light the Way

Words can make a difference; words can change lives. As a teenager living in Stuttgart, Germany, Tobias Merckle's life was changed upon reading a book about one man's efforts to help gang members and drug addicts turn their lives around. This book was Tobias' initial inspiration to dedicate himself to helping juvenile offenders transform their lives.

In 1976 in the United States alone, 22 males under the age of 18 were executed. Twenty-one of them were age 17 when the actual crime occurred. Since 1642, an estimated 364 juvenile offenders have been put to death in the United States. The Justice Department estimates that about 10 per cent of all homicides are committed by juveniles under the age of 18. Nearly every year, the FBI arrests more than 33,000 young adults under the age of 18 for offences.

Tobias Merckle became interested in the idea of providing young offenders with an alternative to juvenile prison after working in a drug rehabilitation centre in Tennessee, USA. He remembers, 'When I visited a prison in the US for the first time I thought to myself: This can't be. We can't treat juveniles like this, leaving them under the influence of the inmate subculture and not preparing them to start a life without crime. Being in this environment people don't have a lot of chances to change themselves. We can't do it to them, but we can't do it to society either.' Tobias had a vision of developing an alternative to prison for German youth; his vision took only 13 years to become a reality.

After working in several prisons, Tobias began his thesis which focused on restorative justice. While attending a conference on this subject, Tobias met Dan Van Ness of Prison Fellowship International and his relationship with PFI began. He was invited to visit a faith-based prison unit in Brazil, which he found inspiring. Then he worked at the Prison Fellowship International Secretariat in Switzerland and in the US as an assistant to Ron Nikkel, the President. During the latter time period, Tobias introduced the idea of an alternative to prison to the German Minister of Justice, and a year later in 2001 Prisma/Prison Fellowship Germany was founded.

At the end of 2003, Seehaus Leonberg, a faith-based youth farm, was launched as an alternative to prison for juveniles. In this 400-year-old converted German hunting lodge, male offenders, aged between 14 and 23, serve their prison sentences in a small family setting. Juveniles live at this open facility for approximately 12 to 18 months, learning to take responsibility for their past, present and future. The launching of this facility marked the first time that a non-governmental organisation in Germany was ever permitted the authority to operate an alternative prison unit.

The young offenders live with house parents and their own children, protected from the negative influence of the adult prison subculture, as 'students' in small family groups of up to seven juveniles, eating together, sharing household responsibilities, and pursuing a program of education, social skills, sport, vocational training and exploration of faith. Under Tobias' guidance, Seehaus has continued to expand, with the facility now housing high-quality woodwork and metalwork shops, a bakery, a mobile graffiti removal service, and educational facilities.

The success of the program can be seen in the Christian lifestyle so many of these men have chosen. In 2008 Tobias organised a work project to assist Prison Fellowship Romania in repairing and renovating three shelters. Men who had once lived at Seehaus took a week from their work and families to help the less fortunate. Acts such as these illustrate the accuracy of the words of the Minister of Justice Ulrich Goll, 'Seehaus is a trend-setting model for the inner security of the state, for peaceful society, and the integration of young men in the state and in the community.'

Tobias contends that many factors have attributed to Seehaus' success. 'We take the juveniles into families where they experience family life and love —often for the first time in their life. We use the power of peers through a Positive Peer Culture, and they educate themselves. We train them in social skills, in taking on responsibility and they can get their school diploma and start to learn a trade. They experience a very strict daily schedule from 5.45am to 10.00pm and therefore learn to structure their lives. They also get exposed to many potential leisure time activities. In addition, as staff we want to pass on the Christian faith by living it as an example. It is also important that they have the possibility to receive aftercare.'

Tobias would like to see the model replicated throughout the country. Ivan Sotirov, PFI's Regional Liaison, comments, 'He has developed the best working model of alternatives to prison which is now attracting the attention of correctional and justice officials across Germany. I admire him for his hands-on leadership and his big heart for juvenile prisoners.

Indeed, the success of Seehaus in the Baden-Wurttemberg state has been noticed; the Ministry of Justice of Saxonia has given approval for Prison Fellowship Germany/Prisma to start a second project. However, the project's commencement hinges on funding.

Tobias continues to work to empower young men to transform their lives. His strategy is simple: instead of locking young people up and surrounding them with others who have made bad choices, society must provide juveniles an alternative to prison which provides real, loving relationships with people who will minister to their spiritual and physical needs. This is the winning approach that Tobias envisioned many years ago and which Prison Fellowship Germany has applied, contributing to countless people's lives being changed.

Acknowledgement:

Thank you to Elizabeth Street, the Communications and Marketing Director of Prison Fellowship International for granting permission to include this story. The world's largest and most extensive criminal justice ministry, Prison Fellowship International (PFI) is a global association of over 100 national Prison Fellowship organisations. PFI is active in every region of the world with a network of more than 50,000 volunteers worldwide working for the spiritual, moral, social and physical well-being of prisoners, ex-prisoners, their families and victims of crime.

Prison Fellowship International – beyond crime and punishment

PO Box 17434 Washington, DC 20041 USA

P +1.703.481.0000 | F +1.703.481.0003

www.pfi.org

26
HOPE

The key to endurance

Hope can mean many different things to many different people. Some hope for good health and prosperity, others simply hope their children will do well in school exams. Most of us hope that bad things won't happen to us or to those we love and, if they do, we hope that despite the difficulties, we will endure. When we experience fear we hope for courage and when we come up against the seemingly impossible, we hope that we can overcome it.

Hope is one of our core human values. We talk about it, yearn for it and celebrate it. Some of us stumble through life hoping our lives will become more enriched or that life will get easier. When we feel pain, we hope that it will end. When we experience fear we hope for courage and when we come up against the seemingly impossible, we hope that we can overcome it.

Hope is what keeps us going in life and what changes with our own individual perspectives. We determine what is important and what we need in our lives to make us happy, prosperous and fulfilled. Perspectives often change as we change and sometimes we get disillusioned with life. Sometimes we feel great elation when our expectations exceed our hopes. Then there are times when we despair because we've set the bar too high.

Our hopes are often born amidst our darkest moments when we, consciously or unconsciously, take that very first step away from our problems. Hope whispers to us that the struggle we are facing is not hopeless, we just need to trust ourselves to find a way through, whatever it is that is threatening to overwhelm us.

Nothing is impossible if we just believe in our capacity to endure and overcome.

When I encountered my darkest moments in Phonthong Prison, when I felt as if life was slipping beyond my grasp, I tried to find that place inside that was like the storage place for all my hopes and dreams. I thought of all those hopes and reminded myself every day that I had so much to live for, that I could live because I had hope. When all else fails, when despair consumes you, when freedom is lost, when there seems to be no way through the darkness, I clung to hope. It was like the last grip on a very long rope and I was determined not to let go.

Having a loved one detained in a foreign prison is a horrendous experience. Often families feel as if they too are serving a sentence with their loved one. Their lives become overwhelmed with incredible despair, trauma and uncertainty. Emotional and economic turmoil completely envelop their lives. They live from day to day never knowing what the next day will bring and doing everything they can in the meantime to prevent their lives from falling apart.

Over the years, I've received thousands of heart-wrenching letters and emails from families who have been plunged into a nightmare, a horrific world they previously knew nothing about. More often than not, they simply want to share their feelings and try to come to terms with everything happening around them. The key to these families being able to endure the turmoil they face is, largely, in the support they receive from family, friends and people in their community. It may be that the emotional turmoil is taking its toll and engaging a professional counsellor might just be the answer to help clarify a particular problem, put things into perspective or introduce coping strategies.

Engaging the right counsellor may be difficult, because it's important to engage someone with whom you can connect. Someone you can feel comfortable with and to build a relationship of trust. What works for some may not work for others. Families have to recognise first that they need help and support before they can go looking for it or before they will accept the advice of a friend telling them they need help. While I could perhaps dedicate an entire chapter to counsellors, I must refrain because I would only be giving advice based on personal experience, not professional qualification.

What I will say, however, is that we should never feel embarrassed by admitting we need help coping or tackling an issue that we just can't seem to move forward with. All of us at some stage in our lives need a helping hand.

Much of the support they need is similar to that which any family would be given when facing any crisis. Helping them collect children from school or checking the post office box. Giving them a hand around the house or taking a load of rubbish to the tip (dump). Never underestimate the little things that can compound existing stresses. Some families stress more if they are used to having order in their lives and then suddenly they are consumed by chaos. Knowing they are not alone can make a huge difference. Particular attention should always be given to child safety and there are some paramount considerations when a child has a loved one detained in a prison, foreign or domestic. Due to the complexity of the topic, I have listed a few valuable resources at the end of this chapter for anyone wishing to know more.

There are countless practical ways of lessening the burden on families who have a loved one detained in prison. People have enormous potential to give. You might have computer skills and be in a position to help them create a website or campaign page to generate practical support for their loved one.

You may be a great organiser and get a group of friends together to plan a fundraising event to help a family member travel overseas to visit their loved one who is a foreign detainee. You might be a great writer and lobby on their behalf to your government, (with the family's permission of course), expressing your concerns in regard to their circumstances.

Various organisations are dedicated to raising awareness of a family's loved one in prison and have vast experience in lobbying issues. You might contact them and seek their willingness to support a particular family, or offer your services to the organisation. Most of the time, simply caring and being a friend is the best support for these families.

I hope that this book helps in some small way to give hope to those who need it most; to humanise the suffering that goes on in the families who have loved ones detained in foreign prisons. To help others understand that those who defend the rights of others do so, not with the intention of seeking the release of prisoners, only that they be granted some sort of human rights status. Many support the idea of creating a society based on the principles of equality and solidarity, that understands and values human rights, and that recognizes the dignity of every human being. Many support the concept of moral rightness based on ethics, rationality, law, natural law, religion, fairness, or equity, along with the punishment of the breach of said ethics. It doesn't take much to make a difference in someone else's life. It simply begins by caring.

No kind action ever stops with itself. One kind action leads to another. Good example is followed. A single act of kindness throws out roots in all directions, and the roots spring up and make new trees.

The ultimate measure of a man is not where he stands in moments of comfort and convenience, but where he stands at times of challenge and controversy.
—Rev. Dr. Martin Luther King, Jr.

USEFUL RESOURCES

Foreign Prisoner Support Service Resources
http://www.usp.com.au/fpss/resources.html

Action for Prisoner's Families
http://www.prisonersfamilies.org.uk/

Anxiety Treatment Australia
http://www.anxietyaustralia.com.au/anxiety_disorders/post_traumatic.shtml

Amnesty International
http://www.amnesty.org/

American Indian Prisoners
http://www.americanindianprisoners.com/

American Civil Liberties Union
http://www.aclu.org

Australian Civil Liberties Union
http://www.go.to/aclu

Assistance Association for Political Prisoners (Burma)
http://www.aappb.org

Australians Against Capital Punishment
http://aacp.wordpress.com/

Australian Prisoners Abroad
http://www.nswccl.org.au/issues/prisoners/abroad.php

Bangkwang Net
http://www.bangkwang.net/

Cageprisoners
http://www.cageprisoners.com

Canadian Civil Liberties Association
http://www.ccla.org/index.shtml

Centre for Crime and Justice Studies (UK Link)
http://www.kcl.ac.uk/ccjs

D.A.R.E
http://www.dare.com/home/default.asp

Death Penalty Information Center
http://deathpenaltyinfo.org

Drug Awareness Video
http://www.mariafullofgrace.com

European Group for Prisoners Abroad (EGPA)
http://www.egpa.org/

Family/Friends of South African Detainees Abroad (FOSADA)
http://www.fosada.za.org

Fair Trials International.
http://www.fairtrials.net/

Get Up
http://www.getup.org.au

Hmong International Human Rights Watch
http://www.hmongihrw.org/

HHUGS
http://hhugs.org.uk

Human Rights First
http://www.humanrightsfirst.org/

Human Rights Watch
http://www.hrw.org/

Innocence Project
http://www.innocenceproject.org

Lao Veterans of America
http://www.laoveterans.com/

Life After Exoneration Project
http://www.exonerated.org

Miscarriages of Justice (UK)
http://www.mojuk.org.uk/

Partners of Prisoners
http://www.partnersofprisoners.co.uk

Paul Wolf, Attorney at Law
http://www.icdc.com/~paulwolf/lawpractice/lawpractice.htm

Prison Care
http://www.prisoncare.org

Prison Legal News
http://www.prisonlegalnews.org

Prison Talk
http://www.prisontalk.com/

Prison World and Prison Land
http://www.prisonworld.nl

Prisoners Abroad
http://www.prisonersabroad.org.uk

Prisoners' Families Helpline
http://www.prisonersfamilieshelpline.org.uk

Reprieve
http://www.reprieve.org.uk/casework_lindacarty.htm

Rights Australia
http://www.rightsaustralia.org.au/

Smart Traveller
http://www.smartraveller.gov.au/index.html

United Nations Crime and Justice Network
http://www.uncjin.org/Laws/extradit/extindx.htm

World Coalition Against the Death Penalty
http://www.worldcoalition.org/

CAMPAIGNS

Foreign Prisoner Support Service
www.usp.com.au/fpss/campaigns.html

Fair Trials International
http://www.fairtrials.net/cases

Innocence Project
http://www.innocenceproject.org/know/

Prisoners Abroad
http://www.prisonersabroad.org.uk/Get-Involved.aspx

Cage Prisoners
http://www.cageprisoners.com/cases

About the Author

Kay Danes is a remarkable woman who has an incredible life story. She is a college graduate with a Diploma in Professional Writing and Editing. Kay is the author of several highly acclaimed books; *Families Behind Bars*, *Standing Ground* and *Beneath the Pale Blue Burqa*.

Kay is a tireless humanitarian with over 15 years aid work experience, in some of the most hostile countries on the planet. In 2008 she embarked on a humanitarian aid mission into war-torn Afghanistan. She travelled the ancient silk route, through Taliban strongholds, in a dusty Toyota Hiace with four fellow Rotarians, delivering life changing aid to people devastated by war. Her journey addressed key humanitarian issues, which became an integral part of a National Debate in Australia on Afghanistan. Kay's commitment to bridging communities through understanding and empathy, is recognised by senior Government officials in Australia and overseas. Kay is recognised as a voice for the voiceless. She has addressed several U.S. Congressional forums on democracy, the US National Press Club, and the Conference on World Affairs with an audience of 91,000, previously attended by Eleanor Roosevelt and US Vice-President Joe Biden.

Kay Danes speaks on a broad range of topics including achievement, motivation, women in the security industry, surviving in a hostile environment, human rights, social justice, resilience. She has overcome many personal challenges, including torture and arbitrary detainment in a communist prison, following a horrific hostage ordeal she and her husband endured in 2000, when working as Security Managers in a communist state. From director of security to humanitarian aid worker, Kay Danes has provided consultation to many groups, including the Australian Institute of Export, the National Human Rights Commission of Australia on the treatment of people under arrest or detained in prison, the Joint Standing Committee on Treaties; and the secretary to the UN Special Rapporteur on Torture.

In 2011, Kay Danes was named one of 50 of Australia's most influential women. Kay's mantra in life is: Hope gives courage to us all and sometimes it is the very thing that enables us to endure!

Useful resources

You can contact Kay through New Holland Publishers Australia
Unit 1, 66 Gibbes Street
Chatswood NSW 2067
Australia
Phone: +61 2 8986 4700
Fax: +61 2 8986 4799
www.newholland.com.au
Kay Danes' website: *www.kaydanes.com*

Also by Kay Danes

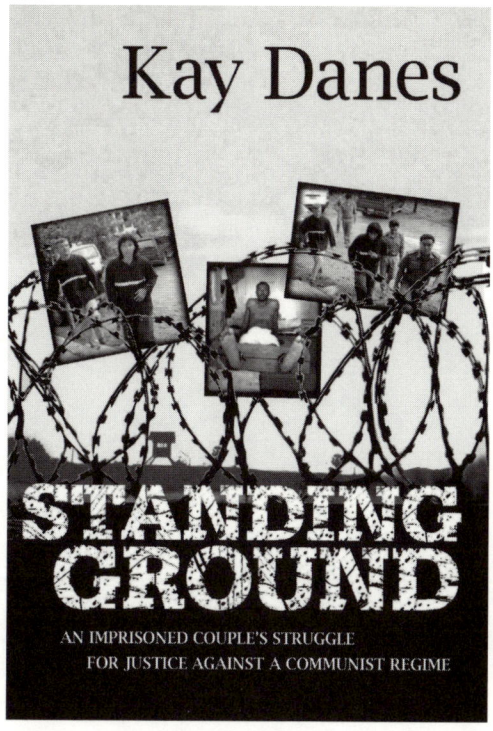

Standing Ground
ISBN 9781741107579